Unanimously Praised for Its Insight
And Scripturally Accurate Information

"Among the best books on cults in print. Should become a best seller to all young people and their parents."

> *The Banner*
> Christian Reformed Church

"Filled with thought-provoking comment and examples."

> *The Standard*
> Baptist General Conference

"A life-saving course for more people than you would guess. Every high school library should have several copies."

> David Poling
> *Viewpoint*/NEA

". . . his wit coupled with his sense of the ridiculous make this book entertaining as well as informative reading."

> *The Lutheran*
> The Lutheran Church in America

"Factually and scripturally accurate. A good book for young people and their parents."

> *The Pentecostal Evangel*
> General Counsel, Assemblies of God

"If you have parents on your gift list, this is recommended."

> *Christian Life Magazine*

"Heartily recommend its reading and study."

> *Presbyterian Journal*

THOSE CURIOUS NEW CULTS IN THE 80S

WILLIAM J. PETERSEN

Introduction by Jay Kesler,
President, Youth for Christ/USA

Keats Publishing, Inc.　　New Canaan, Connecticut

THOSE CURIOUS NEW CULTS IN THE 80s

ISBN: 0-87983-317-3
Library of Congress Catalog Card Number: 72-93700

Printed in the United States of America

Keats Publishing, Inc.
27 Pine Street
New Canaan, Connecticut 06840

CONTENTS

Introduction to the revised edition

I welcome this new help to youth, their parents, pastors, youth workers, teachers. I am impressed with Bill Petersen's book because it is confidently Christian. He believes that when the Christian faith is properly understood it can enter into the arena with all combatants and come out victorious. He doesn't have to tell falsehoods about other religions nor does he have to prejudice us against them. He simply allows them to be what they are and then compares their weakness with the strength of the gospel of the Lord Jesus Christ.

We in Youth for Christ have been working with young people for almost forty years. My own active involvement has been for the last twenty-six. There was a day when the battle for the allegiance of young people was between naturalism and supernaturalism, that is, the Christian church was attempting to convince young people that there is a God and that science is the process of thinking God's thoughts after Him. Ministers and youth workers were telling young people that science could not account for the origin of the universe nor for the existence of the soul, for man's moral nature, or for his eternal destiny. That argument is by and large one of the past. Most young people have either worked out a personal position or they have put faith and science into separate compartments in their heads.

In today's world the battle for the minds of young people is more often between various forms of supernaturalism. These supernaturalisms can cover a wide range from the more bizarre occult groups to seemingly sophisticated mind-over-matter types of Eastern religions.

Petersen has given us an authoritative documented book to help us understand these cults. Oftentimes when parents or clergymen try to struggle with young people over these issues they feel that by simply establishing the lack of credibility of these new religions, the weaknesses of their founder-leaders or pointing out the faulty logic, immoral practices or financial manipulation young people will turn away from them. They are surprised when after all the evidence has been presented, the young people close their eyes and blindly move closer toward error.

In this book we are helped to understand the appeal of these cults, that they are based on the recognition of legitimately felt human needs. The fact that some of these faulty "religions" and cults have adjusted themselves to meet these needs makes them difficult to combat.

Cults can be a salve providing temporary relief for certain symptoms. The Christian faith is not that sort of thing. It goes to the root cause of the human problem and solves it from the inside out. The Christian faith also, however, is a strong personal warm expression that meets immediate human needs.

Those Curious New Cults in the 80s helps us understand the needs of our youth and to incorporate into the expression of our Christian faith the experiences and realities that youth are seeking.

This book has a sense of fairness about it that would allow a parent to ask a young person to read the appropriate section and not fear that he or she would feel that this is merely a propaganda book for Christianity written against their new found friends. The tone of the book, I believe, will make it something not only for parents to read as they try to understand and combat error, but also for young people to read and begin to ask serious questions. I know our staff is going to find it a useful tool in working among youth in today's often confusing youth culture.

Jay Kesler, President
Youth for Christ/USA

A Note from the author

One spring afternoon in Amsterdam, as I was strolling near Dam Square with my family, we spotted some Hare Krishna devotees doing their thing across the street. Curious, my son Ken went over to get a closer look. These chanting, swaying religionists were young people from America too, and about Ken's age. Totally dedicated, they were willing to make fools of themselves for Krishna Consciousness. Apparently, they had finally found something to believe in.

Back home again in the States, I became increasingly fascinated by the hold that these new religions are having upon people today; and I also became increasingly concerned about Christian churches and parents whose examples had inspired youth to boredom and disdain. So I began writing a brief series of sketches on contemporary cults for *Eternity* magazine, and thanks to Nathan Keats and Donald Kauffman this has blossomed into a book.

In the following pages I want you to get a closer look at Hare Krishna and twenty-two other "curious new cults." You may wish that I had added a few more to the list or that my treatment of some of them would have been more exhaustive. But I am writing not for scholars but for young people and their parents who are looking for something to believe in.

This book I am dedicating to my son Ken, who has found Someone to believe in.

WILLIAM J. PETERSEN

THOSE CURIOUS
NEW CULTS
IN THE 80s

I

WHY PEOPLE ARE TURNED ON BY THOSE CURIOUS NEW CULTS

Turning On to Religion 1

I DON'T KNOW when it all started, but it must have been sometime after President John F. Kennedy was gunned down in Dallas late in 1963. Young people seemed to identify with the young President. When he was slain, the blood of many youthful dreams was poured out too.

Other things had also been happening in 1963. Pope John XXIII, the aged Pope with a youthful heart, passed on, and the Roman Catholic Church would never be the same again. He had been called a "caretaker" Pope when the College of Cardinals had selected him only a few years before. But his spirit and the innovations of Vatican II had changed that designation. Pope John had opened the windows of the Vatican, and many were chilled by the draft.

In America, the United States Supreme Court, ruling against the Commonwealth of Pennsylvania, had prohibited state-sponsored Bible reading in the public schools. The ruling itself wasn't as significant as what it symbolized. It was the end of an era. America was no longer to be considered a Christian nation. Many question whether it ever was, but this decision settled the debate.

At Harvard University, a professor named Timothy Leary was dismissed because he had become an evangelist for his LSD religion. LSD, he said, could lead young people to God. Though the university officials could not follow him, hundreds of thousands of young people did. And the publicity that ensued from his dismissal from Harvard made him the most successful guru since the Pied Piper.

In England, four mop-headed youths from Liverpool who called themselves the Beatles created their own music and a new beat known as the Mersey Sound. Young people mobbed them wherever they went.

Also in England, the Bishop of Woolwich shook the Anglican Church, to say nothing of the rest of Christianity, by publishing a little paperback called *Honest to God*. He spoke of "religionless Christianity." Many laymen were shocked by how far the bishop seemed to go to jettison the traditional forms of his faith. He emphasized that God wasn't "out there someplace," but was "inside."

Another religious paperback came out that year too. Entitled *The Cross and the Switchblade*, it claimed no great theological merit, but merely told the story of a young Pentecostal preacher named David Wilkerson, who felt called of God to work among street gangs in New York's roughest ghettos. He told them, "Jesus loves you." Along with *Honest to God*, it made the bestseller lists.

Each of these incidents of 1963 started a chain reaction that is still growing in the 1980s, culminating in the rise of Eastern religions, the occult, the Jesus people, the Catholic Pentecostals, religious revival and ecclesiastical disarray. And that's where we are today.

Let me list a few of the factors:

1. *Disillusionment with America.* Vietnam loomed large as a reason for almost anything. The election of 1964, in the aftermath of the Kennedy assassination, pitted an acknowledged hawk against an apparent dove. The dove won handily, escalated and perpetuated the war, and brought the youth of America into the Slough of Despond.

Whether John F. Kennedy or Barry Goldwater would have done differently or would have done better is not the point. The point is that youth, egged on by revolutionary forces, began to despair in America.

Coupled with this was the fact that young people began to see the hypocrisy of their elders more clearly than ever before. They saw hypocrisy in their government's politics; they saw hypocrisy in their parents' playing with religion; they saw hypocrisy in advertising, in business, in the suburban rat race. Every place they looked they seemed to hear people saying one thing and doing another.

Civil rights marches had accomplished little; the ghettos were smoldering. If it wasn't Watts, it was Harlem that was erupting.

Here was America, the richest country in the world, totally disregarding some of its greatest problems while fighting a war thousands of miles away that nobody wanted to fight. Of course young people were disillusioned.

2. *Dehumanization by science.* It was also the time of the historic robot-like Cape Kennedy countdowns. Man was on his way to the moon. "What has Man wrought" seemed etched on every rocket that forged its way into space. Science had reached the pinnacle of its success. Surgeons were even talking about transplanting hearts. Computers were spitting out information faster than man could absorb it.

But if this was what Western civilization had brought

upon man, youth didn't want it. Only a few years before, the Russian Sputnik had propelled young people into science majors at college; nuclear physics, chemistry, cybernetics, biology courses had been jammed. Now young people were disillusioned by science. All it was bringing was the 1984 that Novelist George Orwell had promised.

Only a few years before, science was thought to be the mighty Savior, the great god of twentieth-century man. Science had suddenly turned into Beelzebub; the more man worked with computers, the more he seemed like a robot himself.

3. *Advent of the drug culture.* Years ago Writer Aldous Huxley had predicted the day when the machine would be worshiped. In his book *The Doors of Perception* he pointed to drugs as the doorway to a new religion. And led by Dr. Timothy Leary, young people followed through the door. The advocates of drugs made sensational claims for such psychedelic drugs as mescaline and LSD. LSD would unlock the secrets of the universe, it was claimed; it would tell you who you really were and also who God was. Said Leary, "The LSD kick is spiritual ecstasy. The LSD trip is a religious pilgrimage."

What LSD seems to do, according to many competent researchers, is to remove "that part of a person which gives him his individual identity—the I of the me." It induces a type of schizophrenia in which inner and outer reality become confused.

As John Lennon sang in "I Am the Walrus," "I am he as you are me and we are all together." The individual blends into the universe and becomes one with it.

This parallels what the Eastern religions are saying and thus it is little wonder that LSD "has become known as a chemical shortcut to enlightenment."

4. *Future fright.* Almost every young person goes

through a time when he has to decide who he is and where he is going. There is nothing unusual about this. Analyst Erik Erikson talks about this period when young people try to find their niches.

But one thing that has aggravated the problem is the cataclysmic future that confronts young people. They constantly hear all types of dire predictions: the population explosion, nuclear warfare, the pollution crisis, the disintegration of society. The list of grave catastrophes that threaten to engulf us within the next twenty-five years is terrifying.

Frantically, the young person is groping for security in a world that gives him very little. Can he find some security in the stars, via astrology? Should he renounce the idea of time and live in an eternal Now, as eastern religions advocate? Should he look eagerly for Armageddon?

Young people have always asked themselves who they are and where they are going. Now they are seeking some alternative questions.

5. *Breakdown of the family.* All of society seems to be at war with the family structure. Corporations move fathers from one corner of the nation to another, and obligingly relocate their families as well. But the wound of uprootedness is not salved. Despite increasing leisure, families seem to use it to spend more time away from each other. TV, that strange living-room Cyclops, has brought the members of the family back into the home and converted them into utter strangers.

A young person may have a car and a guitar, but no real sense of belonging in the home and community. Maybe Mom will miss him when he's gone, but will anybody else on the block even know he's away?

So young people are making their own families. Perhaps the biggest family of all was Woodstock, at a rock festival in August 1969, where 400,000 young people were crammed together in a sea of mud. They had something in common: drugs, music, youth.

Young people turned to communes, experimenting with new patterns of living together. Many of the new religions use the commune idea to provide security and belongingness. Where else can they find it?

6. *Popular culture.* Music is a part of youth today as it never has been before. And the popular rock artists have led young people into Transcendental Meditation, Zen Buddhism, astrology and many more new cults. But even before the Beatles and Bob Dylan, there were the poets Allen Ginsberg and Jack Kerouac talking about Zen and Hare Krishna.

Among college students especially, the greatest influence in recent years has been Herman Hesse, the German-Swiss novelist.

Hesse died in 1962, but American youth didn't really turn on to him until about five years later. Then it was that his short novel *Siddhartha* began selling 100,000 copies a year. *Siddhartha* is a short, romantic account of the life of a young Buddhist, who goes through all the adolescent problems of alienation and searching that young Americans face. His pilgrimage ends as he discovers that "seeking means to have a goal; but finding means: to be free, to be receptive, to have no goal."

Tom Wolfe, author of *Electric Kool Acid Test,* and Kurt Vonnegut, author of *Slaughterhouse Five,* are two other significant authors who have shaped the lives of the young, and have guided them toward new forms of religious experience.

7. *Psychology and the occult.* The psychic research of Duke University's Dr. Joseph Rhine and his ESP laboratories is quite well-known. While Rhine's work was blasted by many scientists, he braved a scientific age to show that maybe there is a sixth sense after all. And it paved

the way for other mind research, such as that at the Dream Laboratory at the Maimonides Medical Center in Brooklyn.

In the past several decades psychologists have become increasingly fascinated with psychic phenomena. While Sigmund Freud himself had little to do with it, his early associate Carl G. Jung was deeply involved in astrology and the occult.

Thus, science, long preoccupied with the material and tangible, has been undercut by its younger brother, psychology.

Along with research psychology's innovations have come new special psychologists and philosophers who have had a profound impact on youth today. Herbert Marcuse's Marxist humanism with its strong revolutionary flavor, Norman Brown's quest for liberation through mysticism and Erich Fromm's Marxist existentialism with its fascination for the East have accentuated youthful alienation without solving the problem.

8. *Decline of the church.* In the 1960s the major denominations didn't go anywhere. The dedicated churchmen built some beautiful vehicles with power steering and power brakes, but the motor had dropped out. First, they streamlined the design, but that didn't help. Then they decided to all get together and build a greater, more monstrous vehicle with all the extras.

To young people who looked on, it was all foolishness. They got the impression that the church was only trying to save itself. Major theologians seemed dominated by rationalism and humanism. Every time they reached for relevance, they dropped transcendence. And as their God shrank, so did their membership and their attendance.

Against the tide, however, some churches continued to grow. Dean Kelley, executive in the National Council of Churches, chronicled the phenomenon in his 1972 book, *Why Conservative Churches Are Growing*. The churches that gave their people something definite to believe in, that called for clear commitment, that built a strong sense of fellowship and that challenged their people with missionary zeal seemed to be surging ahead. Churches that were fuzzy in doctrine and encouraged the notion that everyone should be free to do his own thing were stagnating.

But young people sensed something more. Young people weren't eager to join an institution. They wanted a relationship, a personal relationship. Many churches, however, were building institutions, and young people avoided them like the plague.

9. *The ecology crisis.* It was about the same time that the ecology crisis convinced youth that Mother Nature was one mother who should not be rebelled against but rather should be loved. Somehow man's future was intertwined mystically with the future of the earth. So if they were going to die together, maybe they should learn to live together.

What man loves, he comes to worship. What he worships, he deifies. And consequently, nature with a capital N moved onto the throne.

As this collage of youth-shaking elements was brought together in the mid-1960s, an entirely new religious picture was formed. Some of the new cults which compose this picture may seem almost grotesque; some, sinister; others, naive. Yet the young adherents come with hungry hearts and groping minds for something or Someone to reconcile their alienation and to make sense out of chaos.

In the early 1970s the cults seemed to be faddish like hula hoops to be discarded after the season. Instead, they were more like Frisbees. They stayed in the air much longer than anyone expected.

What Makes a Cult a Cult?

THE CULTS of the late 60s and early 70s were not a passing fancy. They certainly didn't die amid the embers of the Vietnam war as some had predicted. Nor did they fade when the whispers of Watergate ceased.

Some of them evolved (and some devolved); some new ones emerged (and some old ones submerged); some came to be respectable (and others continued to be a spectacle), but, as a whole, cults remained as strong as ever.

They continued to make headlines. Brainwashing, kidnaping and deprogramming charges were splashed across the pages of every newspaper. Celebrities flirted with the cults, and the cults played the romance to the hilt.

But the most sensational headlines—and perhaps it was the story of the decade—were made toward the end of 1978 by a cult that hadn't even existed a decade earlier.

Jim Jones had led his followers in the Peoples Temple movement to Jonestown, Guyana, and together they committed mass suicide. More than 900 bodies were strewn across the jungle clearing. Fruit punch had been laced with cyanide; adults had willingly drunk it, and then they made their children swallow the deadly stuff. The cult leader, who had intended to construct a socialist utopia in Guyana, died from a bullet wound in his right temple. It was self-inflicted.

Those who had previously joked about cults no longer regarded them as a laughing matter. But it baffled many that such a suicidal bloodbath could take place in our enlightened society.

The Jonestown folk were not impressionable teenagers; they were adults; many of them were parents with children. Nor were they all uneducated by any means; nor were they right-wing zealots, as some have attempted to peg other cultists.

Historian Martin Marty explained it this way: "For me, Jonestown brings to a logical conclusion the trends of a decade in which people sought authority, hungered for surrogate family, willingly submitted to leadership of any sort, welcomed religious experience so long as it gave short-range focus to their lives, and on occasion made it possible for them to sustain a kind of idealism so long as they surrendered choice."

Though it may have been the conclusion of a decade, it certainly wasn't the conclusion of cults.

But the shock of Jonestown caused some of the dogs to start barking up the wrong tree.

Not all cults are the same. Few of them have the potential to end up like the Peoples Temple movement. Some do, but most are laced with more subtle dangers than cyanide.

Many cults are blindly authoritarian, as Martin Marty rightly says that the cults of the 70s tended to be.

Fashions in cults tend to mirror fashions in popular thought. The 1960s were the era of "if it feels good, do it,'' and the decade spawned dozens of experience-centered cults with an emphasis on freedom. The experience was the thing.

The 1970s felt the backlash and moved toward discipline and authoritarianism. Even some cults of the 60s that were born with an experience mystique became more strongly authoritarian in the 70s.

And what of the 80s?

Since the mass suicide in Guyana many of the cults have been trending to less organization. In a British newspaper John Allan wrote, "The mood of the 80s is much more for small, less organized, less threatening groups. They range from holistic health groups to astrological groups to pyramid power groups, but they are prepared to work together because of their common conviction that a personal and planetary transformation is taking place."

It's possible then to float from one group to another, picking up a little from a lecture from one, buying cassettes from a second and subscribing to a magazine of a third. You can build your own religion like an ice cream sundae—a scoop of this, a scoop of that and a little of that topping over there, with nuts, whipped cream and a cherry on top. You fabricate your religion for your own desires of the moment.

Thomas Luckman speaks of it in *The Invisible Religion*, "You don't speak of commitment, but you ask, 'What are you into right now?' A cult leader may be more apt to have a clientele than a congregation."

It's getting so confusing that you can't tell a cult when you see one.

And that raises an interesting question: What *is* a cult?

According to a strict dictionary definition, any religion is a cult, because the word is derived from the Latin word for worship.

But the word cult has assumed a specialized meaning in the past two centuries. Today we think of a cult as a deviation from orthodox religion. And it deviates in crucial areas. A religion—whether it is Christianity, Islam or Buddhism—may be divided into denominations or sects, all of which are variations on the same theme. But on the fringes of each religion are cults which diverge from the core of the religion's tenets in vital areas.

Baptists, Presbyterians and Methodists, for instance, may have different views on baptism and how their churches should be governed. While these views are important to members of the denomination—otherwise the denominations wouldn't have become distinct groups in the first place—they are not the central core of Christianity's beliefs.

What is that central core?

Some people would answer, "The Apostles' Creed" or some other similar statement to which all Christians have historically agreed. But for the purposes of this book, I would summarize the crucial areas in answers to three questions:

1. Who is Jesus Christ?
2. What is man's basic problem?
3. How is man's problem resolved?

In the past few decades, the "far-out" cults have received the most publicity and therefore the word cult is often defined as "a crazy group that follows a weird leader and does some wild things."

But that is not a true definition of cult.

Unitarians, for instance, have traditionally been regarded as a cult by the Christian Church, because their answers to the big three questions are at odds with what orthodox Christianity has always stood for. They are certainly not "a crazy group that follows a weird leader and does some wild things." Far from it. Some of our finest citizens in American history have been Unitarians.

Yet the Unitarian Church has been turned down by such an open-minded group as the National Council of Christian Churches. Why? Because it is outside the pale of orthodox Christianity.

The new wave of cults ("those curious new cults," if you will) has swept ashore an assortment of groups with widely diverse beliefs, lifestyles and leaders. Strictly speaking, some are not Christian cults at all, but rather are Hindu, Buddhist and Islamic cults instead.

They are diverse, and yet they have some common markings. In fact, because of these common markings, some people assume that it is the markings that make a cult. Not so. Some Christian groups display the same cultic markings, but while they may be cult-like, they are not cults.

What then are these cultic markings?

1. A cult has a founder-prophet who is revered.

2. It has an authority through which the Bible or God can be understood; in fact, it is impossible to truly understand the Bible or God except through this authority. The authority is often the writings of the founder.

3. It is authoritarian, encourages dependence, and discourages rational thought. Cults of the 80s may not be as notable in this marking as cults of the 70s were.

4. It is separatist, secretive and tends to have a persecution complex.

5. It frequently employs a degree of deception in its recruitment and conversion practices.

6. While the group itself provides a strong supportive and loving fellowship, fear is a powerful motivation in the group's bag of tricks.

Those six cultic markings characterize many—but not all—of the new cults.

Cults, of course, come in all shapes and sizes. Today

there are between 1,500 and 3,000 of them and new ones keep springing up each year. Cults of the 60s and early 70s tended to aim young. The cults of the 80s often have an older clientele in mind. Not only is the population getting older and so there are more people in the older age groups today, but also there is more money in the hands of the older people. And cults, like any business, need money to survive.

Though cults cannot be pigeonholed, most of them seem to fit into one of five different groups:

    (1) Occult interests
    (2) Eastern cults
    (3) Christian aberrations
    (4) Self-improvement religions
    (5) Syncretistic groups

Each variety meets particular needs for its adherents. The occult generally draws people who are frustrated by powerlessness. Eastern cults attract those who are frustrated by their inability to find answers to life's problems. Many of the Christian aberrations lure those who are frustrated by an inability to establish meaningful relationships. The self-improvement cults attract those who are frustrated by their own weaknesses. And the syncretistic groups usually combine an appeal of two or more of the above.

But that's enough of an overview. Now let's take a closer look at some of these curious new cults.

II

WHEN THE FORCES ARE AT WORK OR DID THE DEVIL MAKE ME DO IT?

Astrology 3

THE AGE OF AQUARIUS has dawned. You may not have noticed it; in fact, you may feel no different from the way you felt in the pre-Aquarian age. Perhaps you even feel worse. But it doesn't matter. Astrology is with us.

The rock musical "Hair" signaled the advent of the age. Its featured song gained instant popularity: "This is the dawning of Aquarius." But astrology was on the rise even before "Hair" opened on Broadway.

Almost every newspaper of importance besides the *Wall Street Journal* carries an astrological column; at last count, more than twelve hundred dailies across the country did so. Even Dick Tracy and Orphan Annie of the comics get entwined with astrology. And on the front page you can read of a mysterious San Francisco maniac murderer who identifies himself as Zodiac.

In Philadelphia's prestigious John Wanamaker department store you can buy a computerized horoscope for $20 plus Pennsylvania sales tax. In New York's Grand Central Station, an Astroflash computer can give you an astrological forecast for only $2.50, if your train doesn't

19

leave for ten minutes. And on 200 college campuses there are 24-hour-a-day computers that turn out horoscopes for the younger generation.

You can buy Zodiac cookbooks, Zodiac autograph books and even Zodiac coloring books for children. The publisher of *Astrology and Horse Racing* sold 100,000 copies of his book in a year. And, of course, you can buy a horoscope for your dog if you want to.

Both *Horoscope* and *American Astrology* have paid circulations of about a half million. And that's not all. Astrology is obviously such a big business that it employs 12,000 full-time professional astrologers and keeps 175,000 part-time astrologers busy. (The largest Protestant denomination, the Southern Baptists, has about forty thousand ministers.) According to a 1976 Gallup Poll, thirty-two million Americans take astrology quite seriously. Some 77 percent of American adults know their astrological sign.

But the age of Aquarius isn't uniquely American. In Great Britain, more than two-thirds of the adult population read their horoscopes. In France 53 percent read their horoscopes daily; and in Germany the percentage who take astrology somewhat seriously is 63 percent.

Moreover, many of the popular heroes of youth today refuse to do anything without consulting the stars. As a result, one university professor found out that more than 50 percent of his students "were at least interested in astrology and more or less believed that there was something to it." When he probed into their thinking, the students replied simply: "Astrology works. We don't know how and we don't care." Science, the professor said, always asked How; philosophy always asked Why. But young people today are only asking the question What.

For the past two centuries of science and technology,

we have been asking How. For two centuries before that, taking you back to the mid-1500s, we were asking Why. So it has been 400 years since astrology had widespread acceptance in the Western world.

The blow that seemingly had finished astrology was Copernicus' theory in his book *De revolutionibus orbium caelestium* (published 1543) that the sun and not the earth was the center of the solar system. But astrology continued to have its adherents after that, even including erudite scholars. For example, Johann Kepler, the brilliant scientist at the University of Prague, was both an astronomer in the footsteps of Copernicus and an astrologer because his salary depended on his emperor's superstitious beliefs. Kepler stated in a famous quotation: "Astronomy is the wise mother and astrology is her whoring little daughter, selling herself to any and every client willing and able to pay so as to maintain her wise mother alive." As a result of his lifelong pursuit of astrology, Kepler began to believe it himself. By then, however, the sun of astrology had set in the west.

But the dawn of astrology can be traced back to ancient times.

Perhaps it goes back as far as the Tower of Babel in biblical history. Certainly those Babylonian towers called ziggurats, which date to three millennia before Christ, were erected to survey the heavens. Some 270 feet high on top a series of seven terraces, these towers were climbed by ancient priests to reach the summit of the universe. The priests, who were the go-betweens for the king to the gods, surveyed the skies to discern the will of the deities.

The Chaldean form of astrology was primitive, of course; it applied only to the kings, not to the average man. But it was the first step to what we know as astrology today. Other civilizations also had a form of astrology—the Chinese, Hindu and Aztec, for instance; yet the Babylonians refined it for the western world to appropriate.

In the Old Testament, Daniel, who lived in Babylonian exile, had frequent run-ins with King Nebuchadnezzar's astrologers and magicians. Many important developments in astrology were being made then. For the first time astrology began to relate the birth date of the king to his destiny. Perhaps in Daniel's lifetime the first actual horoscopes were developed. Yet interestingly enough, although Daniel was surrounded by astrologers, he refused to seek his wisdom from that source. Instead, he once told the king, "No wise men, enchanters, magicians, or astrologers can show to the king the mystery which the king has asked, but there is a God in heaven who reveals mysteries."

When the Greeks got hold of astrology they made it into a life philosophy. The Greeks, of course, were philosophers, who loved to discuss what things meant, and had no time to gaze at the stars like the Chaldeans. But after Alexander the Great conquered Babylon, astrology conquered Greece. Actually, astrology fit so smoothly into the Stoic philosophy of pantheistic materialism and of a predetermined universe, that the Greeks almost thought they had invented it.

The big name in astrological history is Claudius Ptolemy, a Greek astrologer-astronomer two centuries after Christ. Ptolemy formulated the Ptolemaic system of astronomy which says that the earth is the center of the solar system and everything revolves around it. Astrology was flourishing throughout the Greek-speaking world in his day, and Ptolemy shaped it into a scientific mold. His *Tetrabiblos* became the textbook for all astrologers from that day to this.

Ptolemy tried to make astrology into an exact science;

actually, he turned it into a pseudo-scientific legalistic religion. For years the early Christian church battled against it; astrology was a more ferocious enemy than the lions in the Circus Maximus.

The greatest warrior against astrology in the early church was St. Augustine, who had played with it prior to his conversion. In his *Confessions*, he warned against the dangers. He said that astrology replaced the will of God with purely mechanical motions of the stars, that it led men to resign themselves to fate and that it denied free will. Said Augustine: "The astrologers say: 'It is from the heavens that the irresistible cause of sin comes, it is due to the conjunction of Venus with Mars or Saturn.' Thus man is absolved of all faults, he who is only proudly rotting flesh. The blame is indeed given to the creator and ruler of the heavens and of the stars."

Shortly after Augustine, with the decline and fall of the Roman Empire, astrology went underground, only occasionally surfacing during the next several hundred years.

How is it that astrology has become popular again in the sophisticated twentieth century after hundreds of years of general disfavor? No doubt there are many contributing factors.

The rise of Spiritualism a hundred years ago, the introduction of Theosophy into America seventy-five years ago, and the popularity of astrology in Germany between the two World Wars set the stage for our modern age of Aquarius.

No doubt, its ascendancy in America goes back directly to Evangeline Adams, a proper Bostonian at the turn of the century, who began studying astrology to the horror of her distinguished relatives. She moved to New York City, made headlines when she predicted a hotel fire, and set up shop above Carnegie Hall. There she read horoscopes for the great and near-great of the theatre profession, and made astrology a legitimate business instead of Gypsy fortunetelling.

Following in her train have come such popular astrologers as Carroll Righter and Sydney Omarr, whose columns can now be found in about five hundred and fifty daily newspapers.

Probably the most circulated religious column, apart from the astrological column, is written by Evangelist Billy Graham. But Graham appears in only two hundred daily newspapers. It is safe to say that no other religion gets as much free newspaper and magazine editorial space as does astrology.

But what precisely is astrology?

Llewellyn George, a prominent contemporary spokesman for astrology, defined it as "the study of life's reactions to planetary vibrations." Or to put it in another way, it is the study of the influence which stars allegedly exert on people and things.

Probably the simplest way to describe how it works is by the use of an object lesson.

Put a piece of masking tape around a basketball and mark off twelve equal sections on the masking tape. According to astrology, the earth would be represented as being in the middle of the basketball, and the course of the sun would be a line in the middle of the masking tape.

The masking tape with its twelve sections would be called the zodiac. This thin strip is the only part of the sky that is of interest to astrologers. The twelve sections are called "houses" and twelve constellations (the signs of the zodiac) move through those twelve houses during the course of a year.

To make things more complicated, astrologers chart the position of the planets which move through the twelve houses every twenty-four hours, and also the relative positions or the "aspects" or angles formed between stars and planets.

Now, theoretically, your horoscope is based on what the heavens looked like the exact moment you were born. According to Llewellyn George again: "Certain vibrations inbreathed by a newly-born babe endow the tendencies of character it will manifest."

In other words, to get an accurate horoscope from a professional astrologer you must know not only the date of your birth but also its precise moment and the latitude and longitude of your birthplace.

Of course, most of the astrological advice you see in the newspapers is absurdly general. Here is Astrologer Sydney Omarr's advice to Geminis for one typical day: "Don't duck responsibility. Go with tide. You will gain if available, ready, prepared and capable. You lose if lackadaisical, indifferent, resentful. One who can pull strings will be observing. Do yourself a favor by being cooperative."

Ben Franklin said some of the same things in his *Poor Richard's Almanac*, but no one made a religion out of it.

Despite the abstract generalities of the daily horoscopes, millions of true believers refuse to clean closets, sign contracts, take a plane trip or be kind to their neighbors until they read the daily columns. And if the newspaper editor inadvertently omits the daily horoscope, woe be unto him. The protest is ferocious.

Though they are vague and meaningless, newspaper columns are much cheaper than professional astrologers. Such a consultation may be as cheap as $25 but more likely would be $100 or more. And if you are unhappy with the way one astrologer describes your personality, you can try another one. Astrologers use a variety of source books to establish their interpretations, and your horoscope will depend on which interpretation book is consulted.

Recently some of the top astrological columnists in the Southern California area were compared for one day. Here is what the researchers discovered:

Virgos were told by Carroll Righter to entertain at home in the evening, but Sydney Omarr told them to go out and attend the theatre. Frances Drake told Libras to plan their day as they wished, but Jeane Dixon told them to watch out because their personal plans would get a temporary setback. Aquarians were told by Miss Drake to shape their plans and then to follow through on them consistently. On the other hand, Omarr's advice to the Aquarians wasn't so optimistic. He told them to "lie low. There is no need to rush, push or cajole."

It is obvious that if you want to keep your faith in astrology, you better not compare one against another.

When did the Age of Aquarius begin? Sometimes we kiddingly say that it began in the second act of "Hair." But astrologers aren't joking when they argue about it. Some astrologers say it began in 1904, others in 1936, others in 1962 and others say that it hasn't even begun yet.

What do they mean by the Age of Aquarius? Astrologers as well as astronomers speak of a star-age as about twenty-two hundred years. It is the age during which the sun rises—on the first day of spring—in the heavenly space occupied by one of the signs of the zodiac.

For the past twenty-two hundred years the sun has been rising in the sign of Pisces (the sign of the fish). But sometime in this century—1904, 1936, 1962 or later—the sun began to rise or will rise out of the space occupied by the constellation Aquarius.

Astrologers say that every time we change from one star-age to another, new forms of worship develop, new governments are in style, new philosophies become popular. The Age of Aquarius, say the astrologers, will be characterized by humanism, brotherhood and astrology. It will be a golden age of love and brotherhood.

Or haven't you noticed?

Does astrology really work? That, after all, is the key question in many people's minds. If it didn't work at all, it is questionable whether it would have any adherents.

First of all, it works just as *Poor Richard's Almanac* works and just as good psychological advice works. Much astrological advice is simply good psychological counsel. If your horoscope for the day tells you to "Look before you leap," and you exercise a little extra caution, thereby saving you much distress, you tend to credit astrology. You could just as well have credited Ben Franklin or King Solomon in the Book of Proverbs where you will find similar good advice.

Second, it is difficult to prove when it fails. *Time* magazine described it like this: "Break a leg when your astrologer told you the signs were good, and he can congratulate you on escaping what might have happened had the signs been bad. Conversely, if you go against the signs and nothing happens, the astrologer can insist that you were subconsciously careful because you were forewarned."

So it is difficult to convince a believer that it is a fake, that it really doesn't work. After all, he knows it has worked in his own experience time and time again.

Yet objective observers disagree. A recent *Redbook* article stated: "Astronomers, psychologists and statisticians who have tried to apply simple, scientific principles to astrology find that it doesn't work at all. A recent study explored the connection between birth dates and a gift for science. The source was a select Who's Who called *Men of Science*. The study came to one conclusion; that the birth dates of scientists are as random as the birth dates of the general population.''

There are a number of other problems with modern astrology, too. The simple fact is that the heavens have shifted in the two thousand years since the original astrological charts were established. Astrology, however, hasn't changed; it hasn't kept up with astronomy. If you were born in early October, astrologers say you are in the sign of Libra. Astronomers who have looked up at the sky a bit more recently say that the sign is Scorpio.

Besides that, astrology has had a hard time knowing how to cope with new planets. Uranus, Neptune and Pluto have finally been added to the order of ruling planets, but astrologers say that those planets had no influence on people before they were discovered.

Many scientists and scientific associations have denounced astrology. One German psychologist wrote: "We can see how dangerous it is by the way in which serious psychic disturbances, a fear of life, despair and derangement are produced by it in sensitive people. Astrology paralyzes initiative and powers of judgment. It stupefies and encourages shallowness. It molds the personality into receiving an underground movement that thrives on platitudes.''

. The Astronomical Society said in 1949: "Whatever hides behind the title of astrology . . . is nothing more than a mixture of superstition, duplicity and business.''

In September 1975, eighteen Nobel Prize winners and one hundred eighty six other prominent American scientists spoke out against astrology, denouncing the "pretentious claims of astrological charlatans'' and saying that "there is no scientific basis for it.''

Bart J. Bok, former president of the American Astronomical Society, said, "It is deplorable that so many newspapers now print this daily nonsense. . . . At the start, the regular reading is a sort of fun game, but it often ends up as a mighty serious business. The steady and ready availability of astrological predictions can over many years have insidious influence on a person's personal judgment."

That summarizes scientific opinion.

And there are many other problems with astrology, which astrologers struggle desperately to answer. Here are some of them:

1. Why do only the constellations of the zodiac have any effect on man? From our scale model, we have seen that the masking tape covers only one inch of the basketball. What about the constellations in other areas?

2. What about Eskimos and Laplanders? Did you know that they may have no horoscope at all? If they are born north of the Arctic Circle, where no planet or sign of the zodiac can be seen for weeks or even months, they are apparently deprived of a destiny.

3. Why are there so many astrologies? Not only are there many different interpretations in Western astrology, but if you would go to the Orient, you would find entirely different symbols with greatly different meanings.

4. What about twins? This is a classic problem for astrologers, and they have ready-made answers. But the answers don't really solve the problem. Two babies born at the same time in the same place should have the same destiny. Yet one may die in the hospital and the other may live to be ninety.

5. And why does astrology refer to birth rather than conception? At birth it would seem that the attending obstetrician exerts a greater influence than any star or planet. Wouldn't it make more sense, if there is any astral influence at all, to say it happened at the time of conception?

But certainly the heavens do have some influence

upon us. There are cycles and seasons to many things in nature and man is influenced as well. Some scientific research is now being done in these areas; thus far, all that has been proven is that the moon and the sun exert gravitational force. No other celestial body apparently exerts any discernible force, according to science.

Yet if there is no scientific basis for astrology, some say, why is it that astrologers can predict events with such accuracy? All you have to do to disprove the theory that astrologers are accurate is to go into a second-hand bookstore, pick up an old astrology magazine and see what it predicts for its current year.

What about those astrologers who predicted Kennedy's assassination? Surely that must prove something.

Writer Harriet Van Horne investigated one such prediction that appeared in *American Astrology* for November 1963. An astrologer was showing it to her as an example of the amazing accuracy of his craft. The key sentence read: "Apart from its direct link to things military, the powerful Mars influence incites much social unrest of the sort that erupts blindly into retaliative violence."

Of course, the Kennedy assassination neatly fulfilled the prophecy. But with a prediction so general, *any* trouble erupting during that fateful month of November would have fulfilled it.

It does seem mysterious for astrology to have arisen so rapidly in our scientific age. But, as a young Japanese astrologer said, young people get interested in astrology because "they've found the material things failing them, and they're trying to find their souls." The growing disillusionment with materialism has come when science and technology have seemingly reached their zenith. Man has gone to the moon. But what does the moon mean to man? Is there meaning in the universe? Astrology is an attempt to make the universe make sense.

It happened first in ancient times when the heavens were mysteriously close at night. Today, it has happened as the moon has become close to us again. In both cases man has attempted to transfer awareness into meaning.

But beyond that, this is an age of depersonalization. You take a computerized test to find your life's vocation and very likely it is a vocation of pushing buttons for the rest of your life. Computers even find your mate. Everything is depersonalized. Does the universe care about you? Are you anything special to the heavens above? It is no coincidence that the "death of God" theology came into vogue at about the same time as astrology. Young people couldn't seem to reach God in traditional religion, so they began to reach out to see if the created universe would speak back to them. They stopped talking to the Creator, and began holding conversation with the creation.

Also related to this is that much of Christianity has become demythologized and secularized. All the mystery and miracle has been stripped from it, leaving it devoid of supernaturalism. But man cannot live without God.

One other thing. Astrology seems to revive in times of fear, anxiety and confusion. It happened in Germany after World War I; it happened in Europe in the seventeenth century after an epidemic of plagues; it is happening today in the Western world where the nuclear bomb, the pollution threat and the population explosion hang like the sword of Damocles over our heads.

Anthropologist Margaret Mead put it this way: "When there is a degree of breakdown in established institutions, there is a proliferation of superstition, an outbreak of astrology, soothsaying, divination, all sorts of things. . . . Whenever there is the end of an epoch, there is a proliferation of this sort of thing."

Occasionally, astrologers try to bring the Bible onto their side, but the Bible is certainly not a friend of the pseudo-science. Back when the Children of Israel were roaming in the Wilderness, Moses warned them about the "abominable practices" of the Canaanite nations. Most of the abominable practices were linked to various types of fortune-telling. Moses told the people not to seek fortune-tellers or false prophets, but rather to wait for The Prophet, identified in the New Testament as Jesus Christ.

The most explicit Old Testament passage regarding astrology is in the Book of Isaiah. There, astrology is chided, and the Babylonians who developed it are mocked for their superstition. Isaiah warns the Israelites, "Astrologers can't save you, for they wander about each in his own direction." The Old Testament writers recognized that astrology was basically a religion and not a science. To the Chaldeans each of the planets was a god to be worshiped and feared, and each planet had a personality.

When Jesus in the New Testament said, "Do not be anxious about your life, what you shall eat, or what you shall drink, nor about your body, what you shall put on," he was undercutting the very basis of astrology. And when He rebuked the wind and calmed the sea from that little boat in the storm-tossed Sea of Galilee, He demonstrated clearly that He was in charge of nature; nature was not in control of God. Thus, for Christians who have a trusting relationship with Jesus Christ, there are no forces in the universe, either natural or supernatural, either real or imagined, which can endanger them.

The Apostle Paul wrote two letters (Galatians and

Colossians) to churches in an area of Asia Minor that was particularly impressed by astrology. In both letters he warns against being ensnared by "the elemental spirits of the universe." He called it bondage.

Paul recognized the contrast between astrology and Christianity. One was enslaving, the other was liberating. "What Christ has done is to set us free" (Galatians 5:1 New English Bible). "Stand firm, then, and refuse to be tied to the yoke of slavery again."

According to astrology, your destiny is in the stars. To some people this gives comfort or at least an excuse. If they can insist that some outer force is in control, they can refuse to accept personal responsibility. While astrologers say that the stars do not compel, but only impel, astrology does encourage the star-struck to evade personal responsibility.

New Testament Christianity is poles apart from that view of life. Paul told the Romans that "every one of us shall give account of himself to God," as he spoke of the coming Day of Judgment. God insists on personal responsibility.

I Ching 4

SUPPOSE YOU WANT GUIDANCE.

You have a big decision to make, and you don't feel capable of making the right choice all by yourself. What do you do?

You could go to a psychiatrist, lie on a couch, spend $50 to allow him to ask questions.

You could go to an astrologer to have your horoscope read for $25.

Or you could practice I Ching, the mystical ancient Chinese form of divination.

More and more young people today are opting for I Ching. Many of them have already tried professional counselors and even astrologers. Many of them have dabbled with Tarot cards, Ouija boards and other types of fortune-telling. I Ching seems to have a strange attraction for youth today. And it is an alluring first step into the religions of the East. Actually, it is probably the second step; usually, astrology is the first step into the occult.

Jacob Needleman in *The New Religions* wrote, "Where before one heard talk of anxiety, guilt, anal and oral

34

personalities, superego and so forth, one now hears of 'working out one's karma,' 'past incarnations,' 'rising signs' and 'sun signs.' The language of existentialism with its concepts of 'the absurd,' 'dread' and 'radical freedom' is also giving way to the language of astrology, psychism and mysticism. Even Marx and Chairman Mao now have to compete with the I Ching and the Tarot cards.''

In *The Occult Explosion*, Nat Freedland writes, ''As a fad, astrology has probably already hit its peak, although it will level off at a much higher plateau than ever before in an industrialized Western society.''

And what has taken its place, according to Freedland, as the leader in the occult explosion?

I Ching.

Basically, I Ching is not a religion; it is a book. Translated from Chinese, it means Book of Changes. But the book is so obtuse that you need an interpreter to help you interpret the interpretation of the translation.

In New York and Los Angeles, a Hollywood actor named Khigh Dhiegh has established branches of his International I Ching Studies Institute. Khigh Dhiegh, who usually plays Chinese roles on TV and in films, was actually born in New Jersey of mixed Anglo-Egyptian-Sudanese parentage, but on the side he promotes I Ching.

On the surface, I Ching seems so simple that it sounds ridiculous. According to I Ching, you can obtain guidance by tossing sticks or coins. The reason is, its followers say, that if you know the question, your subconscious mind already contains the answer.

And if you still think it is silly, just remember that the great Swiss psychiatrist, Carl G. Jung, Freud's early associate, thought it serious enough to write a lengthy preface to the first Western translation of the Book of

Changes. Jung felt that the ancient Chinese knew some secrets about modern depth psychology that twentieth-century man has forgotten. He tied these long-forgotten secrets into his psychological concepts of the "collective unconscious" and "synchronicity."

The strange thing about I Ching is that it too was almost forgotten even by students of Chinese culture and philosophy. You can search through some fairly exhaustive works on Chinese culture and not find a word about I Ching.

Why?

Because it seemed "just too inscrutable to be able to place it in any 'rational' picture of Chinese civilization."

Only in the past few years, then, has it been resurrected. To Jung and his ilk, it is a means of uncovering "mythic" subconscious patterns. But to thousands of young people, it's a game, like an Ouija board, and American young people like to play games, especially when they have some mystical element attached to them.

From 1949, when Jung's introduction to I Ching was published, until 1967, the book sold slowly, about a thousand copies a year. But then in the late 1960s Poet John Cage took up I Ching, Author Tom Wolfe wrote of it, and Singer Bob Dylan praised it in an interview. Almost overnight sales of the book began to soar.

How do you play?

You can either use fifty yarrow stalks or three coins, whichever are the most available. So in China, you use yarrow stalks; in America, you use three pennies. Supposedly it helps the image if you use Chinese coins, but most American young people today don't have Chinese coins.

By tossing the sticks or the three coins, you are led to a chapter in the Book of Changes which supposedly is most appropriate for your particular need. There are sixty-four chapters in the book, and that pretty well covers all the possibilities.

In more primitive days, there were only eight chapters, but that was changed some two thousand years ago. Life became more complicated and so did I Ching.

To us, the flip of a coin is the most random way of deciding anything. But to the Chinese, nothing is accidental; everything has meaning. It was this idea that fascinated Psychologist Jung. What we call "accidental may be the exact picture of the moment."

This is what fascinates young people today, at least those who look at I Ching under the surface. So much of life seems computerized and programmed that it is exciting to find that even a coin toss has deep symbolic meaning.

What is so deeply symbolic about coin-tossing?

It is deeply symbolic because it is based on the old Chinese notion that the universe is divided into two forces, the yin and the yang. The yang is the male force that begins things; it is the idea that impregnates things with its pure spirit-substance. The yin, on the other hand, is the female that completes things; it gives form and substance to what the yang has begun.

The symbols are carried on at length. Yang stands for shining, strong, male, sunny, heaven, above, front, hard, and light. Yin stands for cloudy, yielding, female, shadow, earth, below, back, soft, and heavy. Heaven rose out of yang and earth out of yin, and as they cooperated together all organisms and plants were brought forth. At first, Chinese pictured yin and yang as opposites warring with each other, but gradually yin and yang were considered as complements, interacting with each other, affecting each other, and sometimes even changing into one another.

Now, the Chinese weren't content to talk philosophically; they also had to draw pictures to illustrate. So the yang became a solid, unbroken horizontal line, and the yin became a broken line, like two bold dashes.

What does all this have to do with tossing three coins?

Well, the coin-tossing, believe it or not, is to enable you to draw a picture of yins and yangs. And this picture becomes a rather philosophical fortune-telling device.

Let's see how it works. First, you have to assign two points to the heads side of each coin and three points to the tails side. Now you throw the three coins and come up with two heads and a tail, a total of seven points. According to I Ching reckoning, a seven is a yang, so you place an unbroken line at the bottom of your pictograph. If on your next toss of the three coins, you totaled eight points, you would have a yin. So then you would draw your broken-line yin on top. A six is called a yin, but it's a changing line, so it will change into a yang with a value of seven. And a nine is called a yang, but it too is a changing line, so it will change into a yin with a value of eight.

(If this sounds complicated in English, you can imagine how confusing it would be in Chinese.)

After six coin tosses, you have a picture of a six-story building, some of the stories being solid lines and some broken lines. Your next step is to hunt through the Book of Changes with its sixty-four chapters for the chapter that matches your pictograph.

Suppose your pictograph (or as they say in I Ching, your hexagram) was a solid-line yang at the bottom and five broken-line yins above it. This corresponds with Number 24 in the Book of Changes, and there you read under the heading "The Turning Point":

Return. Success.
Going out and coming in without error.

Friends come without blame.
To and fro goes the way.
On the seventh day come return.
It furthers one to have somewhere to go.

If that isn't immediately clear, you look for guidance in accompanying notes. There you might read an explanation of your six-story picture: "After the dark (broken) lines have pushed all of the light lines upward and out of the hexagram, another light line enters the hexagram from below. The time of darkness is past."

Of course it has deeper significance than that, but that, in a very condensed form, is how I Ching works.

As its believers say, "In each hexagram we have a symbol: the hexagram itself. The hexagram often speaks to us simply, through our intuitive faculty, giving us information and answers whose meaning can rarely be expressed rationally. What the symbol speaks to is the heart.

According to the *Great Commentary* on the I Ching, if you follow the course of action recommended by the I Ching you will come to "resemble heaven and earth." No longer will you be in conflict with heaven and earth and no longer will you be "tossed about by the conflict of the opposites." "When man finds the measure of heaven and earth within himself—the measure of his own heaven and earth—the conflict is nullified by their marriage and peaceful union."

As you become more adept in analyzing the I Ching pictograph or hexagram, you recognize that certain lines represent heaven, certain lines represent man and certain lines represent earth. In fact, there are almost countless ramifications on reading the pictograph, and that's why schools are established specializing in I Ching.

Scholars don't know exactly when the Book of Changes

was written. Some say it goes back to 3000 B.C., although most would say it was started around 1000-1200 B.C.

If this were all there was to I Ching, we might dismiss it as an innocent little parlor game. But there is more.

Through their intricate and often mysterious interpretations, the ancient Chinese instilled into I Ching their deepest religious, ethical and philosophical concepts. Perhaps Tao is what they built into it.

Tao is one of those Chinese words that is hard to translate. Originally it meant a road or a way and it began to symbolize the way of man and nature. Yet in another way, Tao became the Chinese impersonal god.

When you think of China's religion, you may think of Buddhism, but actually Buddhism is a later import into Chinese religious thought. The two ancient Chinese religions are Confucianism and Taoism, both founded by men who lived about twenty-five hundred years ago.

Confucius was more a teacher of ethics than anything else. Perhaps he was to the Chinese what King Solomon was to the Hebrews.

Incidentally, Confucius once said, "If some years were added to my life, I would give fifty to studying the I Ching."

The founder of the Taoist system is usually considered to be Lao-tse, who according to legend was a contemporary of Confucius. But these two leaders didn't see eye to eye at all. Confucius was a vigorous teacher whose aim in life was to be a political power so he could guide his nation toward his high ethical standards. Lao-tse was a mystic who recommended that his followers lead a peaceful, desireless existence. To Lao-tse, it was senseless to follow a strict moral code and to interfere with the course of events. Rather, you should sink into the stream, "into the depths of the primal ground of all being," and do what comes naturally and spontaneously.

In *Tao-Te-Ching*, the most important book of the Taoists, are these lines:

> Great Tao is a boat that drifts,
> It can go this way; it can go that.
> The ten thousand creatures owe their existence
>   to it and it does
> Not disown them;
> Yet having produced them, it does not have
>   possession of them.
> Tao, though it covers the ten thousand
>   things like a garment,
> Makes no claim to be the master over them,
> And asks for nothing from them.

According to the ancient Chinese philosophers, in the beginning was Tao. But then Tao separated into the two prime principles, yang and yin. And from the many combinations of yang and yin everything else that is in the world has emerged.

Yang and yin produced the "five elements," which are metal, wood, fire, water and earth. Everything in life is in a constant state of flux; in fact, the only thing that you can be sure of is that it will change. The I Ching itself speaks of change as that which does not change. The purpose of the I Ching (remember that this means Book of Changes) is to show you how you can drift along with the changes, to help you transform tension from conflict into a smooth flow. You must adapt yourself to the flow of the world in order to live in harmony with the universe.

One Taoist writer tells this story: "There was once a man who was so afraid of his shadow and so disliked his own footsteps that he determined to run away from them. But the oftener he raised his feet the more footsteps he made, and though he ran very hard his shadow never left him. From this he inferred that he went too slowly, and ran as hard as he could without resting, the consequence being that his strength broke down and he died. He was not aware that by going into the shade he would have got rid of his shadow, and that by keeping still he would have put an end to his footsteps. Fool that he was."

That, in a nutshell, is the philosophical viewpoint of I Ching.

But that is not the viewpoint of Christianity.

It is understandable why young people are attracted to such a philosophy. They have seen the most advanced civilizations of the world threaten to bomb each other out of existence. The steel and concrete societies of our day care nothing about nature. So nature is raped and ravaged, soil is eroded, rivers are polluted, air is contaminated. And the older generation, sometimes their own parents, are obsessed with greed, striving insanely and violently for material gain. It's understandable, then, why young people would rather drop out of the sacrilegious rat race and become a part of the rhythm of nature.

But neither the materialistic culture of the Western world nor the impersonal unity with the Tao is the way set forth in the Bible of Christianity.

The Bible, from its opening pages, tells of a God who is an all-powerful Creator but also a personal friend for man. God made man for fellowship. And if fellowship is broken, it is man's fault, not God's. If guidance is needed, you don't need to get in tune with the creation; you need to get in touch with the Creator.

Ancient Chaldeans studied the stars abstractly to learn how the heavens went, and thus to learn how they should go. But according to the biblical book of Genesis,

God revealed himself personally to one man in Chaldea, Abraham, who became known as "the friend of God." When his contemporaries were led by the stars, Abraham was led by God.

In the New Testament, the Gospel of John begins with the familiar words, "In the beginning was the Word." This seems to resemble the Taoist view of "In the beginning was the Tao." The big difference comes when the Apostle John declares, "The Word was made flesh and dwelt among us." The big impersonal, philosophical Tao never did that. Later John tells us that Jesus was the Good Shepherd who gave His life for His sheep. The Tao never did that either.

The truth is that followers of I Ching are forsaking the possibility of a personal relationship with Jesus Christ in favor of impersonal, mystical guidance of I Ching.

Along with the proponents of I Ching, the Christian agrees that nothing in this life is accidental; everything has a purpose. But behind all of life's happenings stands an omnipotent and loving God. If the God of the Bible is sovereign, there is nothing beyond His jurisdiction. If it is true, as the New Testament says, that God is love, then even the smallest most happenstance details of life have meaning and significance.

But while I Ching tends to merge you into the cosmos and thus cause you to lose your distinctive identity, the Bible indicates that God's plan for you is unique and takes advantage of the distinctive qualities that are you.

Suppose you want guidance.

You have a big decision to make, and you don't feel capable of making the right choice all by yourself. What do you do?

You could go to a psychiatrist.

You could go to an astrologer.

You could consult the Book of Changes.

Or you could seek a Friend.

Edgar Cayce and the A.R.E.

JEREMIAH in the Old Testament was nicknamed the weeping prophet; Edgar Cayce (pronounced Casey) was called the sleeping prophet. And while they lived twenty-five hundred years apart, both of them gave prophecies that shook up thousands of their countrymen.

Who was Edgar Cayce?

Born in 1877 on a farm near Hopkinsville in south-western Kentucky, Cayce discovered early in life that he was clairvoyant. And from 1901 until his death in 1945, he gained international attention by putting himself to sleep in a self-induced hypnotic trance and then talking in his sleep. What was particularly remarkable about Cayce's talking in his sleep was that he could diagnose illnesses of people thousands of miles away and prescribe effectively for their treatment while in a trance. Yet Cayce had only a grammar school education and certainly no medical training.

Besides his medical "readings," mild, bespectacled Cayce also answered questions in his trances on religion, metaphysics and ancient history, and occasionally he prophesied regarding the future. All told, there are nearly fifteen thousand such "readings" neatly catalogued, classified and computerized in Virginia Beach, Virginia, where Cayce eventually made his headquarters. The $100,000 Remington Rand information retrieval system and the 200,000 indexed topic cards provide his followers with "one of the largest and most impressive records of psychic perception ever to emanate from a single individual."

In 1931 Cayce formed a foundation called the Association for Research and Enlightenment, Inc., to preserve the readings which are made available only to members. Today A.R.E. has more than thirteen thousand members (at $35 a year) but thousands more meet in weekly "Search for God" group sessions across the country. In New York City alone there are sixty such groups, plus others that also study Cayce's readings though unaffiliated with the national group.

A.R.E. claims that its study groups "do not propound a religion"; but they "do offer a contemporary and mature view of the reality of extrasensory perception, the importance of dreams, the logic of reincarnation, and a rational or loving personal concept of God, the practical use of prayer and meditation and a deeper understanding of the Bible."

One of the approved biographies of Edgar Cayce says, "The system of metaphysical thought which emerges from the reading of Edgar Cayce is a Christianized version of the mystery religions of ancient Egypt, Chaldea, Persia, India and Greece."

Besides the study groups, A.R.E. holds annual workshops in seven states, conducts a summer youth camp, operates its own press and has its own clinic and medical research division in Phoenix, Arizona.

Back in 1928 Cayce had a hospital of his own in Virginia Beach, where his medical readings could be tested under his own supervised conditions. Two years later he also began a university, Atlantic University. But for some reason, this psychic seer failed to foresee the effects of the stock market crash of 1929 and both institutions were lost in the depths of the Depression.

Yet, although he did not see how disastrous the stock market crash would be for his own organization, he did predict in a vague way an economic depression four months prior to the crisis. A.R.E. disciples claim moreover that he forecast every major crisis in the world between World War I and World War II. However, they admit that he erred slightly about Adolf Hitler, whom Cayce saw as essentially good.

But the "religion" of A.R.E. does not focus so much on the psychic predictions of Edgar Cayce as on his belief in reincarnation, a teaching that is reiterated repeatedly in his readings.

The teaching of reincarnation, one of his biographers hastens to say, "does not mean the return of human beings to animal form. . . . Reincarnation means evolution, the evolution of the spirit of man through many successive lifetimes on earth—sometimes as a man, sometimes as a woman, now as a pauper, now as a prince, here belonging to one race, there to another—until finally the spirit has reached a perfection enjoined on us by Christ." So, according to A.R.E., your present life on earth will determine what you will be when you return to earth again in your next existence. While a man who chooses to waste time in his present existence will not return as a turtle or a two-toed sloth, he might return as a housewife condemned to have fourteen children.

Once Cayce told a wheelchair-bound mother of three that she had suddenly been stricken with polio as punishment for having persecuted Christians in Nero's Rome.

The strange thing about A.R.E. doctrines is that Cayce

was a Bible student as a young man. For forty-six years he read through the Scriptures once a year and was an active church member and Sunday School teacher. He was not the only member of his family with a sixth sense, however. His grandfather had been able to find water by using two forks of a witch-hazel tree, and his father seemed to be a Pied Piper of snakes, believe it or not. But even as a lad, Edgar Cayce seemed to hear voices, have visions and dream strange dreams. When he told his parents about visions he had had, they thought he had been attending too many dramatic revival meetings. When he was still a teenager he had even discussed his dreams and psychic experiences with Evangelist Dwight L. Moody, who simply didn't know what to make of his strange gift.

Then in 1901, when Cayce was twenty-four years old, he suddenly lost his voice. For an entire year he could hardly speak above a whisper. He had to quit his job as a salesman and begin training as a photographer, a job that didn't require that he talk. Physicians were summoned, but to no avail. Finally it was suggested that Cayce put himself into a trance and that he be asked to describe his problem while in that state. So Cayce gave his first medical reading and it concerned himself. The medication and therapy which he prescribed restored his voice in a few minutes.

Until 1923, Cayce's hypnotic trance-talking continued primarily in medical areas. He was called a miracle-man because of his fantastic cures for everything from hay fever, arthritis and hemorrhoids to epilepsy, ulcers and cancer. Yet he refused to commercialize on this mysterious gift. He was offered money to assist speculators and fortune hunters; Cayce was not interested.

But in 1923 a wealthy printer named Arthur Lammers of Dayton, Ohio, was intrigued by Cayce's gift and summoned the forty-six-year-old photographer to his home. Lammers had been exploring astrology and an Eastern cult known as Theosophy. A branch of this cult had been founded in America in 1875 by a Madame Blavatsky and included reincarnation, karma and 11,000-year-old pyramids in its beliefs.

Lammers was obviously not interested in physical healing but rather was seeking confirmation of his newly acquired religious views. Cayce consented to check out Lammers' beliefs. While Cayce was in his self-imposed trance, Lammers asked a number of leading questions and Cayce responded by confirming his theories on reincarnation and astrology. At first, Lammers asked the psychic to provide him with his horoscope, but in subsequent readings he asked for his previous life incarnations. Soon such readings became known as life readings to Cayce devotees and were distinguished from Cayce's previous readings regarding physical health.

Initially, Cayce was disturbed by what he had told Lammers. He could not square the idea of reincarnation with the Bible. He feared that "his subconscious faculties had suddenly been commandeered by the forces of evil." Once he said, "If ever the devil was going to play a trick on me, this would be it."

But instead of following these intuitions, Cayce turned to Lammers for guidance and away from the New Testament teachings. Lammers soon convinced him that reincarnation might not be unbiblical if you interpreted some passages very symbolically.

Cayce's life readings frequently referred to the legendary lost island of Atlantis. Part of Lammers' theosophical system presumed that all souls that ever existed had been created in the beginning and reappeared periodically on earth. Since there are three billion souls on earth now, there must have been a heavily populated civilization very early in the earth's existence. Hence, the importance of Atlantis. Cayce's life readings indicate that many souls on earth today have been reincarnated from that fabled spot. According to Cayce, a glorious civilization (with TV, death rays, atomic power and laser beams) inhabited by a superhuman race developed on Atlantis nearly ten million years ago and lasted until about fifty thousand years ago. Perhaps even more startling was Cayce's prediction that the island of Atlantis would begin to reappear in 1968 or 1969. People are still looking for it.

But Cayce's haziness on the subject of Atlantis adds to the intrigue. His followers ransack his readings for clues and then seek to make them fit into current archeological discoveries.

When Cayce bought the idea of reincarnation, it drastically affected his outlook on Jesus Christ. Prior to his meeting with Lammers in 1923, Cayce held an orthodox Christian view that Jesus of Nazareth was the unique Son of God. But later in his readings he distinguished between Jesus and Christ. Sometimes he refers to "Jesus who became the Christ." In previous incarnations (at least those that were spoken of in the Bible) Jesus had been Adam (thus he sinned in the Garden of Eden), Enoch (who walked with God), Melchizedek (the mysterious king of Salem in the time of Abraham), Joseph (who was Pharaoh's right-hand man in Egypt), Joshua (who fought the battle of Jericho), and Jeshua (a high priest in the time of Ezra and Nehemiah). Actually, according to Cayce, when Christ became reincarnated in Jesus, it was his thirtieth incarnation.

One Cayce book puts it this way:

"In one reading an individual asked if he could gain perfection in his lifetime. (So as not to have to return to earth again.) The sleeping Cayce flippantly replied, 'Why should you expect to do in one lifetime what it took the Master thirty lives to attain?' ''

In Cayce's reconstruction of the life of Jesus, the sect of the Essenes plays a fantastically prominent role. His list of Essenes includes John the Baptist, Jesus, Joseph, Mary, Martha, Zebedee, the Bethlehem innkeeper and many more. If the Essenes were as prominent as Cayce imagined, it indeed is surprising that the Bible says so little about this group. Where the historical evidence of the Dead Sea Scrolls or of Josephus conflicts with A.R.E. teachings, the problem is brushed aside by saying, "No doubt there were many sects among the Essenes." No doubt there were.

According to Cayce, Jesus was tutored in prophecy on Mount Carmel. He was still in his early teens at the time, when a leader of the Essenes named Judy took him under her wing. There is no record that the Essenes ever congregated on Mount Carmel, but that doesn't matter.

After Judy got through with him, he journeyed to Egypt, then to India where he stayed for three years and finally to Persia. Incidentally, in Egypt, he allegedly was initiated into the secrets of the Great Pyramid, along with John the Baptist.

Much of Cayce's life of Christ is extraneous to the biblical account, and so it is impossible to check on it. Can you prove, for instance, that Jesus didn't go from Mount Carmel to Egypt and then to India when he was fifteen or sixteen years old? It's at least a three thousand mile walk across the Arabian desert and the Indian desert, but you can't prove that Jesus didn't do it.

At times however, Cayce blatantly contradicts the writers of Scripture. Luke, for example, must have been mistaken when he says that Jesus grew up in Nazareth; Cayce says that Capernaum was his hometown. Cayce apparently didn't like Luke, for in another place he states that Luke never wrote the Acts of the Apostles as has been traditionally believed. Instead the author was Cayce himself in a previous incarnation when he was known as Lucius, Bishop of Laodicea. In another incarnation, Cayce even got closer to Jesus. That was in Persia where Cayce was the grandfather and Jesus was the father of Zoroaster in the seventh century B.C. It's a small world.

It is also an amazing thing how people who happened to consult Cayce about their previous incarnations just happened to be relatives or friends of noted New Testament characters.

Even the New Testament characters themselves are wondrously interrelated by Cayce. Nicodemus was a brother-in-law of Peter. Martha was the wife of Nicodemus. Cleopas was the mother of blind Bartimaeus although Cleopas is a man's name. Jesus had a sister named Ruth who studied in the best schools of Greece and Rome. Most of these convenient identifications cannot be proven wrong, no matter how preposterous they may seem.

Yet to anyone who takes the Bible seriously, Cayce's imaginative distortion of Bible stories is not as serious as what he does in manipulating cardinal doctrines. God is depicted by Cayce as a creative force or the "universal creative energy."

Was Jesus the only begotten Son of God? Cayce in some classic circumlocutions says both yes and no. God had many Sons in the land of Atlantis but they "went astray." Thus, Jesus was not the only begotten Son of God. But Cayce explained it this way:

"When there was the beginning of man's advent into the plane known as earth, and he became a living soul, amenable to the laws that governed the plane itself, as presented, the Son of Man entered the earth as the first man, the son of man, the Son of God, the Son of the First Cause, making manifest in a material body. This was not the first spiritual influence, spiritual body, spiritual manifestation in the earth, but the first man—flesh and blood; the first carnal house, the first body amenable to the laws of the plane in its position in the universe."

Then neatly summing it up, Cayce said in his sleep, "Hence ... he became indeed the Son ... as the development came to the oneness with the position in that which man terms the Triune. . . . Thus, from man's viewpoint, becoming the only, the first begotten of the Father." It was amazing how Cayce could clarify things in his sleep.

If you have trouble following Cayce's semantics, perhaps this statement from Gina Cerminara's A.R.E.-approved book, *Many Mansions*, will state the position for you more plainly:

"For almost twenty centuries the moral sense of the Western world has been blunted by a theology which teaches the vicarious atonement of sin through Christ, the Son of God. . . . All men and women are the sons of God. . . . Christ's giving of his life . . . is no unique event in history. . . . To build these two statements, therefore—that Christ was the Son of God and that he died for man's salvation—into a dogma, and then to make salvation depend upon believing that dogma, has been the great psychological crime. . . . It is a psychological crime because it places responsibility for redemption on something external to the self; it makes salvation dependent on belief in the divinity of another person rather than on self-transformation through belief in one's own intrinsic divinity."

Such a teaching is not only diametrically opposed to twenty centuries of Christian doctrine, it is also opposed to the Bible and to the words of Jesus Christ Himself. Repeatedly the Bible declares that man cannot save himself; he must have help from the outside.

"No human being can be justified in the sight of God for having kept the law," says the Apostle Paul in Romans 3:20 (Living Bible). "Law brings only the consciousness of sin. . . . All alike have sinned and are deprived of the divine splendor. . . ."

How then can a man be saved? Paul goes on to say, "God designed him [Jesus Christ] to be the means of expiating sin by his sacrificial death, effective through faith."

But that's just it, Cayce would say. Or as he actually did say, "Since we all have sinned and come short of the glory of God, we would be doomed if we had only one life for making ourselves acceptable to the Father." That's why reincarnation is necessary. And since it took Jesus thirty reincarnations to make it according to Cayce, it will take most of us quite a few incarnations longer.

What evidence is there for reincarnation?

You have to take Cayce's word for it. And his word is reinforced by his psychic insights into the past, present and future which are sometimes right and sometimes wrong. Perhaps he deserves to be known as the most powerful psychic of modern times, although one observer says "the evidence is shrouded in fiction, faith and exaggeration." But even if he was, that doesn't prove that Cayce's sleep-talking is right about reincarnation.

Does the Bible support reincarnation? Cayce and his followers distort a couple of Bible references such as the appearance of Elijah and Moses on the Mount of Transfiguration to prove their point. But this really disproves their point. For even after many centuries these two Old Testament characters were the same people they always were. They weren't reincarnated at all.

The Bible never gives a clue that there is a second chance for any individual. Decisions that you make in this solitary life apparently determine your eternal destiny. Perhaps the Scripture verse that decimates the A.R.E. position most strikingly is Hebrews 9:27, 28: "It is the lot of men to die once, and after death comes judgment, so Christ was offered once to bear the burden of men's sins."

Yet what is puzzling to many people is the fact that Cayce had a psychic, almost supernatural gift. If he could be trusted to diagnose the illness of someone who lived thousands of miles away, shouldn't he be trusted to tell the truth in religious areas?

J. Stafford Wright, author of the book *Mind, Man and the Spirits*, made this assessment of Cayce, "It would seem that Cayce had a very rare psychic capacity, an extension of what is sometimes called psychometry, in which a person can perceive something of the past, present and future of the owner of some object which the sensitive handles. Cayce's deep mind worked by a telepathic identification. He could identify with another's body, and perceive what that body realized to be its true state. He could perceive what the body was needing to assist its recovery."

Frankly, we don't know much as yet about such psychic power, except we know that some people have it in a much greater degree than others.

Despite Cayce's undeniable psychic powers, he certainly doesn't bat a thousand as a prophet. Even his dating of the Great Pyramid is about eight thousand years too early, and that isn't even prophecy. A.R.E. fans are trying to make the best of his predictions regarding Atlantis, but thus far that hasn't reappeared either.

Then, looking ahead, Cayce predicted that North Carolina and Georgia would disappear into the Atlantic

Ocean sometime after 1960 and those two states would be followed by New York somewhere in the early 1970s. About the same time the West Coast would slide into the Pacific. (Other seers have been saying the same thing about the earthquake-prone regions and eventually maybe one of them will be right.) Besides a few spots in the Midwest and in Canada, Cayce also predicted that the safest place in North America will be Virginia Beach, Virginia, which has since that prediction become a boomtown and the headquarters of the A.R.E. movement.

And one other thing. Anyone who puts his mind in neutral should check to see who is behind the wheel. Whenever Cayce went into a self-induced trance, he was at the mercy of outside forces. How much Cayce was unconsciously misled by Lammers and others, we will never know.

Not everything that you say in your sleep is inspired by God. It can also come from the intricate workings of the subconscious mind or it can come from a demonic source.

For a good portion of his life, Cayce was a commercial photographer. He understood very well the mechanics of his trade. A blank film is developed in the dark.

The nature of a photograph, whether it is a formal family picture or pornography, depends not on the film but on the photographer who uses the camera. During his trances, Cayce's mind was like a blank film that would be developed in the dark.

I believe that Cayce allowed his camera to get into the wrong hands.

Spiritualism 6

JUST WHEN WE thought Spiritualism was dead and buried, it rose up again. Today it is just as hale and hearty as it was a hundred years ago. Some of the credit for its resurrection goes to Arthur Ford, a Disciples of Christ minister who doubled as a medium for about fifty years.

Some of the rest of the credit goes to Episcopal Bishop James A. Pike, who was so strongly influenced by Arthur Ford that he wrote a book, *The Other Side*, a bestseller for many months. Then in 1967, Pike had a televised seance with Arthur Ford which took Spiritualism into the living rooms of millions of Americans.

Actually, only 150,000 Americans officially list Spiritualism as their religion. Dr. Charles Braden says five hundred thousand to seven hundred thousand might be a more accurate total. But in addition, Gallup polls have revealed that millions of Americans believe that man can communicate with the dead.

In America, it all began one fateful night in Hydesville, New York, March 31, 1848. Hearing strange noises upstairs, Mrs. John Fox went to investigate. Her two daughters, Margaret, fifteen, and Katie, twelve, said that they were in communication with the dead. When they asked questions, they were answered by rappings. One tap meant No; two taps meant Doubtful; three taps meant Yes. In the nights that followed, the Fox girls said that the friendly ghost was a murdered peddler named Charles B. Rosma, who allegedly had been murdered in the basement of their home some years earlier.

Neighbors were called in to listen to the dialogue. Soon as many as three hundred visitors were crowding the little wooden house for the nightly rap sessions. Scholarly committees were brought in to "test the spirits," and while they refused to admit it was genuine, yet they could not prove it to be a fraud. In the next six years, Spiritualism spread like an epidemic across the country. By 1854, 15,000 Spiritualists petitioned Congress for an impartial investigation of the Hydesville happenings.

Some investigators claimed that the noises were made by "deliberate snapping of toe joints," or by a maid who was in cahoots with the girls, but by that time Spiritualism was a wildfire out of control.

In Millfield, Ohio, a farmer named Jonathan Koons built a log cabin "under spirit direction." At night, lights flashed, spirit hands played musical instruments and furniture floated through the air. It is said that "By 1857 the majority of western Ohio's population were Spiritualists, and for some years the orthodox churches stood empty each Sunday."

Spiritualist lecturers, including the Fox sisters, were roaming the country like revivalists. And they won many converts, including such prominent names as William Lloyd Garrison, James Fenimore Cooper, William Cullen Bryant and Horace Greeley. In fact, there were even rumors that President Abraham Lincoln himself was a secret believer in Spiritualism.

After the Civil War, however, magicians learned how to duplicate the Spiritualists' tricks. Everything the spirits could do, the magicians could do better. Gradually, the American public became dubious of Spiritualism itself.

But the real blow to Spiritualism came in 1888 when Margaret Fox, then fifty-five years old, oft married, poverty-stricken and an alcoholic, claimed to be converted to Catholicism and confessed in a newspaper article that she had really been snapping her toes for the past forty years and that accounted for everything. A year later, she reversed her position again, and withdrew her confession, but by then the Spiritualism balloon had been punctured. It seemed that Spiritualism was dead and buried.

During the roaring 1920s Spiritualism enjoyed a brief revival, as seances, table-rappings and fortune-telling were naughty but exciting excursions. During that decade Arthur Ford became caught up in the practice. Ford claimed to have a spirit-guide named Fletcher, who was a French-Canadian killed in World War I. But the revival of Spiritualism was short-lived. The Depression seemed to force it to retreat again until the mid-1960s.

Today, there are eighteen different Spiritualist denominations in America; it is obvious that unity is not one of their cardinal doctrines. Yet all of them are tied together by the belief that it is possible to have "communication between this and the spirit world by means of mediumship," as the National Spiritualist Association stated fifty years ago.

Spiritualism should not be confused with spiritism, which is the worship of spirits as practiced in many of the more primitive countries of the world. Voodoo, black magic and macumba are outgrowths of spiritism.

Many Spiritualists are interested in communicating with a recently departed loved one. Those bereaved friends may consult a Spiritualist medium for a brief period in their lives, although sometimes the consultation becomes a habit if the contact is particularly satisfying.

Many others scorn the sentimentalities of a seance but try to discover from the "advanced spirits" a philosophy of the universe. And somewhat surprisingly, considering the assortment of Spiritualist denominations and the number of independent mediums who claim no allegiance to any particular group, there are more similarities of teaching than many people realize.

But the prevalent characteristic of all those is the communication with the dead by means of a spirit.

What is a Spiritualist seance like?

Spiritualists say there are six types of seances: passivity, vocal reality, trumpet revelation, lights, transfiguration and levitation. In one sitting, several of these might be witnessed. One former medium, Victor Ernest, describes it like this: "Seances are noted for quietness. As the participants enter and meditate, they block out their tensions, worries, anxieties and problems. . . . Lights are turned down at every seance. Shades are drawn in the daytime and at night."

Seances always begin on time. If you come late, the spirits might be offended.

After a time of meditation, an object may move. Sometimes it is a glass on the table. Sometimes it is a small board on which a message is automatically written. Then the medium may go into a trance. His body may seem to be possessed by the spirit. When he opens his mouth, the voice you hear is different from the medium's voice. In fact, the entire personality of the medium seems to have changed.

Usually, the medium claims to be controlled by one

spirit-guide repeatedly, although some say that three or four different spirits speak to them and through them. These spirit-guides are their contact with the spirit world. During the course of many seances, the mediums get to know their spirit-guide quite well.

Besides the seances, the Spiritualist Church also has its regular church services. The spirit-guide, rather than the medium, preaches the sermon. During the service, there may be the recitation of the Twenty-third Psalm, an offering, silent meditation, and the singing of hymns. While the hymns may resemble Protestant hymns, significant changes are made. For instance, the traditional "invitation" song, "Just As I Am," is stripped of all reference to the death of Jesus Christ and His atonement on the cross.

The Spiritualist version reads:

> Just as I am, without one plea,
> But that, O God, Thou madest me,
> And that my life is found in Thee
> O God of love, I come, I come.
>
> Just as I am, nor poor, nor blind,
> Nor bound by chains in soul or mind,
> For all of Thee within I find
> O God of love, I come, I come.
>
> Just as I am, Thou wilt receive,
> Though dogmas I may ne'er believe,
> Nor heights of holiness achieve,
> O God of love, I come, I come.

In the Spiritualist version of this old hymn, such lines as "But that Thy blood was shed for me" are omitted. Also gone is any reference to man's inadequacy to save himself. And from the last stanza it is obvious that neither doctrine nor holiness is integral to Spiritualistic religion.

Yet despite its disclaimers to dogma, a core of Spiritualist doctrine is well accepted not only by the mediums but also by the spirit-guides who speak through the mediums. Many years ago the National Spiritualist Association set forth these "Seven Principles":

1. The Fatherhood of God
2. The Brotherhood of Man
3. Continuous Existence
4. Communion of Spirits and Ministry of Angels
5. Personal Responsibility
6. Compensation and Retribution Hereafter for Good or Evil Done on Earth
7. A Path of Endless Progression

In his book, also titled *Many Mansions*, Lord Dowding wrote, "The first thing which the orthodox Christian has to face is that the doctrine of the Trinity seems to have no adherents in advanced circles of the spirit world. The divinity of Christ as a co-equal partner with the Father is universally denied. Jesus Christ was indeed the Son of God, as also are we sons of God."

Furthermore, the *Spiritualist Manual* declares, "every human soul born into life is a child of God and the opportunities for development will at some time be realized and taken advantage of by each one. Spiritualism proclaims 'The doorway to reformation is never closed against any soul here or hereafter.' "

It goes on to say, "Merely leaving the physical body does not change the condition of the spirit, which is the actual personality. It must learn to desire and to progress to higher and better conditions, just as we do on earth."

While many Spiritualists claim that they practice a high form of Christianity, yet obviously Spiritualism cannot rightly claim to be Christianity at all. Christian concepts are used. But if the heart of Christianity is removed—if Jesus Christ is not the unique Son of God, if his death on the cross is not the unique means of reconciliation between God and man, if there is no heaven and no hell, but only astral spheres of progress, if there is no importance placed on man's decision in this life affecting his eternal existence—then Spiritualism is not a version but rather a perversion of Christianity.

The spirit-guides are amazingly uniform in their religious and philosophical moorings. Red Cloud, the spirit-guide for Medium Estelle Roberts in England, says, "God is not a being but a force of good which permeates the universe and is infinite. . . . Never forget that we are all individual parts of God, which is the Whole. It is not to be expected that we can achieve perfection within the span of one lifetime. After death we go to the astral plane, on which there are many worlds of consciousness. After a period we incarnate once again on this earth, or some other interpenetrating world, for the further progress of our souls."

The Rev. Ellen Resch of the Spiritual Science Mother Church in New York says, "Spiritual science believes in the universal spirit, the teachings of the Scriptures (Christian, Indian, Buddhist), reincarnation and love between neighbors." Her spirit-guide is another Indian. For some reason, American Indians seem to make good spirit-guides.

Many Spiritualists today are Spiritualists with a lower-case s. They don't want to identify themselves with the Spiritualist Church in any of its eighteen denominations. Ena Twigg, Arthur Ford, and George Daisley, the three mediums whom Bishop James Pike used, all operated independently. Said Ford, "I give the Spiritualist Church credit for keeping the subject alive until the scientists were compelled to look at it." Daisley, who originally had been in the Spiritualist Church, left it, saying, "Spiritualism could no longer give me the high-minded religion I wanted—too much ego and hanky-panky."

Yet, although these three are not members of the Spiritualist Church, their beliefs are certainly similar to it. Mrs. Twigg gave Bishop Pike this message from his son: "Don't ever believe that God can be personalized. He is the Central Force." As for Jesus, young Jim's spirit allegedly declared: "They talk about him—a mystic, a seer, yes, a seer. Oh, but Dad, they don't talk about him as a Saviour."

According to Ford's spirit-guide Fletcher: "Jesus is just another person, been here longer."

And Daisley: "I haven't heard anything personally about Jesus. Nobody around me seems to talk about Him."

While the messages were a bit contradictory, it was obvious that they were certainly not Christian.

Pike's son, who had committed suicide on a bad LSD trip, is supposed to have appeared to Daisley in his Santa Barbara office, and said, "I am Jim Pike, the bishop's son. . . . I want you to help me communicate with my father."

In Bishop Pike's first sitting with Daisley, the spirit told Pike personal things that no one else would have known. "I was with you the other day," the spirit said, "when you could not find a book in your library."

The "spirit" of the young Pike also explained the reason for his reappearance. "I want to do all I can," he said, "to bring forth the knowledge of life after death. I have a role to fulfill by becoming more effective in this type of communication."

Hardly a year had passed when Bishop Pike met with Medium Arthur Ford in Toronto as TV cameras ground away. Ford announced calmly that the bishop's son was in contact with Fletcher, Ford's French-Canadian spirit-guide. Fletcher, using Ford's vocal cords, referred to places and events in the life of young Jim Pike that neither the medium nor the bishop had any conscious knowledge about. But when the spirit started explaining what the afterlife was like, it sounded very much like the interpretation given by the Spiritualist Church.

Of course, the big question is: Is all of this really on the level? Or is it a big fraud? Do the mediums really contact the spirits of the departed? Or do they just think they do?

There are probably three answers to the question.

1. In the 125-year history of modern Spiritualism, there has been undeniably a great deal of fakery.

One notorious case in Great Britain concerned a medium named Mrs. Helen Duncan. She was convicted for fraud because photographs of her "materializations" showed them to be made out of cheesecloth.

Many people who come to mediums are already in a disturbed state of mind because of bereavement, and desperately want to hear from their loved one again; so it is relatively easy to play tricks on the mind. Of course, trickery comes easier because the seance takes place in a darkened room.

Sir Arthur Conan Doyle, creator of Sherlock Holmes and an ardent supporter of Spiritualism, was himself taken in by a book of fairy photographs that sixteen-year-old Elsie Wright had snapped.

One of the most notorious frauds regarded Madame Blavatsky, the founder of Theosophy (then living in India), who claimed to communicate with the masters of her religion, two Tibetan mahatmas, by astral telegraph. Investigators from the British Society for Psychical Research uncovered forgeries and secret panels that explained everything. Madame left hurriedly on the next boat; the slow boat ride to Europe gave her time to plan a textbook for another religion.

Even the mediums who brought Jim Pike back to his father might have been fraudulent, according to Milbourne Christopher, a past president of the Society of American Magicians. He said that the "telekinesis and subsequent events might have been contrived. On the surface, it almost looks like a conspiracy by someone trying to play on the feelings he had after his son's death, possibly to draw him into Spiritualism."

Joseph T. Bayly, in his book, *What About Horoscopes?* suggests, "Pike was a public figure. Research could have uncovered many things about his past that he'd forget had ever been printed or spoken. By his own admission, for instance, he had been on hundreds of television shows."

2. While a percentage of spiritualistic phenomena may be traced to trickery or fraud, much of it cannot be explained that way. Even former mediums who have renounced the craft say this.

Psychologist Lawrence LeShan says that there is "no question" that mediums and other sensitives do produce facts that they could not otherwise know through investigation or normal sensory perception. "This does not necessarily mean, however, that messages come from the dead. As scientists, we must choose the simplest explanation, so we prefer to assume that there is such a thing as extrasensory perception."

Dr. Stanley Krippner, noted researcher in this field, believes that the findings of modern physics on the interrelation of mind and matter might also eventually explain many of the things that go on in Spiritualism.

Many mediums recognize this fact also. Eileen Garrett, a medium who has investigated her gift more honestly than many others, wrote, "In examining my own process of clairvoyance, I have become aware that I draw knowledge which helps me build the images of the dead relatives and friends of those who need help, from the subconscious minds of the sitters."

Dr. J. Stafford Wright, Anglican clergyman and student of psychic phenomena, says, "When one has eliminated occasional trickery, there is nothing here that could not be ascribed to nonspiritualist ESP. . . . There may be something like a psychic switchboard which may link one person to another at a deep level, so that feelings and information concerning past, present and future can be recovered, experienced and shared. We may accept this as an unusual part of the human situation and have no need to introduce the concept of spirits as conveyors of the information."

He goes on to say, "There is a strong probability that communications of this kind are not directly from the departed, but are latent memories of him or her, clothed with whatever the medium believes about the nature of the next world."

While most mediums are convinced that they are communicating with the spirit world, many psychic researchers have their reservations. But how do they explain the spirit-guide who speaks through the medium?

Allen Spraggett, author of *The Unexplained*, says that in his more than fifty sittings with various mediums, he has talked to a variety of spirit-guides. "They've included Egyptian priests, Chinese sages, more Red Indians than I can remember, an Arab sheik or two, a Negro mammy, a garrulous child named Ivy, a German doctor, a Scots Highlander, and others." And that doesn't even include Fletcher.

As far as the medium is concerned, he is usually in an unconscious state and doesn't know what is coming out of his mouth until he wakes up and someone tells him. Is it possible, though, that the medium by self-hypnosis has convinced himself that he is a disembodied spirit?

Word-association tests given to Mrs. Garrett and Mrs. Gladys Leonard, another well-known British medium, seemed to indicate that spirit controls represented aspects of the mediums' unconscious minds which were repressed in the normal state.

Mrs. Garrett also allowed medical tests to be made on her, first when she was in a normal state and then when she was in her mediumistic trance. Because she had two spirit-guides, one an Arab, and one a Persian named Abdul, each was tested. The surprising thing was that blood count, blood clotting time, blood sugar tests and electrocardiograms all indicated striking differences among the three states of Mrs. Garrett's existence. In fact, the cardiologist who examined the electrocardiograms said he "didn't think it was possible for the three readings to be of the same person."

The evidence would seem to indicate that a high percentage of what goes on in a seance is psychic phenomena, which includes clairvoyance, psychokinesis and telepathy. The medium, whether she knows it or not, is probably also the message.

3. The third possibility, of course, is that Spiritualism is just what the mediums say it is—contact with those who have died, by means of a spirit-guide.

Obviously, most mediums sincerely believe this to be the case. The fact that they are surprised by much of the information revealed would attest to this idea.

But many things are wrong with the notion. While the spirits often reveal little-known facts, they can often be surprisingly inaccurate. People who are still living are called dead; and an imaginary person who is in the mind of the sitter can be conjured up in a seance just as readily as a real person.

Then there is the strange fact that this whole religion started only in the mid-1800s. Where were the spirits before that? Couldn't they find receptive mediums through whom to communicate their messages?

And then there are the statements of former mediums. One such was R. B. Davenport, who was quoted in the *New York Daily Tribune* and *New York World* back in 1888 as saying, "I am here tonight as one of the founders of Spiritualism to denounce it as an absolute falsehood from beginning to end, as the flimsiest of superstitions, the most wicked blasphemy in the world."

But what other possibilities are there? If there is a spirit world as the Bible declares, then the distinct possibility exists that some contacts are made, not with the departed spirits as alleged, but with evil spirits.

While most mediums admit that both good and bad spirits exist, they naturally insist that their control spirit is a good spirit. However, former mediums who have been converted to Christianity allege that all the spirits of Spiritualism are evil.

In *I Talked with Spirits*, Victor Ernest declares: "Just what are these spirits and how do these spiritualistic phenomena occur? I cannot emphasize too strongly they are part of Satan's strategy to deceive Christians and to enslave those who as yet do not know God."

Besides the testimony of former mediums, the testimony of the spirit-guides themselves condemns the practice. The fact that its teachings undercut the basic Christian beliefs regarding Jesus and why He came to earth is enough to pronounce a verdict of anti-Christian upon it.

In addition, there are the harmful aftereffects that psychiatry knows about. A leading psychologist from the

University of Freiburg in Germany wrote, "People who try to discover what life after death is like through spiritism and superstition are in danger of falling prey to the dark and hidden side of their own minds and souls. . . . I have quite a number of patients who have suffered serious psychic disturbances through the misuse of such practices. Their personalities have been split and they have been utterly confused by the spirits on which they have called."

Another researcher has commented, "Involvement often results in subjection to such a degree that the individual is almost, if not totally, dependent upon the mediums for information and advice, until the victim is hopelessly entangled in a labyrinth of evil influences and control."

All of this can hardly result from "good spirits."

One medium wrote about his relationship with his control spirit: "I am aware that my guide loves me. He usually refers to me, when speaking in a trance, as 'my beloved one,' or 'my beloved instrument.' At times of depression or disappointment in my life he has come to comfort me. And I have been aware at those times of a great love, waves and waves of it, pouring over me from the spirit world."

The King James Version of the Bible has an interesting translation of the Hebrew word *ob*. It translates the word as "familiar spirit." Most modern translations use the word "medium" or "spirits of the dead," but apparently today's mediums do have familiar spirits. However, the Hebrew word *ob* was sometimes used of a ventriloquist, someone who spoke with different voices and personalities. Dr. J. Stafford Wright says it "clearly refers to a medium with a control spirit." And the Bible warns repeatedly against such people who are possessed of familiar spirits or who allow their voices to be used by spirits.

Listen to these biblical warnings:

"Do not turn to mediums; do not seek them out to be defiled by them" (Leviticus 19:31).

"There shall not be found among you anyone who . . . casts a spell or a medium or one who calls up the dead. . . . The Lord your God has not allowed you to do so" (Deuteronomy 18:10, 14).

The Living Bible's translation of Isaiah 8:19, 20 puts it plainly: "So why are you trying to find out the future by consulting witches and mediums? Don't listen to their whisperings and mutterings. Can the living find out their future from the dead? Why not ask your God?"

The only contact with the spirit world which is endorsed by the Bible is contact with God, and this contact is made through prayer. There is no hocus-pocus about prayer, no darkened rooms, no floating objects. And millions of Christians testify that it establishes an intimate contact with God Himself.

Just prior to His death on the cross, Jesus taught His disciples much about prayer, but He also told them about the Holy Spirit, the third Person of the Trinity, who would come and dwell within them. He would be their Comforter, He would be their Spirit-Guide as He would "guide you into all truth," He would be the presence of God living inside them. Consequently when Christians believe that they have the Spirit of God within them, why then should they need to seek out any lesser spirit?

The Bible also urges Christians to test the spirits. Spiritualists talk much about this, but they omit the key biblical test. According to the Bible the key test is what the spirit says about Jesus Christ. Here is where Spiritualism flunks the test utterly.

Most of the sophisticated older generation today smile at the idea of a spirit world, of unseen powers and forces in the universe. Most of the younger generation are quite serious about the possibility and are interested in exploring.

As Spiritualism is examined, some of it must be ascribed to fakery, and much of it to psychic phenomena, but there is still some left that cannot be easily ascribed to anything but a supernatural source. That leaves the two other possibilities: either it comes from the spirits of the departed dead, as the Spiritualists would have it, or from evil spirits, as the Bible would have it.

That is the choice that confronts many young people today.

Since Spiritualism seems to thrive in darkness, the Apostle Paul's words seem appropriate: "Be not ye therefore partakers with them. For ye were sometimes darkness, but now are ye light" (Ephesians 5:7,8).

But why not check it out?

For the same reason you don't check the contents of a gas tank with a lighted match. Too many people have already been irreparably burned.

For the same reason you don't check the rim of the Grand Canyon on a dark night. Too many people have fallen and it's a long climb back up.

NOBODY BELIEVES IN witches any more, do they?

Nobody except the witches themselves, that is. And their numbers are multiplying faster than you can shoo them away with a broomstick.

In Germany, according to the German Medical Information Service, 10,000 people are engaged in witchcraft, with the numbers increasing steadily since 1968.

Back in 1951 in England, the British Parliament in a neighborly gesture rescinded an ancient witchcraft act. After all, why have a law on the books to prohibit something that really doesn't exist anyway? Today there are 30,000 practicing witches in England.

How many witches are there in America? One witch says there are nearly ten million practicing witches in America. The same supposedly authoritative source within witchcraft says that of these, four million are officially registered with witchcraft centers. That would mean there are more registered witches in America than there are registered Episcopalians or Presbyterians. We think that is a case of witchful thinking.

Since the U.S. Census Bureau doesn't take a count of

witches, it is hard to get accurate figures. Sybil Leek, a self-styled British witch as well as a medium, says that the witch population has exploded 40 percent in the past five years. Today more than four hundred covens are scattered across the country, according to Sybil.

On the other hand, you can take the conservative estimate of Nat Freedland, author of *The Occult Explosion*, who says, "From the visible manifestations of the witchcraft scene it's doubtful if there are more than six or seven thousand really active practicing witches around today—three thousand in England . . . perhaps two thousand in North America, and another one or two thousand scattered around the globe." So you can take your choice as to whom you wish to believe.

Best known among witches is probably Sybil Leek, who claims to be 560 years old if you count previous incarnations. Besides being an antique dealer and part-time newspaper columnist, she is a medium, astrologer, psychic, numerologist and witch. A prolific writer, she has done more than anyone else to publicize and legitimatize witchcraft in America. Today she is making so much money on other things that she has almost forgotten how to cast a spell.

But of course there is also Louise Huebner, attractive mother of three, who has been proclaimed the Official Witch of Southern California. No doubt it was all a mistake, but a public official, Eugene Debs, gave her a ceremonial scroll bestowing upon her the dubious honor when she cast a spell aimed to "increase the sexual vitality of Los Angeles." When Debs realized how much free publicity he had given to witchcraft, he disavowed the scroll. Promptly Mrs. Huebner revoked her spell.

Where that leaves the future of Los Angeles nobody knows. But it certainly left Louise Huebner with a lot of publicity, a weekly column in twenty community newspapers, a book, *Power Through Witchcraft*, a record album, "Seduction through Witchcraft," a witches' cookbook and maybe even a TV series.

But that's the way it is these days in California. You can enroll in courses in witchcraft in many high schools and colleges there. Midpeninsula Free University, for instance, offers five such courses. Both San Francisco's Heliotrope Free University and San Diego State College have courses in witchcraft with real witches as professors. In the San Diego area alone there are more than two dozen covens including two high school covens with fifty members each.

But you don't have to go to California to find witchcraft courses being taught. New York University, the University of South Carolina and the University of Georgia have all had popular courses in the sinister subject. In fact, sixty-eight institutions of higher learning now have courses in it.

Make no mistake about it, witchcraft is gaining a wider and wider following. It used to be assumed that it was a religion for superstitious, uneducated folk. No more. In New York today, a doctor, a teacher and a businessman as well as several housewives and college students compose the thirteen members of one coven. Another coven on Long Island includes a hardware clerk, a sign painter, an airline employee and an Air Force officer.

You must keep in mind, of course, that the classic text in the field of witchcraft by E. E. Evans-Pritchard, *Witchcraft, Oracles and Magic,* published by Oxford University Press a generation ago, says flatly, "Witchcraft is an imaginary offense because it is impossible."

One of the biggest blots on American history was the Salem witchcraft trials, when nineteen alleged witches were hanged in a climate of mass hysteria. The problem, as most scholars have seen it, was not with the supposed witches but with the ordinary citizenry that allowed itself to panic. There is no such thing as witchcraft, so how can it be prosecuted?

This has been the accepted viewpoint for the past hundred years with very few exceptions. One exception was British anthropologist Margaret Murray who claimed that witchcraft had an objective reality. But she wasn't taken seriously.

Then in 1969, Historian Chadwick Hansen in his significant study *Witchcraft at Salem* concluded: "Witchcraft actually did exist and was widely practiced. . . . It worked then as it works now."

And even more recently, Dr. John Charles Cooper, chairman of the department of philosophy at Eastern Kentucky University, wrote: "There is such a thing as witchcraft; it exists and it works. I have seen the fear that it inspires in college students enrolled in large universities, fear that passes over into clinical paranoia in some instances. . . . And I have seen it work on white, middle-class, well-educated people in the heartland of the United States."

B. G. Parrinder in his book *Witchcraft* states, "There is little sign of a decrease in witchcraft belief with increasing education."

But why is there so much confusion about witchcraft? Why doesn't anyone seem to know how many witches there are? Why can't scholars agree whether it actually exists?

Part of the problem is in definition. How do you define a witch?

A dictionary might say that a witch is "a person who practices witchcraft." And what's witchcraft? It is "the art practiced by witches."

Another dictionary says a witch is "a person who practices magic."

An encyclopedia says witchcraft is "the use of supposed supernatural power for antisocial ends."

A more scholarly treatise defines it: "Witchcraft is the process of one rational being willing evil against another. Witchcraft takes many forms, but in every case it is antisocial."

Now if you ask a witch, you will be told that there are different kinds of witchcraft. There is black witchcraft and white witchcraft. A black witch practices magic that will aid himself no matter how it affects others. Unfortunately, the white witches don't wear white hats, so you can't tell them apart.

Furthermore, you will be told that witchcraft is "the Old Religion." By "Old Religion," witches mean that it is the original religion, going back long before Christianity. Hans Holzer, a very sympathetic commentator on witchcraft, explains it like this:

"The early religion of western and northern Europe was a nature religion in which the forces of the world around man were considered manifestations of divine power. In this respect, the early religion was pantheistic. . . . The image of the Mother Goddess, representing the forces in nature, developed and was eventually given a companion in the Horned God, representing the male principle. To the contemporaries of this civilization, the faith was simply 'religion,' but after the advent of Christianity it became known as 'the Old Religion' to emphasize the contrast."

The Horned God, the witches hasten to explain, isn't really Satan, although he certainly looks the part. He is probably Pan, the Roman god of nature, who was half-god and half-man. But it doesn't help the witches' cause when they speak of him as Lucifer, a name that the Bible bestowed upon Satan. The ancestry of the Old Religion can no doubt be traced to Artemis of the Greeks and Diana of the Romans, and perhaps even to the moon goddess of the Egyptians and the fertility goddesses of the Canaanites.

Through the Dark Ages, witchcraft thrived in Europe and particularly Great Britain. In the Celtic language it was called *wicca*, from which we get the word witch.

Quoting Hans Holzer again, "The priestess and the priest of the Old Religion were referred to by just that name, not by anything as fancy as head witch or such, and the members of the community did not originally call themselves witches, but merely members of the coven." *Coven*, like the word *covenant*, can be traced back to the Latin, meaning "to come together."

Holzer insists that witchcraft "is not a mockery of any other faith nor does it include in its service any element even remotely similar to actual Christian practice or worship." He contrasts it with Satanism, which is definitely a perversion of Christianity. White witches are supposedly good and noble. Yet worshipers of the Old Religion may use drugs, herbs, ESP and other psychic influences as well as incantations to cast their spells. While some of them will cast a spell at the drop of a hat, most of them will defer such drastic action until the next meeting of their coven.

Members of a coven, usually thirteen in number—the priest or priestess, plus six men and six women—meet once a month, on the night of the full moon. The monthly meeting is called an esbat. In addition, there are eight sabbats: one at the beginning of each season, one for Halloween, one for the Maypole dance on May Eve, one on February Eve and one on August Eve. The Bible of the Old Religion is called *The Book of Shadows*, which describes their rites, cures, charms and spells, and it is read at every esbat and sabbat.

So far witchcraft may seem quite innocent and you

may wonder why witches would be persecuted in ancient times. But let's look at it a little more carefully:

"The Old Religion is a nature religion," says one of their priests. "And sex between men and women is an integral part of our ritual. . . . Witches have always used drugs."

Raymond Buckland, high priest of about a score of covens from Boston to San Francisco, explains that witchcraft is a "religion of freedom, joy in the sensual appetites and in nature." In the Buckland esbats, which are a bit more subdued than those of the typical coven, the witches go down into the Buckland basement, take off their clothes (they call it becoming "skyclad,") and immerse themselves in saltwater to become purified. Then stark-naked they form a nine-foot circle and sing ("Yod He, Van He—Blessed be"), chant and dance to tape-recorded music until they work up a good ecstatic sweat, while incense is burning in a brass censer. Broomsticks are sometimes used, following an ancient fertility ceremony, but the witches don't fly away on them. Finally, as they drink wine and tea, they hear readings from *The Book of Shadows*.

Why is it necessary for the group to be naked? One wizard explains, "The human body has tremendous energy forces but clothing can cut them off."

Each new member is initiated into the coven in a traumatic ceremony. Blindfolded with hands tied behind her back, the new member is led naked (or sometimes clad in a light robe) into the midst of the ring of witches and wizards. After the high priest reads the charge, which usually refers to the belief in reincarnation and the worship of the "powers of nature as represented by the female principles of fertility and creation and the male principle of procreation and providing the necessities of life," the postulant is scourged, then lifted to her feet and given the witches' five-fold kiss, including the feet, the knees, the sexual organs, the breasts and the lips. Finally, after taking an oath, the initiate has the blindfold removed and has passed into the first degree of witchcraft. If it is a man who is being initiated, the ceremony is conducted by the high priestess.

Second and third degrees in witchcraft often involve sexual intercourse. But there is a surprising lack of uniformity among covens as to proper procedure. In some covens, sexual intercourse is a part of all three degrees.

But why do people join a coven? No doubt for various reasons. Sometimes it is for sexual thrills or for vicarious thrills, but usually it is for power. They believe there is great power in the spells they cast. Hans Holzer writes: "Witches believe and are taught that their dancing and chanting raises 'the power,' which is an electric force emanating from their bodies and which they can release under the direction of the high priest and high priestess. . . . Witchcraft takes this [force] and organizes it, and thereby multiplies the results, controls the direction, and turns a hit-and-miss attempt into an effective weapon for good. Occasionally, of course, a coven is dominated by a black, or evil, priest—but what human group isn't? The power inherent in witchcraft is neither white nor black, but it can be used either way, depending on the one invoking it."

In other words, if the high priest decides that he wants a person to change his ways, his coven forms its witchly circle, dances and casts its spell to accomplish its purposes.

"They become witches," Holzer concludes, "because of the promise that together with others like themselves they can work spells, make things happen, in the here and now."

As you see, a lot depends on the goodness of the high priest, who is usually an autocratic individualist who shapes witchcraft into his own image. Most high priests do not recognize rival high priests, and this helps to explain why the estimates of witches vary so greatly. But even beyond that, there are many freelance witches who don't believe they need the organized communal power of the coven to accomplish their purposes. They can "whomp" up a perfectly good spell all by themselves, and besides, this prevents them from being vetoed by the high priest.

Besides the free-lance adult witches, thousands of self-made teen-age witches read every book they can on the subject in order to change their drab everyday lives into something exhilarating and exciting.

"The fact is," writes Martin Ebon, in his survey *Witchcraft Today*, "anybody can now buy any one of the increasing number of books on this subject, from the simplest how-to book on magical rites to esoteric treatises on the Kabala or Satanic rites." This allows young innocents to become deeply involved in a variety of sometimes psychologically harmful rituals.

Even pre-teens often get hooked on witchcraft. In New York City one group of sixth-grade girls read *Rosemary's Baby* and started to experiment themselves. Their parents thought they were having pajama parties, but actually they were going through the old ritual.

When you realize how upsetting and unnerving the secretive witchcraft rituals and spells are even in our supposedly sophisticated age, it is no wonder that the Roman Catholic Church in the Middle Ages panicked.

For many centuries the Church had thought of witchcraft as a "delusion," and smiled benignly at the practice. But then in the wake of the plague of the Black Death, people sought every charm they could to spare them. The Church itself, riddled with corruption, inspired no confidence so witchcraft became prevalent throughout Europe. St. Thomas Aquinas finally concluded that it wasn't an illusion after all; it was a reality. In the late fifteenth century Pope Innocent VIII vigorously condemned witchcraft and forbade Christians to turn to witches for help. It was too late. One single witches' sabbat in Italy was attended by 25,000 worshipers. In desperation, the Church, as if fighting for its life, lashed out at witches and supposed witches. The battle lasted for three centuries; some scholars estimate that hundreds of thousands were put to death in the witch hunts. Some of them were witches; some were not. The remedy may have been more disastrous than the disease.

In America, the Salem witchcraft trials were merely an echo of the explosions that had been rocking Europe for three centuries.

Now for the past three hundred years, scholars have been telling us how primitive and hysterical it all was. There is no such thing as witchcraft, they said.

But not long ago, the General Cigar Company petitioned the National Labor Relations Board to void a union election. Why? Because of the unfair use of witchcraft. According to General Cigar, the union hired a coven of witches to make sure the employees would vote in favor of the union.

Psychological and parapsychological studies in the past generation have indicated that the mind may have powers—be they natural or supernatural—that cannot be explained by scientific principles. And modern youth is turning toward the occult to explore these powers.

Many modern American witches don't feel wicked about what they are doing. Many even continue their membership in the local church. They look at witchcraft as a "mind over matter" affair, and all the hullabaloo about esbats and sabbats is only to help them get the mood. Louise Huebner virtually admits this: "What you are doing is psyching yourself into believing that because you do one action another will result. If you do it often enough, like using candles, you become very confident in that action and it works for you. A very strong person can do without the candles and other objects. I know I'm becoming more and more able to cast spells without props."

"What makes the magic happen," explains one young witch, "is the group's focused psychic power. A coven that knows its business can make almost anything happen." The rituals, she would say, are a kind of psychic supercharging.

Does it really work?

Of course, it sometimes works. It wouldn't be attracting such a following if it didn't. On the other hand, it fails just as often as it works.

But how does it work?

To that question, you get many answers.

First, sometimes it works by seeming coincidence. If the coven casts a spell on a young man who has been ignoring a cute little witch for weeks, and then suddenly the next day he smiles at her, does that mean that witchcraft works? Or does it mean simply that he finally got around to noticing her?

Second, it often works by superstition. If the wife has been threatening to go home to mother, but the husband tells her he has cast a spell preventing her from going, what happens? She may have an asthma attack and go up to bed. Witchcraft thrives on fear and superstition.

Third, sometimes it works from psychic phenomena. So say many witches today. Is it possible for a powerful mind to exert pressure on a weaker mind without a word being spoken? There is some evidence that this can happen.

Fourth, sometimes it works by a supernatural power. The Bible indicates that there is more than one power in the universe. Besides the power of God, there is also a demonic force. Any person who seeks a spiritual power for his own gain is in danger of encouraging a takeover by such a force. And the frenzied, hypnotic dance of the witch coven opens the mind for such an invasion. It should be clearly understood, however, that witchcraft and demonism are not identical.

One of the biggest loopholes in the thinking of modern witches is their lack of understanding of human nature. While some of them differentiate between white and black magic, yet at the heart of the Old Religion is the belief that man is basically good and innocent. Evil is merely the absence of good. So witches contrive to gain power over other individuals as well as material things, assuming that what they themselves want is necessarily what is needed.

Power corrupts. And there is no reason to assume that it takes any longer for power to corrupt a witch than any other mortal. In fact, C. S. Lewis wrote, "I am very doubtful whether history shows us one example of a man who, having stepped outside traditional morality and attained power, has used that power benevolently." Witches, take note.

Another problem for witchcraft is that their religion is earthbound. Their god is the god of this world. This religion holds to a hope of reincarnation, but most of its adherents are more interested in power and happiness now than in any afterlife.

While in ancient days early followers of witchcraft had their pagan deities to worship, modern witches worship nature. What god there is is impersonal. Historically, witches trace their lineage to Diana of the Ephesians, whose worshipers the Apostle Paul confronted in Acts,

Chapter 19. The upshot of that confrontation was that "Many of those also who used magical arts brought their books together and burned them before all men; and they counted the price of them and found it fifty thousand pieces of silver."

It is easy to see why the Bible condemns witchcraft. There was never any thought about accommodation or compromise. In three of the first five books of the Bible it is seriously condemned. It is repeatedly called an "abomination unto the Lord." And in Revelation, the final chapter of Scripture paints the beautiful picture of God's eternal paradise, but says, "Outside are sorcerers. . . ."

For anyone who takes the Bible seriously, witchcraft is nothing to play around with.

Why has witchcraft grabbed hold of our young people?

There are many opinions on this. Says Arthur Lyons, author of *The Second Coming: Satanism in America:* "Witchcraft is alluring and psychologically satisfying for the reason that it offers itself as a way of manipulating the environment, thus helping the individual to conquer any feelings of inadequacy he may experience. Its secret tradition is also attractive in that it adds a provocative scent of mystery, supplying the practitioner with a means of identification in a society of anonymity."

Psychologist Carl Jung would place the blame on religion for failing to give young people meaning and purpose in our increasingly complex society.

Historian Oswald Spengler would say that whenever a society shows abnormal interest in such aspects of the supernatural, it is a sign that the entire society is degenerating. A missionary-anthropologist Donald Jacobs agrees: "When witchcraft activity is intense, the entire social fabric is in danger of disintegrating."

In his book *The World of the Witches*, Julio Caro

Baroja writes that the historical circumstances of the communities that believe in witchcraft are situations of pestilence, war and other disasters.

But perhaps there is still another reason. Dr. Donald Nugent of the University of Kentucky believes that young people are turning to witchcraft today because they need some sense of mysticism in their lives. Never before in history has so much been logically and rationally explained. Even religion itself has lost its mystery. To many people, God doesn't answer prayer; instead, you answer your own prayers. God is no longer worshiped; He is studied. Churches today are filled with study groups, but the celebration and delight of the early Church is missing.

Instead of allowing young people to enjoy their faith, we make them memorize their catechism. We have squeezed out the mysticism and pumped them full of rationalism.

What can be done in this disintegrating, rationalistic age?

First, allow God to answer your prayers. Expect Him to do it, and rejoice in it.

Second, make your faith a celebration, not a dull drudgery.

Third, don't panic. A disintegrating society, if that's what we're in, needs something that's stable. If Salem, Massachusetts hadn't panicked in 1692, America's early history would have been a lot brighter. Some of those alleged witches might even have been redeemed. And if you don't panic, and meanwhile practice the first two steps, you might be able to redeem some twentieth-century potential witches.

ONLY SINCE THE mid-1960s has Satanism been making a comeback. The catalyst of the revival was a Paramount Pictures box-office smash named *Rosemary's Baby*.

Anton Szandor La Vey, self-styled high priest of San Francisco's First Church of Satan and author of *The Satanic Bible*, played the role of the devil. Later, he called the film the "best paid commercial for Satanism since the Inquisition."

No doubt it was.

The film shockingly concludes with a scene in which the heroine, Mia Farrow, accepts to her bosom the child that was implanted in her by the devil. At the close, the witch-leader Castavet triumphantly cries out:

"God is dead! God is dead and Satan lives!

The year is One, the first year of our Lord!

The year is One, God is done!"

The film was easily the box-office hit of the year. It grossed forty million dollars and became one of the top fifty moneymakers of all times.

Somehow if credit is to be given for bringing back

Satan, Aleister Crowley shouldn't be forgotten. Crowley, who honored himself with the title "the wickedest man in the world," was born in 1875 as the son of a wealthy British brewer. His parents, however, were converted to Christianity through the Plymouth Brethren, who take the Bible a lot more seriously than they take the organized church. A child prodigy, young Aleister got a fiendish delight out of shocking his parents and playmates, until his mother finally was so outraged that she called him the Great Beast prophesied in the Book of Revelation. When his father died, his uncle symbolized Christianity to the boy: vicious, unyielding, brutal but always respectable.

Crowley has been called other things besides the Great Beast of Revelation. A biography makes him out to be a silly egomaniac; a disciple calls him a Victorian hippie. But more than anything else he liked to shock people. He hated stuffy respectability.

He made a pact with Satan, wrote odes to murderers, called Queen Victoria dirty names, seduced a housemaid and played around with homosexuality. He wrote a collection of pornographic poems and dedicated them to his uncle, advocated the free use of drugs and finally established his own villa in Sicily for continual orgies.

A master magician, Crowley made his craft his religion. His creed was summed up in the words: "Do what thou wilt shall be the whole of the Law." He called God a "figure in Jewish mythology," but nevertheless felt that Satan was quite real. Sex, an integral part of both his magic and his religion, became increasingly degraded throughout his life.

Finally his obscene exhibitionism failed to attract either money or disciples. World War II made a shambles of "Crowleyanity," as he called it. When it came to being a personification of the devil, Crowley looked like a cheap and lurid trickster compared to Adolf Hitler.

At the age of seventy-two, in a cheap boardinghouse in Hastings, England, Aleister Crowley, injecting eleven grams of heroin into his wasted body each day, begged for morphine to kill the pain. But the pain wasn't assuaged, and Crowley passed on to meet his Maker.

Technically, Crowley wasn't a Satanist himself, but he did more to popularize Satanism in this century than any other man. And today, especially on the West Coast, there is a revival of Crowleyanity. His writings are once again being avidly read by the young. His delight in shocking the older generation and his disgust with stuffy hypocritical respectability are shared by youth today.

The best-known proponent of Satanism today, however, is Anton La Vey, who often gives the impression, like Crowley, that he is trying to shock people, not convert them. Yet he converts them too. Today he claims to have more than ten thousand active members of his church in the United States and thousands more in other countries. Totally, the Satanist movement has been estimated at about one hundred thousand in America, although an estimate is hardly any more than a guess.

Born in 1930 of Russian, Rumanian and Alsatian ancestry, La Vey dropped out of high school to join the circus when he was sixteen. After two years of feeding lions and playing the circus calliope, he left the Clyde Beatty Circus and became a magician's assistant in a carnival. Quitting that, he became a police photographer for three years and after that he played the organ in nightclubs. All the while, he was studying more about the occult, and eventually started classes in black ritual magic in his home.

Finally in April 1966, La Vey shaved his head, grew a Mephistophelian beard and announced the formation of his Church of Satan. All other churches, according to La

Vey, are based on worship of the spirit and a denial of the flesh. So he decided that his church would be "a temple of glorious indulgence that would be fun for people. . . . But the main purpose was to gather a group of like-minded individuals together for the use of their combined energies in calling up the dark force in nature that is called Satan."

Satanism, La Vey admits, "is a blatantly selfish, brutal religion. It is based on the belief that man is inherently a selfish, violent creature, that life is a Darwinian struggle for survival of the fittest, that the earth will be ruled by those who fight to win."

La Vey is an inveterate showman, a sensationalist who grabs headlines however he can. At the same time, he keeps current his long-time contacts with the police, and until recently housed a pet lion as a remembrance of his circus days.

His *Satanic Bible*, which outsells the Holy Bible in many bookstores, is inscribed to a motley collection of fifty people including Rasputin, P. T. Barnum, Marilyn Monroe, Tuesday Weld, Jayne Mansfield, Horatio Alger and Howard Hughes. Sometimes you feel that La Vey is P. T. Barnum, who said "A sucker is born every minute." At other times you have the feeling that La Vey is dead serious about his satanic craft.

But what does La Vey believe?

Listen to his own words: "We hold Satan as a symbolic personal saviour, who takes care of mundane, fleshly, carnal things. God exists as a universal force, a balancing factor in nature, too impersonal to care one whit whether we live or die. . . . We literally want to give the Devil his due. There has never been a religion before that has given him credit. . . . We believe that man is sometimes lower than the animals, that he is basically greedy and selfish, so why feel guilty about it? We accept ourselves as we are and live with it."

While La Vey's church has no doctrinal statement as such, it does have a list of nine Satanic Statements to which a prospective member is expected to subscribe.

These nine statements declare that Satan represents indulgence, vital existence, undefiled wisdom, kindness only to those who deserve it, vengeance, responsibility only to those who are responsible, the animal nature of man, all the "so-called sins," and "the best friend the church has ever had, as he has kept it in business all these years."

When La Vey appeared on the Johnny Carson show, he wore a horned hood and brandished a ceremonial magic sword. He shocked his national audience when he said that on his church altar was a live and naked woman to symbolize the pleasures of the flesh. Because the Church of Satan is recognized by the Internal Revenue Service, his income, far in excess of $25,000 a year, comes tax-free as dues from his church members.

But La Vey is not the only Satanist leader in circulation. Actually, despite his hucksterism, he may be one of the more harmless ones. In three years, California alone reported more than one hundred murders that were somehow related to occult involvement. The most notorious, of course, were the Manson murders, Sirhan Sirhan and the Zodiac killer; but in other places as distant as Miami, Florida and Vineland, New Jersey, Satanism also played a prominent role in violent death.

In June, 1970 a devil-worshiping pack of young people killed a gas-station attendant and a schoolteacher who was the mother of five children. The following month another pair of Satan cultists murdered a Montana social worker near Yellowstone Park. They shot him, hacked his body into six pieces and then ate his heart.

When Charles Manson was interviewed following his arrest for a multiple murder, he claimed, "All my women are witches, and I'm the devil." The reporter kidded him and responded, "Sure, that makes two of us." But Manson wasn't joking. "No," he said, "I really am."

Satan worship goes back hundreds of years in Europe. Whether it developed because the peasants were frustrated with the church-state link that dominated their lives or whether it began in order to bring power to man instead of to God is a matter of controversy. Hans Holzer, in *The Truth about Witchcraft*, casts his lot toward the latter idea: "The devil-worshipers couldn't care less about Christ as such. They were reversing the symbols and rites of Christianity purely because they believed that these symbols and rites had power and in reversing them the power would go to them, into their ritual, rather than flow out toward the God of the Christians."

At any rate, the most infamous blasphemy of Satanist ritual is the Black Mass. In the Black Mass, the participants try to reverse everything they know about Christianity. The crucifix is hung upside down, the altar is covered in black instead of white, hymns are sung backwards, the rite is performed by a defrocked priest, and whenever the Lord or Christ is mentioned, it is spat upon or worse.

In addition, sexual rites were added to make the blasphemy even more complete, and sometimes even a child was slain or an animal was sacrificed. During the ceremony, the worshipers would renounce their faith and acknowledge Satan as Lord. As in La Vey's ceremonies today, a naked woman was on the altar. And of course, when the ritual finally concluded, the high priest closed with a curse, rather than with a blessing.

In the late 1600s the Black Mass scandalized the royal court of Louis XIV as well as Paris social circles. The king's mistress sought help from a high priestess of Satanism in order to help her rise in the king's favor. A Black Mass was celebrated, an infant was slain, and a wafer made of flour and blood was given to the oblivious king as a love potion. Three times the Mass was tried without success; finally the high priestess decided to try a Mass of Death to poison the king. And that's when the whole plot was discovered. The high priestess confessed that she had burned in the furnace of her house and buried in her garden the bodies of over twenty-five hundred infants. As the police investigation continued, several Catholic priests, as well as many other prominent Parisians, were also implicated.

The horror of the revelation swept Europe, and Satanism went underground. During the nineteenth century and into the earlier twentieth century, it was practiced more as an excuse for sexual perversion than to worship the devil.

In America, Satanism had never had much of a following. No doubt, some devil worship did exist in backwoods areas, but it never seemed to spread to more populous parts of the country.

Today it is different. Arthur Lyons reports that there are "several interstate religious organizations dedicated to devil-worship which have ecclesiastical hierarchies and central headquarters acting as overseers of dispersed local covens. I have been informed confidentially by reliable private sources that there are organizations set up secretly for training and ordaining ministers into various Satanic priesthoods in New York, Philadelphia, Chicago, and Los Angeles."

While some elements of the Black Mass may be present in these groups, it is not painstakingly copied. Young people are not revolting against the domination of the church as much as the frustration of society. But, make no mistake, Satan is the object of worship. "In the modern groups," says Lyons, "the immediacy of Satan and his concern for man's earthly existence has frequently become the dominating factor in their ritual and doctrine. . . . They seem to be striving for communication with some ascending power who is sympathetic to their needs; it is the striving for affection from a cosmic father-figure. God may be too busy to talk with them, but Satan is not."

Lyons may be romanticizing the nature of Satan worshipers a bit, but the quest for communication is there. Yet free sex still plays a major role in attracting new members. And that doesn't apply merely to young people. In fact, according to Occultist E. J. Gold, the wife-swapping clubs that are springing up in middle-class suburban neighborhoods across the country "are increasingly being converted into Satanic covens."

So Satanism takes many strange twists. Some groups are vicious and violent; others are sex-crazed; some are rebelling against religious restraints, such as those in Salt Lake City in the heart of Mormon country; some are seriously studying the occult.

Anton La Vey and his Church of Satan in San Francisco are hardly typical. He denies any link with the rest of the Satanic movement, and insists that members of his church be stable, sincere individuals. Our members, he says, "are accomplishment-oriented people, who believe that the Satanic magic they perform will assist them in gaining money, lovers, better positions." So La Vey is not fighting society. He is seeking to use Satanism to climb the ladder. He opposes the use of drugs and is reluctant to perform a Black Mass.

Lest that make him sound too noble, you should remember that La Vey takes credit for the death of Actress Jayne Mansfield, who was a member of his church. "Jayne and I were very close," La Vey says, but Attorney Sam Brody was Jayne's boyfriend at the time and "Sam Brody hated my group." So La Vey put a ritual Satanic curse on Brody and told him that he would see him dead within a year. Within a year, Brody was killed in a car crash near New Orleans. Jayne Mansfield, who was with him, was decapitated.

Either La Vey is hopelessly naive or devilishly vicious. How can you encourage indulgence and vengeance and not expect to reap debauchery and mayhem? Satanism may seem like fun to start with, but it doesn't stay fun for long. The fact that La Vey's group has already had several splits indicates that those interested in complete indulgence want more than La Vey can give.

While La Vey takes pride in his respectable adult clientele (his magic formula is "one part outrage to nine parts social respectability"), most of the Satanic covens are frequented by young people.

A fourteen-year-old girl in Fort Lauderdale was married in a Satanic ceremony. On her wedding night she was forced to have sexual relations with five young men. A seventeen-year-old boy in Rochester told of a Black Mass in which all thirteen male members of the coven performed "every type of sexual perversion" on the naked girl on the altar.

A San Diego coed had the assignment of hacking off a limb from a male student's body.

A Los Angeles police captain told writer Stan Baldwin: "Unfortunately, it appears that Satan worship, including the sacrificing of animals, is on the increase. Information from reliable police informants has described in detail the sacrificing of dogs, cats, and various other animals during weird witch-type rites. One informant recently described an incident wherein the blood of a sacrificed dog was mixed with an LSD preparation and drunk by the participants."

La Vey calls it hedonism, the abandonment of yourself to the pursuit of self-gratification. He calls it "glorious indulgence that would be fun for people."

"So it was," wrote Apostle Paul to the Romans of the first century, "that when they gave God up and would not even acknowledge him, God gave them up to doing everything their evil minds could think of. Their lives became full of every kind of wickedness and sin. . . . They were fully aware of God's death penalty for these crimes, yet they went right ahead and did them anyway, and encouraged others to do them too" (Living Bible translation).

It was Jesus Christ Himself, who, according to the Gospel of Matthew, was led by Satan to a high mountain peak. There Satan showed Jesus "the nations of the world and all their glory."

"I'll give it all to you," said Satan, "if you'll only kneel down and worship me."

But Jesus told him. "Get out of here, Satan. The Scriptures say, 'Worship only the Lord God. Obey only him.' "

Jesus faced the temptation of hedonism and Satan worship very squarely. He understood what the alternatives were. On the one hand, He was offered pleasureful self-indulgence; on the other hand He was offered an ignominious death by crucifixion. For some reason, He chose the latter.

But for what reason?

Probably there were two reasons. First, He recognized that true happiness is found only when man submits to God's direction. Second, He loved you so much that His own desires were forgotten. If He chose a cross to save you, it is unthinkable that you should callously turn your back on Him and choose Satan and self-gratification.

In his book *Man in God's World*, Helmut Thielicke, the German theologian, recalls that when Christ walked this earth, "the demonic powers gathered themselves together in one last effort" to preserve their doomed kingdom. Now Thielicke advances the idea that "the nearer we come to the end of this present age, the more energetically the Adversary mobilizes his last reserves, until the demonic excesses reach their climax and Christ returns and the new age of God begins."

If that is so, the second coming of Satanism may foreshadow the second coming of Jesus Christ. And one thing is sure: he who has welcomed Satan will not be anxious to welcome Christ.

III

EASTWARD HO OR WHICH WAY IS THE GURU GOING?

Hare Krishna 9

ON THE BUSY street corners of almost every major city in America and Europe, you could see them chanting, dancing, swaying to the drumbeat of their mantra. Robed in saffron, the young men had shaven heads except for an isolated pigtail. On their foreheads and coming down on their noses were Hindu marks of ashes. The girls, whose faces like the men's might be striped with white, wore saris. Prayer beads were contained in cloth bags that hung around their necks.

For hours they chanted themselves into ecstasy, their eyes lowered, and lips curled, their faces expressionless.

What were they chanting?

"Hare Krishna, Hare Krishna, Krishna Krishna, Hare Hare, Hare Rama, Hare Rama, Rama Rama."

What does it mean?

These are their names of God.

Why were they chanting?

Because they believe that they can realize God by chanting His names in order and that they can liberate their souls from the evil influence of their bodies by this discipline of yoga.

As they chanted in the 70s, so they continue to chant in the 80s. As they begged in the 70s, they continue to beg in the 80s. On the surface, you might think that everything's the same as it always was. After all, their little begging bowls make you think you are in Calcutta or Benares. Of course, you are aware, that unlike many Eastern religions, Krishna devotees are aggressively seeking converts. Sometimes, very aggressively. Usually, they have some literature that they are peddling. Perhaps it is called *Back to Godhead*, one of their most popular publications.

While Krishna worship or ISKCON (International Society of Krishna Consciousness), as it is officially called, is not the largest Eastern religion in the Western world, it is certainly the most visible. Krishna followers have invaded Africa and Europe with their street-corner chanting and their train terminal peddling, and Western disciples have even staged an international convention in New Delhi, India.

But things have been changing in the ISKCON world. Not all their disciples are dressed in those saffron robes any more. And some of the changes are much more significant than that.

Of course, Krishna worship is not new in India, where it has been a popular sect of Hinduism since 1486. But it began its current vogue in America in 1965 and 1966. Those were the years the Swami A.C. Bhaktivedanta, guru of the International Society of Krishna Consciousness, quietly strolled through New York's Greenwich Village making converts of hippies and young intellectuals.

Seventy years old, the Swami had taken a slow freighter from Calcutta to New York to spread his gospel. He slept in a Yoga Center at night and wandered the streets during the day until a young admirer finally gave him a month's rent to set up a storefront headquarters.

The Swami was a strange sight in his yellow gown and ash-marked forehead even in Greenwich Village. He had been counseled to westernize a bit, but was holding true to advice he had received thirty years earlier in India from a spiritual mentor. At that time he had been told to go to America and convert the West. Thirty years later, he was seeking to do just that.

The hippies were responsive to the way-out guru. Soon classes were started in the storefront and in a few weeks the new converts were out on the street corners chanting "Hare Krishna, Hare Rama."

Beat poet Allen Ginsberg, who in the 1950s had befriended Zen Buddhism, now nurtured Krishna Consciousness. Another early convert was Howard Wheeler, a lecturer in English at Ohio State University, who took the name of Hayagrivadas. Like other Krishna followers, he was on drugs before he met the Swami.

While the Swami left his mark on Greenwich Village, the Village also left its mark on Krishna Consciousness. Soon the *Village Voice* was carrying stories on the movement, and flyers were distributed on the streets, saying, "Stay high forever. No more Coming Down. Practice Krishna Consciousness. End all Bringdowns. Turn-on through music, dance, philosophy, science, religion, and prasadam [spiritual food]."

Though the rules were strict, Krishna Consciousness gained a quick following among the young. It hopped across the country to San Francisco and became a hit in Haight-Ashbury, and from New York and San Francisco it spread to a score of other cities in the next four years.

George Harrison wrote a Hare Krishna song, "My Sweet Lord," which went to the top of the popularity polls, and soon Krishna Consciousness spread across the Atlantic to Europe. Amsterdam, Paris, Rome, Copenhagen and other major cities became very much aware of the strange new American missionaries with their strange new religion.

It is certainly amazing that the Krishna disciples have been remarkably successful in their evangelism. Members not only shave their heads, wear saris, and become vegetarians, but they also voluntarily give up sex except for the purpose of having children in marriage. Women must accept the principle that men are superior to them. Yet Krishna is growing slowly but effectively. If it makes a thousand converts a year, half of them will continue to be devotees of Krishna at the end of the year, and all of those who continue will be missionaries for Krishna.

The name of "Krishna" is rather common to devotees of Hinduism. And most Krishnas are not related at all to Krishna Consciousness. There was, for instance, a Krishna Venta in southern California three decades ago, who declared himself to be the Messiah. He proved to be a fraud, an ex-convict and a bigamist many times over. Unfortunately for this Krishna, he tried to appropriate his followers' wives once too often. Two irate husbands blew up Krishna Venta with twenty sticks of dynamite.

Krishnamurti is another Krishna who has nothing to do with Hare Krishna. He was the Indian youth who was adopted by Theosophists in the 1920s and was termed a reincarnation of Christ. After several years of parading around the country speaking in riddles, he finally denied he was the Messiah and repudiated Theosophy, thus embarrassing the Theosophists, but confirming the notions of everyone else.

A third Krishna is a Ramakrishna, a famed Indian holy man of the last century who was a forerunner of the Vedanta Society in America. His basic innovation was that man in his true nature is divine and all religions lead to the direction of truth. But because all religions were true, there was no need to convert anyone and, consequently, Vedanta has been gradually petering out.

But all of these are only distantly related, if at all, to Hare Krishna, the most colorful of the modern youth cults.

To get a clearer understanding of Krishna Consciousness, you need to go back to the deities of Hinduism, the religion of India without founder and without creed.

Hinduism, somewhat like Christianity, has its own Trinity, though Hinduism's Trinity is three separate gods. The three are called Brahma (the Creator), Vishnu (the Preserver) and Shiva (the Destroyer). According to the Hindus, Vishnu, the second god in their Trinity, has been incarnated nine times, sometimes as an animal, sometimes as a man. The eighth incarnation (or avatar, as the Hindus would say) was Krishna (a legendary hero who directed a battle in which 640 million Indians were killed). The ninth incarnation, incidentally, was Buddha.

The story of Lord Krishna is told in *The Bhagavad Gita,* an eighteen-chapter Hindu poem. The *Gita,* as it is called, is a dialogue between a man and a God. The God is Krishna, the man is a warrior named Arjuna. Arjuna's problem is that he is about to enter a battle in which his relatives are on the other side. So, rather than kill his own kin, he is considering the possibility of quitting the fight. But Krishna tells him to go ahead and fight, not to think of the consequences of his actions, but to do what must be done. It is his duty (or *dharma*). What must be done, must be done. Arjuna is urged to act, without seeking the fruits of his action.

Though the setting of the *Gita* is war, the main teaching seems to be "Kill desire, the powerful enemy of the soul."

Krishna counsels Arjuna: "The dweller in the body of every one, O Arjuna, is eternal and can never be slain;

therefore thou shouldest not grieve for any creature. . . . When a man puts away all the desires of his mind, O Arjuna, and when his spirit is content in itself, then is he called stable in intelligence. . . . He who abandons all desires and acts free from longing, without any sense of mineness or egotism, he attains to peace."

A summary of Krishna's thought is expressed in these words from the *Gita*: "When a man dwells in his mind on the objects of sense, attachment to them is produced. From attachment springs desire and from desire comes anger. From anger arises bewilderment, from bewilderment loss of memory; and from loss of memory the destruction of intelligence and from the destruction of intelligence he perishes. But a man of disciplined mind, who moves among the objects of sense, with the senses under control and free from attachment and aversion, attains purity and spirit."

But Krishna goes one step further in the *Gita*. Besides telling Arjuna that he shouldn't seek reward for work or good deeds and besides telling the warrior to cultivate an indifference to pain, pleasure or gain, he also tells him that the path to salvation lies in devotion and love for him: "Whoever surrenders to me is not destroyed."

This emphasis on love and devotion (or *bhakti*) is quite unique in Hindu writings and sets the *Gita* apart. Henry David Thoreau said that the *Gita* was one of two books that had made his mind, and the Mahatma Gandhi praised it highly in shaping his life and conduct. However, Krishna followers accept only their Swami's special translation of the *Gita*. All the others, they say, are full of "mental deceptions," and "mental speculations."

The *Gita* is actually part of the huge epic of 90,000 double verses called the *Mahabharata*. In it Krishna is credited with having 16,000 wives, although he is popularly pictured in the company of his mistress Radha. Thus, Krishna has a rather checkered career.

But despite his shady past, Krishna, as one of the nine incarnations of the god Vishnu, has generated a distinct Hindu sect, one of many sects within Hinduism.

Krishna Consciousness traces its ancestry to Chaitanya Mahaprabhu, who was born in India in 1486. He became a great holy man and was even regarded as another incarnation of God. Because he lived in what is called "the yellow age," he wore a yellow robe. And because the age was so corrupt, he felt he was called to save it by chanting Hare Krishna.

Incidentally, Prabhupada, the Swami who brought Krishna Consciousness to America, claimed to have descended from both Krishna and Chaitanya, and hinted that his followers might ascertain some day that he was an incarnation of Krishna.

While most of Hinduism tends to have a rather impersonal feeling about God, Krishna Consciousness stresses the importance of a personal relationship with Krishna. One disciple said, "If you live a life of Krishna Consciousness, Krishna says that when you leave your body, if you think of Him you will achieve bliss."

Because Krishna Consciousness believes that the body is ruled by passion and the soul by serenity, it, like all Hindu sects, attempts to liberate the soul from the body. Other sects may concentrate on fasting, walking through fire, or other types of asceticism and austerity. Some emphasize knowledge, meditation and realization. But Krishna believes that the best way to liberate the soul from the body (which is as close as Hindus ever come to the Christian concept of salvation) is by devotion and in particular the Hare Krishna chants.

Through the constant chants of the various names of his god, the Krishna convert eventually goes into a state of trance-like ecstasy. He feels that he is liberated from his body and is suspended in a state of pure spirit. But it is the repetition of God's name and total abandonment of self to him that accomplishes it.

In Hinduism, this is called *bhakti* yoga, or the achieving of union with God through the discipline of devotion. Of the four main roads to God in Hinduism, this is the one that is closest to Christianity, for its basic direction is outward, not inward, Godward, not manward. Its devotion is to a personal God, not an impersonal concept. One scholar commented that the goal of the follower of Krishna Consciousness is "to adore God with every element of his being. . . . In such a context, God's personality, far from being a limitation, is indispensable. Philosophers may be able to love pure being, infinite beyond all attributes, but they are exceptions. The normal object of human love is personality, however exalted its attributes of wisdom, compassion, and grace may be. . . . Insofar as we succeed we will know joy, for no experience can compare with that of being authentically and fully in love."

In an old classic of Russian orthodoxy called *The Way of the Pilgrim*, an unnamed peasant is desperately seeking to obey the biblical injunction, "Pray without ceasing." He wanders throughout Russia and Siberia, asking one religious authority after another for the way to do it. Finally a holy man teaches him that praying without ceasing means "a constant uninterrupted calling upon the divine Name of Jesus with the lips, in the spirit, in the heart . . . during every occupation, at all times, in all places, even during sleep." And so the peasant learns how to repeat the name of Jesus more than twelve thousand times a day without strain.

Hare Krishna is similar to this, only with more of an emphasis of ecstasy, of dropping out of the world. The world, says the Swami, is unreal. The whole of the world is really a grand illusion. By practicing Hare Krishna, you will eventually come to see the world as only a dream which has reality just for those in the dream.

In November 1977, the founder of ISKCON, Prabhupada, died, and the young movement with its many young followers had to adjust. Eleven gurus, several of them Americans, were anointed as "spiritual masters." Technically the eleven are all equal, but those who control more money and power seem to be "more equal" than the rest.

Emerging as one of ISKCON's new dominant forces is Keith Ham, known as Kirtenanda Swami, an American who is in charge of New Vrindaban, the 1500 acre West Virginia property with a magnificent palace. James and Marcia Rudin, in *Prison or Paradise*, describe the palace this way: "The building is crowned by a twenty-four carat gold-leaf dome, has terraces, moats and gardens and is decorated with two hundred tons of marble from forty countries, crystal chandeliers, stained-glass peacocks, and teak-wood floors."

Not bad for a decade or so of begging and selling *Back to Godhead* in train stations and airports.

But that isn't all. They've also built a two million dollar temple in Bombay; they own large holdings in urban properties in Los Angeles, and they own and operate large farms around the world.

But breaking into the tranquility are the charges that ISKCON forceably cuts off its members from their families and then moves them from temple to temple so parents cannot find them. Others have alleged that Krishna chanters often end up as "basket cases" because of their chanting. One former member told the authors of *Snapping*, "There are people cracking up all the time."

But the technique of ISKCON that has aroused the most controversy is the way they ask for money. In earlier years you could always identify members by their distinctive garb. No more. At Christmas, they may dress up in Santa Claus suits. They have been known to say that they are collecting for Muscular Dystrophy or a Roman Catholic mission. They have posed as park rangers at a national park. "There is no harm," they say, "in transcendental trickery." Or as one Krishna devotee explained it on national TV, "It's all right if we're doing it for God."

Obviously, what they have been doing is lucrative. One Krishna official estimated that their "U.S. street missionaries collected $75 million during the 1970s." No public accounting is made of the use of the funds, although recently even some of the members have raised questions about it.

Authorities also have been asking questions, and not only about finances. Despite the statement of ISKCON that it is against its policy "to keep any stockpile of weapons or ammunition for any reason," there have been repeated instances of Krishna-ites being arrested on weapons charges, and caches of arms being discovered on Krishna turf. According to the *Wall Street Journal*, "One cache of their weapons and ammunition was discovered out in California, but now it turns out there are others. Police on both coasts have discovered three other loads. The haul to date includes not only conventional arms and ammunition but such exotica as a grenade launcher and a sub-machine gun. . . . A spokesman for the group contends that 'the armament isn't for ourselves. . . . We're here to protect our God.' "

In addition, one of the four highly-touted principles of Krishna is that its members "abstain from all intoxicants and drugs, including alcohol, tobacco, tea and coffee."

Yet in recent years members of the Hare Krishna movement have been convicted of smuggling and trafficking in heroin, hash oil, morphine, cocaine and marijuana in Holland, Canada, Hawaii and various parts of continental United States. Of course, whenever a sect member is charged with such a violation, the movement disavows him or her, but the frequency of the violations is curious, to say the least.

So ISKCON may be changing. But it continues to gain new members, mostly among the young. The logical question to ask is WHY?

1. Because it is anti-materialistic. Reacting against the hard-driving, success-oriented culture today, youth realizes that money and material possessions haven't brought satisfaction to their parents. Science has brought us the H-bomb; materialism has brought us an endless chase after unhappiness; competition has brought us ruthlessness and failure. Krishna says, "Why worry about material things? They are all unreal anyway!"

2. Because it is the ultimate drop-out. Not having answers to the complex problems of the world, youth decides that the easiest thing is to negate the physical by Hare Krishna chants, which are certainly less dangerous than LSD trips. Drugs, as more and more young people are discovering, are not the answer. But they still want to drop out some other way.

3. Because it is the ultimate protest. It seems ridiculous to think of Hare Krishna as a protest movement, but perhaps that is what it is in America. Young people have protested violently against the system, and they have participated in active politics against the system. But their protests have seemed to be to no avail. Perhaps Hare Krishna is just a simple way of thumbing their noses at the system that refuses to change.

4. Because it is as close as Hinduism ever comes to

Christianity. Lord Krishna has evolved into a pale imitation of Jesus Christ, although Krishna's liberation is not Christian salvation, and Krishna's reincarnation is not Christian regeneration.

However, Krishna Consciousness evades the most important issues. The key problems are not solved but dissolved. Writer Alan Watts said as much when he stated, "The solution for us is not solution, but only solution via dissolution." Krishna's liberation is a "liberation from" not a "liberation to." It is a liberation from yourself. Everything that you need to be saved from is declared to be an illusion.

Yet the problems of the world are not solved. You do not help those who need help. You are concerned only with achieving your own mantra-induced ecstasy. If you are separated from the problems of living to such an extent, anything is liable to happen. In fact, it is said that the founder of the Krishna sect, Chaitanya, "danced in such ecstasy, repeating the name of Hare, that he danced on into the sea at Puri and was drowned." Is this the ideal toward which Krishna followers today are heading?

The chief problem of living today is what we call sin. To the Hindu, sin is caused by ignorance; once ignorance is removed, man is restored to oneness with God! But Christianity says that sin is caused by man's own willfulness. Krishna says that man can save himself; Christianity says that man needs outside help.

A recent convert to Christianity, Paul Krishna, wrote recently, "As a Hindu I endured self-discipline and much study for one purpose—to better myself, to achieve heaven by my own deeds. Christianity starts with man's weakness. It asks us to accept our selfishness and inabilities, then promises a new nature. Christ came to heal the sick, not the well or self-sufficient."

Krishna Consciousness twists reality into unreality and

asks you to accept temporary states of ecstasy as reality.

The Sopwith Camel once had a song that said, "Stamp out reality before reality stamps out you."

And that is exactly what Krishna Consciousness has been trying to tell young people today.

IF YOU REALLY want to know what Zen Buddhism is, don't ask a Zen Master.

If you do, you will really get confused.

One old Zen Master, whenever he was asked what Zen Buddhism was all about, merely lifted one of his fingers. That was all; he said nothing.

In response to the same question, another Master kicked a ball; a third slapped his inquirer in the face.

No wonder people have trouble understanding it.

In his book *The Religions of Man*, Dr. Huston Smith wrote: "Entering the Zen outlook is like stepping through Alice's looking glass. One finds oneself in a topsy-turvy wonderland in which everything seems quite mad— charmingly mad for the most part—but mad all the same. It is a world of bewildering dialogues, obscure conundrums, stunning paradoxes, flagrant contradictions, and abrupt non sequiturs, all carried off in the most urbane, cheerful, and innocent style."

As Smith says, at first blush it looks like horseplay.

"Can they possibly be serious in this kind of spiritual doubletalk or are they simply pulling our leg?"

So if you want to quit now and jump to the next chapter, go ahead, because Zen is impossible to explain. And if this explanation makes any sense at all to you, then I have failed utterly to help you understand Zen.

It doesn't help matters any to realize that Zen's big thrust in America came through the beatniks of the 1950s.

In *The Dharma Bums*, Beat writer Jack Kerouac tells how he and Poet Allen Ginsberg trekked to San Francisco in the early 1950s and learned Zen from another poet named Gary Snyder. Another influence upon them was Alan Watts, who had only recently become enamored with Zen himself. Today, however, Watts is known as its foremost popularizer in America; in fact, some have tabbed him as "The Norman Vincent Peale of Zen."

Kerouac's brand of Beat Zen was not held in high repute by the Zen purists, but he did garner a lot of disciples, and he gave many more a first taste of this exotic and sometimes erotic Eastern cult. Sal Paradise in *The Dharma Bums* asked the question, "Why do Zen Masters throw their disciples into a mud puddle?" and he got the response, "Because they want them to realize mud is better than words." In Beat Zen, mud was often better than words.

The experience of the Now was degraded into "Live it up Now," and finally Alan Watts himself recognized that Beat Zen was "a pretext for license . . . a simple rationalization." "To this extent," Watts explained, "Beat Zen is sowing confusion in idealizing as art and life what is better kept to oneself as therapy."

While Beat Zen may have been a perversion, it certainly attracted publicity. The usual image of the time was a coffee-house in New York's Greenwich Village inhabited with bearded beatniks sipping Espresso coffee quoting poetry vaguely related to Zen.

In *The Making of a Counter Culture* Theodore Roszak says, "If the young seized on Zen with shallow understanding, they grasped it with a healthy instinct. And grasping it, they bought the books, and attended the lectures, and spread about the catch phrases, and in general helped to provide the ambiance within which a few good minds who understood more deeply could speak out in criticism of the dominant culture."

Many of the young never thought of it as a religion or a theology, but rather as a way to get the most out of the Now. What counts, says Zen, is how you react instinctively to the Now.

Since the late 1950s, the faddishness of Zen Buddhism has worn off; instead of the coffeehouses of Greenwich Village, Zen has moved into Zen Centers, where it is practiced on a serious basis. Today there are about a score of these centers scattered across America with more than two thousand dedicated students enrolled.

What is called the "center of gravity of Zen practice in America" is a monastery located at Tassajara, 150 miles south of San Francisco. Founded on the site of a former hot-springs resort, the stone-and-masonry monastery compound was purchased for $300,000 by a group of wealthy Zen enthusiasts. The Japanese roshi or headmaster is Shunryu Suzuki, now in his seventies. Short, slight and possessing a good sense of humor, Suzuki Roshi, as he is often called, left Japan for America in 1959, because the Japanese "come to the temple only if you give them food and have a Zen Party." In America he became the priest of the Zen Buddhist congregation in San Francisco and now devotes full time to American students of Zen at Tassajara. His role is to teach his students how to find within themselves the answers of life. But a Zen teacher is an unusual teacher, for the old Zen saying goes, "I owe everything to my teacher because he taught me nothing."

What then is Zen Buddhism?

If you ask Suzuki, he will probably shrug his shoulders, spread both his palms up and give you a beatific smile. But that's always the problem about asking a Zen Master anything.

Three key words, however, will give you a little insight into this puzzling religion. The first word is *Zazen*, which in Japanese means roughly to "sit and meditate."

Through meditation in the characteristic cross-legged lotus posture, with the soles of your feet facing upward on your thighs, you try to find union with the Ultimate Reality of the universe. Your eyes, half open, are staring at the floor a few feet in front of you. And you sit there, hour after hour, trying to develop your intuitive powers. You sit erectly, in deep concentration, breathing deeply from your abdomen (because physiologically your intuitive powers are related somehow to your abdomen).

Why this unique posture? To relax your body, to rid you of impure thoughts and to prepare you for *satori*.

What's satori? Christmas Humphreys in *Zen Buddhism* states, "Satori is the goal, the meaning and the heart of Zen. . . . Satori is the world of perpetual now and here and this, of absolute, unimpeded flow."

Satori is the unique aspect of Zen Buddhism that sets it apart from other forms of Buddhism. The founder of Zen insisted that you must have an immediate experience of truth and not merely an understanding of what truth is. And satori is the flash of light, the sudden intuition of what it's all about, the "Eureka, I've found it!," the realization of the basic principles that hold the entire universe together. It is the mystic state in which you appreciate your own "original inseparability with the universe."

"Though its preparation may take years," says Huston Smith, "the experience itself comes in a flash, exploding like a silent rocket deep within the experiencer and making everything look different thereafter."

But how do you achieve satori? By sitting and meditating.

What do you meditate upon?

That's where the third key word of Zen Buddhism comes in. You meditate upon a *koan*. A koan is a problem, sometimes paradoxical, that cannot be answered logically.

Here are a few koans:

What is the sound of one hand clapping?

When the Many are reduced to the One, to what is the One to be reduced?

What was the appearance of your face before your ancestors were born?

Have you had enough? Actually in Zen literature, there are 1,700 of these koans.

Dr. D.T. Suzuki of Japan, who has become the most important interpreter of Zen to the West, says, "When the importance of the koan is understood, we may say that more than half of Zen is understood."

Now you can meditate on the koan for hours in your lotus posture and you probably won't find a solution. The reason is, according to Zen, that you are depending too much on your logic. That's the trouble with Western man; he tries to figure out everything logically. But koans can't be figured out by your logic or by your intellect.

Huston Smith says it well: "By forcing reason to wrestle with what, from its normal point of view, is flat absurdity, by compelling it to conjoin incompatibles, Zen tries to reduce it to the frantic condition of throwing itself against its walls with the desperation of a cornered rat."

Finally, when your mind is exhausted and bewildered with the total illogic of the koan, satori can break through. Suddenly, you are no longer thinking about, you are experiencing. Suddenly, you are no longer locked in the closet of your own reason; now you burst into the sunlight of total Enlightenment. At least, that's what Zen says. If you have lived all your life in the desert and have never seen water, the best thing for you to do is not to read what the encyclopedia says about water, but to jump into the ocean. That's what Zen says.

Zen Buddhists aren't even concerned about the Buddhist Scriptures. Consequently, they are called the "Wordless sect." Most religions have holy books and creeds but Zen has no verbalized codes at all. What Zen seeks to do is to go "beyond words in order that the original insight of the Buddha may be brought back to life."

Buddhism, of course, is not new. It began in the sixth century B.C. on one full-mooned May night in Gaya, India, "while the Bo tree rained red blossoms." An introspective prince named Siddharta Gautama sat and meditated through the night until he gained enlightenment. He had tried luxury on one hand and self-mortification on the other. Neither had brought him contentment. Finally, says Clarence Hamilton in his book *Buddhism: A Religion of Infinite Compassion*, lotuses bloomed on every tree and the entire universe turned into a "bouquet of flowers sent whirling through the air." Gautama had achieved satori. His eyes had been opened to Ultimate Reality, and for forty-nine days he remained deep in rapture from the experience. Thus he was given the name of Buddha, which means "the Enlightened One."

Afterward, his followers published what Gautama had allegedly learned in his meditation.

In a way, Buddhism must be understood as a reaction against Hindu perversions. Gautama himself is called by the Hindus the ninth avatar or incarnation of the god Vishnu.

Huston Smith characterizes Buddha's religion as a religion without authority, without ritual, without theology, without grace and without the supernatural.

In his *Introduction to Zen Buddhism*, Suzuki says, "Zen has no God to worship, no ceremonial rites to observe, no future abode to which the dead are destined, and last of all, Zen has no soul whose welfare is to be looked after by somebody else and whose immortality is a matter of intense concern with some people."

While Buddhism took away much that seems essential to most religions of the world, it is best known for its four sublime truths and its Eightfold Path.

The four sublime truths of Buddhism are that pain is universal, that pain is caused by desire, that the cure for pain comes through the overcoming of your desires, and that you can achieve this victory through following the eightfold path.

The eight steps in the path are (1) Right knowledge; (2) Right aspiration; (3) Right speech; (4) Right behavior; (5) Right livelihood; (6) Right effort; (7) Right mindfulness; and (8) Right meditation. And that, of course, would lead you into Zen Buddhism. In fact Zen begins where the rest of Buddhism ends. It starts at the eighth step, and some Zen Buddhists don't even bother about the other steps.

Like Christianity, Buddhism split into two main divisions. One, called Mahayana Buddhism, was more or less the liberal branch; the other, called Hinayana, or sometimes Theravada, was the conservative or fundamentalist branch. The first emphasized Buddha's spirit; the second emphasized his writings.

Then each of these divided into denominations, Zen coming through Japanese Buddhism from the Mahayana branch, Zen Buddhists deriving their inspiration from Buddha's well-known Flower Sermon. One day, 2,500 years ago, as his disciples stood around him awaiting instruction from the Great Buddha, their teacher said nothing. Instead, he simply held up a golden lotus.

A thousand years later in A.D. 520, a man named Bodhidharma carried the insight from the uplifted lotus into China, and he became the father of Zen Buddhism. According to legend, he went directly to the court of the Emperor Wu in Canton, because Wu had been a warm supporter of Buddhism in China. However, Wu was not a warm supporter of strangers from India who walked unannounced into his palace. So Bodhidharma left the emperor's court unsatisfied and spent the next nine years "gazing at the wall" in a monastery.

According to another legend, when Bodhidharma was quite elderly, he decided to look for the Western Gates of China. He was last seen with one of his sandals on his head, "scowling and lost in self-absorption."

When Zen Buddhism began to wane in China in the thirteenth century, it seemed to "catch on" in Japan, where it split into several different sects depending on how much emphasis you wanted to place on the koan to achieve your satori. In this century as Zen is beginning to wane in Japan, it seems to have caught on in America.

Many of the American young people now pursuing Zen were once on drugs. Jacob Needleman, in *The New Religions*, states, "Almost all of the American students I interviewed [at the Zen Center] spoke with respect of drugs such as LSD. Some said that without the drug experience they would never have been opened up to the the possibilities in themselves which are being realized in the Zen practice. Drugs gave them, so to say, a taste or glimpse of enlightenment." Satori then becomes a sub-stitute for drugs.

But there are other reasons why Zen is attractive. It contains no talk of morality, no commandments, no mention of sin. In fact, it stresses the idea that you must accept yourself as the Buddha.

One scholar stated, "If you wish to seek the Buddha, you ought to see into your own nature, for this nature is the Buddha himself.... The Buddha is your own mind...." Thus, you are one with the ultimate.

This is the way it is with Zen. It tries to break down your thinking of life as a dualism—soul and body, right and wrong, matter and spirit, God and man, life and death. Where contradictions occur, it doesn't worry about solving them, it only accepts them. It teaches that all of life is a unity, including God and man, heaven and earth, and eternity and now.

In fact, the deeper you go into Zen, the more you feel that you are an "it," not a you.

Of course, there is no God in the Christian sense. Since there is really no sin and no God, man is not separated from God, because he himself is part of the Ultimate. And there is no Savior, only Buddha, the Enlightened One, the Way-Shower. Salvation comes through understanding your true self.

It supposedly brings to you the realization that all of life is good and is to be accepted because it is a part of you and you are a part of it. But coupled with it is "an attitude of total agreeableness."

A Zen poem expresses it this way:

"We eat, excrete, sleep and get up;
This is our world.
All we have to do after that—
Is to die."

Zen does not address itself to problems of good and evil, life and death. It merely accepts what is and does not try to change it. Man suffers, says Zen, because he wants to possess forever things that are temporary, including his own personality. So Zen tries to cultivate a total detachment from all of life.

It advises, "Do not seek after truth; merely cease to hold opinions." A Zen poem entitled "Trust in the Heart" says:

"If you want the truth to stand clear before you,
Never be for or against.
The struggle between 'for' and 'against'
Is the mind's worst disease."

Zen is not only detached from a search for truth, it is also detached from concern for one's fellow man. It revels in awareness but it lacks a social awareness, a social concern for the needs of others. The Christian ideal is to give to the beggar. The Zen Buddhist ideal is to beg. In Eastern lands Zen Buddhists support themselves by begging. On certain days all the Zen monks form a long line and go out on the streets, trudging slowly and crying "Ho," with their bowls outstretched, seeking either money or rice.

All of this is a far cry from the Christian ideal of the West. A convert from Zen Buddhism, Lit-Sen-Chang, now a professor at Gordon Divinity School near Boston, states, "Zen is a revolt against any authority and it does not affirm the existence of God nor the need of a Saviour. It has no object of faith. It purposes to discipline the mind and make it its own master, through seeing into one's own nature. . . . Zen thus distorts the biblical truth by ignoring the gravest factor in the history of mankind, namely the fall of Adam, by which the ground is cursed and our sorrows are multiplied.''

The assessment of Dr. Walter R. Martin in *The Kingdom of the Cults* is bold and straightforward: "Zen Buddhism is the most self-centered, selfish system of philosophy that the depraved soul of man can embrace, for it negates the two basic principles upon which all spiritual reality exists: 'Thou shalt love the Lord thy God with all thy heart, with all thy soul and with all thy mind . . . and thy neighbor as thyself' " (Matthew 22:37, 39).

Some say that the satori experience is similar to Christian conversion. Yet it is more dissimilar than it is similar. According to the Bible, Christian conversion results from God's reaching down into man's dilemma and man's realization that he cannot save himself. Salvation must come from God. Zen's satori is man's own reach into his inner self to find ultimate oneness there.

Why are so many young people turning to Zen today?

Probably because life seems even more senseless than Zen Buddhism's koans. When life makes no sense, when everything seems hopeless, and when every avenue of escape is a dead end, then young people turn to Zen. Just as the koan is a frustrating dead end, so life makes no sense and is devoid of hope. Life is a great big koan.

But Christianity centers on hope. This does not mean that the Bible is blind to the paradoxes of life, the inscrutableness of God or the mystery of God's dealings with us. Yet Christians can face the heaviest blows of life (as in the Book of Job) and still look in faith to a God who ultimately proves His love and trustworthiness. Zen knows nothing of the confidence of the Apostle Paul who wrote, "And we know that all things work together for good to them that love the Lord" (Romans 8:28).

Transcendental Meditation and the Maharishi Mahesh Yogi 11

ANY RELIGION that makes converts out of the Beatles, the Rolling Stones, Mia Farrow, Donovan, and Shirley MacLaine can't be all that bad, can it?

Some have called it "instant Nirvana"; others have pooh-poohed it as a happiness-hungry fad; others have wondered if it were merely a money-making scheme for a diminutive guru.

But Transcendental Meditation, the unwieldy name by which the religion is usually called, has indoctrinated more than a million meditators and has been making additional disciples at a rapid pace both in the United States and in Europe.

In America the movement has also gone under two other names; Spiritual Regeneration Movement Foundation of America for adults and Student International Meditation Society—(SIMS)—for students.

Obviously, the religion doesn't believe in short names. Perhaps that is because the Eastern guru who started the ball rolling is a gentleman with a rather lengthy name himself, Maharishi Mahesh Yogi.

Maharishi means "Great Sage" and Yogi means "a

practicer of yoga." So that leaves him with only one name Mahesh, which is his family name. The remainder of his name is Prasad Warma, but he never uses these parts of his name any more.

Maybe a psychoanalyst would say the real reason that Transcendental Meditation likes long names is because it believes the secret of all of life may be contained in a short meaningless syllable of only two or three letters.

Let's take a closer look at Maharishi Mahesh Yogi, who stands barely five feet tall in his sandals and travels in a chauffeured Mercedes limousine.

Born in north central India ,in 1911, the Maharishi studied physics at Allahabad University and graduated when he was thirty-one years old. For about five years he worked in a factory, while dabbling in Yoga and the ancient Vedas on the side. After World War II he retreated into the Himalayan foothills, where he meditated under the watchful eye of a Hindu swami, Jagadguru Shankracharya of Badrikashram.

Then in 1959, at the age of forty-eight, he emerged from his Himalayan hideout, ready to reveal his exciting new religion to the world.

He sprung it on the citizenry of Madras, India's third most populous city, but to the residents, he was just another swami. Undaunted, he decided to go worldwide and announced a nine-year plan for spreading his message via an organization known as International Meditation Society. Later the same year he headed for London, England, because, he said, "New ideas get better acceptance in technologically developed countries."

So the one-time physicist with a businessman's approach to Eastern religion and an aptitude for public relations that would be a credit to Madison Avenue put up his shingle in front of a London apartment.

For several years, Transcendental Meditation didn't

seem to mix with the British temperament, but then in 1967 it happened. One of the Beatles, George Harrison, who had been studying Indian music, came in contact with the Maharishi. His enthusiasm convinced the other members of the group to see the sensational Indian guru. So off they went to a remote spot in Wales and studied Transcendental Meditation with the Maharishi.

They were quoted as saying, "Even from an early age we have been seeking a highly spiritual experience. We tried drugs and that didn't work." So they tried the Maharishi.

When they returned to public life again, Paul McCartney exclaimed, "Transcendental Meditation is good for everyone."

Ringo Starr said, "Since meeting His Holiness, I feel great."

And John Lennon responded: "This is the biggest thing in our lives."

That was all the publicity the Maharishi needed. *Time* magazine reported, "With their endorsement, the Maharishi hit the big time, winning such show-business disciples as Shirley MacLaine, the Rolling Stones and Mia Farrow." It seemed to be the "in" thing to do; show-business personalities were expected to make a pilgrimage to the Maharishi.

Mia Farrow even took her sister Prudence and jetted to the Maharishi's air-conditioned Meditation Center in India's Himalayas in 1968. When she returned, she said that now she had learned how "to love and to love to love. Everybody wants to love."

It was a fantastic blast-off to instant fame. Maharishi's picture adorned every major magazine you could think of. He seemed almost omnipresent, always appearing in his simple white Indian dhoti, rubber-thonged sandals, a string of beads, and, always in his hands, a flower. One reporter described him as "gentle, bearded, apple-cheeked, soft-spoken and displaying a beatific smile."

The evening talk shows fought for the honor of his appearance on TV, and he received warm welcomes from Harvard University students as well as from throngs at Madison Square Garden in New York City. When he flew to the capitals of Europe, his reception was just as enthusiastic.

His religion seemed simple enough and all he asked for was a week's pay for private instruction. Of course, a week's pay from each of the Beatles, the Rolling Stones, Mia Farrow, Shirley MacLaine, Donovan and numerous other movie stars and recording artists enabled the simple holy man to hire PR men and publicity experts. His nine-year plan to acquaint the world with his new religion seemed utterly successful.

Thousands of young people began to think about something else besides drugs. Half the world seemed to feel that this Eastern guru could whip up instant happiness as easily as a morning cup of instant coffee.

"Life can be bliss," he taught. "It can be easy. You don't have to deprive yourself of wanting things." And the way he said it you firmly believed that happiness was only a syllable away.

Allegedly the Maharishi not only brought instant happiness in his knapsack but world peace as well.

Said the Maharishi, "Even if only one-tenth of the adult population of the world were regularly to meditate for short periods every day, and so produce these infinitely peaceful influences that arise at the deepest level of consciousness, it would take not more than a few months to remove the entire accumulation of tension in the world. War would be impossible for centuries to come. . . ."

And not only world peace. "If young people would accept my mind, the hospitals would be emptied."

But then the charm wore off. One by one the Beatles got bored: publicly they said they had "made a mistake." Mia Farrow, then others, dropped off the bandwagon to Nirvana. Overnight, the crowds lost interest. The Maharishi had undertaken a nineteen-city barnstorming tour of the United States as part of his quest to "regenerate the world," but no one seemed interested any more. An advance man muttered, "He couldn't even draw flies."

The man from Allahabad climbed onto a jet heading East with the sad announcement, "I know that I have failed. My mission is over," and he vowed never to bother the West again.

The little guru with the lovable, laughing brown eyes and the contagious giggle had packed his bags and gone home.

To many it was the end of a daydream, a cute little ephemeral religious fad.

But it wasn't. Working out of his fifteen-acre, fifty-eight room, $750,000 air-conditioned ashram in Rishikesh, India, the Maharishi rebuilt his business.

In 1970, when an inquiry into his financial affairs seemed to become embarrassingly unbearable, he moved to the Italian resort community of Fiuggi Fonte and set up shop there.

But then he developed a new "World Plan" in which he envisioned 350 teacher-training centers (eventually to become universities of Transcendental Meditation) around the world in order to "bring to everyone everywhere the means of realizing his full potential." Financially, the movement grew to be surprisingly prosperous, with substantial Swiss bank accounts; and although the Maharishi's movement seemed dead and buried in 1968,

Time magazine in 1972 reported that "the guru has generated what may well be the fastest growing cult in the West."

The secret of the turnaround in TM's success seemed to be concurrent with a change in the Certificate of Incorporation. By changing a few words, TM tried to become secular instead of religious. This opened the door for work in schools, prisons and other institutions across America.

In New Jersey, as in other states, TM was introduced in public school classrooms and supported by public tax money. But in 1977, TM was dealt a serious blow. A U.S. District Court concluded TM was "religious in nature" and had no business in the public schools.

Since that time, TM has had its ups and downs—some of them quite literally, because it has attempted to teach its devotees the art of levitation.

In order to maintain a steady volume of traffic, the Maharishi has to keep pulling something new out of his bag of tricks. Meditation about nothingness has a tendency to become boring after a while.

In 1982, a professor at TM's Maharishi International University in Fairfield, Iowa, wrote that the longer a person practices TM, the younger he or she becomes biologically. Some meditators, he said, were as much as twenty-seven years younger biologically than the average person their age.

Thus, TM claims to overcome not only the law of gravity, but also the law of aging.

But what is this cult all about?

It all sounds simple enough. The Maharishi says that all the disciplines and arduous effort of most Eastern religions are a big waste of time. No need to contort yourself into that lotus posture. All you have to do is to sit comfortably for a few minutes a day and silently repeat your own special mantra. A mantra is simply a little phrase or syllable that is selected to fit your personality by one of the teachers of Transcendental Meditation.

The teacher looks you over and on the basis of your appearance and actions gives you the secret Sanskrit word for your meditation mantra. If you tell it to someone else, you will spoil everything. So no one really knows how many different mantras the Maharishi has up his sleeve. The best-known Hindu mantras are *Rama* and *Om*, but the Maharishi has said publicly that he doesn't think much of Om for a mantra. He thinks that if you keep saying that over and over again to yourself, you are apt to withdraw from life. And that may be the purpose of other Eastern religions, but that isn't the purpose of Transcendental Meditation.

What you do with your mantra is think it over and over for about fifteen minutes twice a day. Maybe you will need to do it thirty minutes twice a day at the start. In no time at all, your life will be changed. You will feel more energy and less tension. You will become more efficient, more alive, less negative, healthier and happier. Not bad for one little syllable.

The important word in the Maharishi's scheme of things is the word "happier." The happier you are the more you are fulfilling your purpose for existence. So the Maharishi had to find out what brought happiness. Right off, he knew that happiness does not come from external things. That's what he told the Beatles; money and material possessions don't bring happiness. And they knew he was telling the truth.

Now most of the Eastern religions will tell you to discipline your mind, that your mind has to be controlled and regimented. Nonsense, says the Maharishi. All you have to do is to expose your mind to the bliss of the subtler levels of thought. You simply put your mind in neutral, then let your thoughts rush in and finally sic your mantra onto your thoughts. Now if you have the proper mantra, this process "expands the conscious mind and . . . brings it in contact with the creative intelligence that gives rise to every thought."

Then once you are in tune with the universe, your inner conflicts lessen, you become happier and easier to get along with and all personal problems vanish. Since "the wars that break out in the world are the result of the buildup of tension generated by tense, irritable people," pretty soon war will disappear too, along with poverty, injustice and crime.

While critics ridicule the simplicity of the Transcendental Meditation system, its advocates revel in how easy it is. The big drawing card to many people, according to *Life* magazine, is that "it requires no repudiation of the past and no promises to behave in the future."

The Beatles liked it because there was no fuss and no bother; it hardly dented their lives at all. The frequent testimony of almost all the followers of the Maharishi is "It's easy. And it works."

What upsets other Hindu gurus is that the Maharishi has accused them of interpreting their sacred book, the *Bhagavad Gita*, wrongly. At the heart of Hinduism has always been the necessity of renunciation, even of asceticism. But along came the Maharishi and said, "You can eat your cake and have it too." Happiness and material prosperity are not incompatible. In fact, his religion wants to help you enjoy your material possessions even more.

He explained it once this way. It is "like the inner juice of the orange, which can be enjoyed without destroying the outer beauty of the fruit. This is done simply by pricking the orange with a pin again and again and extracting the juice little by little, so that the inner juice is drawn out on the surface, and both are enjoyed simultaneously." In other words, you can drink the juice and enjoy the beauty of the orange too.

Buddhism tells you how to eliminate suffering; you do it by eliminating your desires. As the old saying goes, "Blessed is he who wants nothing, for he will never be disappointed." But Transcendental Meditation says that you can eliminate suffering merely by meditating on your mantra for a few minutes a day. TM unshackles your mind and allows it to attain its natural state of bliss.

Happiness or bliss consciousness is the preeminent goal of the Maharishi. How can a person find happiness? In a way it is the goal of all religion and all psychology, but the Maharishi seems to be crassly forthright in his approach.

Not only the Eastern religions but Christianity as well is concerned about happiness. Jesus' great Sermon on the Mount begins with the Beatitudes, each epigrammatic statement opening with the word "blessed," or as some modern translations put it, "happy."

"Blessed are the poor in spirit: for theirs is the kingdom of heaven.

Blessed are they that mourn: for they shall be comforted.

Blessed are the meek: for they shall inherit the earth . . ."

But the biblical teaching about happiness includes the fact that there is a problem. There is sin in this world, says the Bible; not only is there sin, but man himself is a sinner, and thus estranged from the Holy God. Since man was made for fellowship with God, he can't find happiness until that breach, that cosmic rift, can be repaired.

So the Bible addresses itself to the question of how God repairs the cosmic rift between man and Himself, and thus restores happiness to man. Christianity says that you were made to be related to God and that relationship, like a power line in a devastating storm, has been dramatically severed. Who will repair the cosmic rift? Who will repair the severed power line? That is the message of the Bible. That is the thrust of the Christian gospel.

When the Bible explains why Jesus Christ came into the world, it uses phrases like "The Son of Man is come to seek and save that which was lost." Man is in a bad predicament, and it does not help the situation to say there is no problem. Evil exists, whether the Maharishi wishes to recognize it or not.

Jacob Needleman, usually a sympathetic commentator in *The New Religions*, declared, "When held against the torments of grief, loneliness, pain, disease, self-doubt and anxiety, the Maharishi's talk about bliss-consciousness seemed romantic, even cheap. . . . Had this diminutive, giggling Hindu left his monastery in the Himalayas only to bring to the West the rosy cosmic optimism which had gasped its last in Auschwitz, Hiroshima and Vietnam?"

Just because people say that his system works is no proof that it is good and proper. Needleman cryptically writes, "There had always been methods which hundreds of thousands, even millions, of people had successfully tried—and the result was, if anything, more war, brutality, confusion, and personal misery in the world. Such methods had all come bearing similar promises."

Obviously, then, as Needleman implies, the Maharishi doesn't give any guidance for morality nor any standard of ethics. Transcendental Meditation says that your mind is naturally good. All you need is to sink a shaft of light to it and your mind will gravitate to the light to find "absolute bliss." That shaft of light is, of course, the secret mantra which the Maharishi or one of his disciples will give you. Then "without our having to observe or struggle with ourselves, quite spontaneously our natural inclinations begin to come into greater harmony with the natural laws of the evolution of life. Our desires become increasingly life supporting and simultaneously increasingly fulfilled."

In other words, when the mantra penetrates to the depths of your mind, you don't have to worry about morality any more. While many Eastern religions are largely negative, the Maharishi's cult most definitely is not. There are no taboos at all. It fact, you can almost infer that if you have guilt feelings over your pattern of immorality, you can practice meditating on your mantra for a while, and your guilt feelings will disappear so you can enjoy your pattern of immorality without any guilt feelings.

In Fedor Dostoevski's book, *The Possessed*, one character says, "Man is unhappy because he doesn't know he's happy . . . that's all."

That's just about the way the Maharishi sees it. According to the Maharishi, deep down inside of you you are really happy, and the secret mantra will cover up that surface unhappiness.

Newsweek once called Transcendental Meditation "a vague mixture of self-therapy, Hindu teaching and flower-power."

Perhaps, it would be better described simply as a big aspirin tablet for the headache of unhappiness. Aspirin usually does a good job of curing headaches, but it sometimes fails to get to the root of the problem. If you have appendicitis or a broken leg or an abscessed tooth, aspirin will make you feel happier; but in the long run, the cure is merely delusion. You had better see a doctor.

The Maharishi's contention that there is nothing wrong

with man that an *Om* or a *Rama* or another simple syllable won't cure is bad medicine.

The prescription that Jesus Christ gives is just as easy and is a lot safer in the long run—yes, especially in the long run.

Baba-lovers and the Meher Baba 12

LISTEN TO THIS STATEMENT:

"There is no doubt of my being God personified. . . . I am the Christ. . . . I assert unequivocally that I am infinite consciousness; and I can make this assertion because I AM infinite consciousness. I am everything and I am beyond everything. . . . Before me was Zoroaster, Krishna, Rama, Buddha, Jesus and Mohammed. . . . My present Avataric Form is the last Incarnation of this cycle of time, hence my Manifestation will be the greatest."

Who said it? A little old man named Merwan Sheriar Irani, better known as Meher Baba (which means "Compassionate Father"), who died in India in 1969.

But it isn't quite true that he actually said it, for Meher Baba decided to stop talking when he was thirty-one years old. All his communication after that was through an alphabet board or through hand gestures.

Why did he stop talking? Well, he figured that his previous incarnations—Zoroaster, Krishna, Rama, Buddha, Jesus and Mohammed—had said enough. All Meher Baba wanted to do was to get people to act upon what his predecessors had said.

135

His followers, called Baba-lovers, and a number of prominent celebrities are numbered among them, keep photographs of Meher Baba close to their hearts, enlarged on their walls and reduced microscopically to fit in their rings. But no matter the size, the portrait is unmistakably Meher Baba, "an avuncular older man with warm, soft eyes, a wide and startlingly beaked nose, descending over an enormous moustache that spreads out in an all-engulfing grin." Quite often the photograph is accompanied by his most oft-quoted saying, "Be happy, don't worry."

At times the sentimentality of the Baba-lovers is so saccharine it is almost sickening in our cold, computerized age. The language seems affected, and their prayers seem to have come from the last century: "Oh God, most Beloved Baba, may we show our gratitude for Your Supreme Gift of Yourself by receiving Your Love and giving Your Love and living Your message of Love in our lives."

Or when they speak of what Baba means to them, it gushes out in the same way, "Being in beloved Baba's presence was to be in the presence of pure Love. One experienced . . . the purity of Love. There was a radiance of countenance that no words can express. Compassion . . . true compassion . . . flowed from Baba's eyes. . . . The sweetness of expression was unbelievable. The embrace was not a physical touch. . . . Baba's love enveloped me in a very deep inward way."

And often when they quote the words of the great Meher Baba, the emotion is just as obvious: "Gatherings and meetings in my name should be a channel for the expression of my love, and to give them any other importance is to misunderstand my cause. . . . My office should be the heart of everyone who loves me. The heart of each should be my shrine, and my lover the priest of that temple of love."

With all of Meher Baba's unbelievable personal claims and with the unbearable gushiness of his followers, you would wonder who would want to become a Baba-lover anyway.

Yet the Meher Baba movement has gained wide acceptance among college and university students; many campuses have chapters of Meher Baba Lovers meeting regularly. Meher Baba Centers have now been established on both the East and the West Coasts as well as in Florida. The largest Center is in Myrtle Beach, South Carolina, where a 500-acre plot contains the site of the Meher Baba Spiritual Center and several sacred or near-sacred buildings.

Peter Rowley (*New Gods in America*) visited the place, so let him describe it: "Baba's car, a 1958 blue Ford sedan, up on cinder-blocks, is still shiny. There is a sign in front of it. A large meeting hall which Baba used for audiences of two or three hundred people and two chairs where he once sat are now roped off (they were being worn out from too many Baba-lovers sitting in them). And then Baba's house, *his* house, a redbrick bungalow of about six rooms, fully furnished. He visited the Center three times, the last in 1958. The longest period he spent there was three months. In one room were reliquaries under a plastic top—his robe, white underpants, a lock of hair, gray from his old age, a black lock from younger years, and another, deep brown as a young man. There is an alphabet board by which he had communicated, and nearby, the pillow with the blood-stain where his head rested after the automobile accident in Prague, Oklahoma."

About two to three thousand people visit the Meher Baba shrine each year; most of the visitors are young.

Among the early prominent followers of Meher Baba was Elizabeth Patterson, an unusual woman who had been an insurance broker, an ambulance driver during World War I and an explorer on a Soviet expedition to the Arctic. Then suddenly in the mid-1960s young people started to become Baba-lovers too. Some hippies became Baba-freaks to break the drug habit. Several rock stars, including Peter Townshend, who wrote the rock opera *Tommy*, also became followers.

Although Meher Baba himself opposed the formation of a religious hierarchy and a formalized religion, there is a quarterly magazine called *The Awakener* that ties Baba-lovers together, and a publishing house called Sufism Reoriented which keeps paperbacks by and about Meher Baba on the bookshelves.

Let's take a look at Meher Baba, who was born in 1894, stopped speaking in 1925 and "dropped the body" (the Baba-lovers' euphemism for his death) in 1969, just short of his seventy-fifth birthday.

Born in Poona, India, near Bombay, to Persian parents, he was reared in Zoroastrianism, before attending a Christian high school. While in college, he was riding on his bicycle one day when he met a woman described as a great Sufi saint, "who kissed him on the forehead, thus tearing away the veil which obscured his own God-realization."

(Sufism, incidentally, grew out of a mystical Islam, or an Islam more directed by the heart than by the head. But as it emerged in India, it became syncretistic, adopting views from Hinduism, Buddhism and Christianity as well as Islam. However, it remained more emotional and mystical than rational and mental.)

Baba recalls his "unveiling" by the Sufi saint this way: "With just a kiss on the forehead, between the eyebrows, Babajan made me experience thrills of indescribable bliss which continued for about nine months. Then one night in January 1914, she made me realize in a flash the infinite bliss of self-realization." With that kiss Meher Baba began to appreciate his deity, that he was an avatar, the last and greatest of the divine incarnations.

Not everything he did seemed either loving or compassionate. At one time in 1925, he remodeled an abandoned military camp in Meherabad, India, and provided free hospital services and other facilities to the needy citizens in the area. Thousands flocked to him; at least twenty thousand people helped him celebrate his thirty-second birthday. Then suddenly with no apparent explanation he closed the entire operation.

One of his followers admitted the dilemma: "One of the characteristics of Baba's activities which often puzzles people is the manner in which he will suddenly stop a project in apparent mid-career, regardless of the degree of evident success it is experiencing. In November-December 1926, he did this to the institutions and services which were thriving at Meherabad, closing them all lock, stock and barrel."

Baba's cryptic explanation was, "Often my external activities and commitments are only the external expression of the internal work I am doing."

It was during this time that Baba suddenly stopped speaking. First, he wrote out answers to questions which were addressed to him; then he began using an English alphabet board and spelled out the words of his reply in this painstaking manner.

In 1931, Baba made his first of six trips to the West, stopping first in England and then in America. In New York, the newspapers fought for stories of this self-proclaimed Messiah from India who never said a word. Extensive meetings were arranged for him, but after two days in New York he decided to go to California. Hollywood stars were anxious to meet him, and the Hollywood Bowl was rented for the occasion. But Meher Baba changed his mind again and suddenly left for China, "leaving his American disciples the task of canceling all the engagements that had been made for him."

Baba didn't appreciate the colder climate of England and America. He felt it necessary to explain: "Some of you might ask why, being the Avatar, I could feel or catch cold. . . . Once the God-realized soul comes down with his God-consciousness to normal consciousness of the illusion of duality, then the physical body of even such a God-realized Perfect Master is subject to ordinary contagion and disease. Simultaneously I exist at every level, and as I am therefore on a level with your consciousness, then I suffer, experience and enjoy just as you all do."

He seemed even more susceptible to automobile accidents in America than he did to the common cold. One of his followers explained that these accidents fulfilled his prophecy: Baba had told his disciples in India years before that he would have to shed blood on American soil.

The most bewildering thing about Baba was his self-imposed silence. Coupled with that was the amazing way that his interpreters could translate his gestures when the alphabet board became too tedious. At times they seemed to interpret faster than the little old man could give his hand signals.

But to Baba-lovers what is more baffling is the fact that Baba had said he would break his silence before he died or "dropped the body." Some thought he would break the silence in that Hollywood Bowl engagement in 1931. Others thought he might do it at the special 1962 East-West gathering which he had called "strictly for My

Lovers." Some 137 had come from the West and about 3,000 from the East, but Meher Baba said nothing.

Then he announced another East-West gathering for 1969. It would be the last given "in silence, the last before He speaks His world-renewing word."

He had humbly said in his "universal Message," "When I break my silence, the impact of my love will be universal and all life in creation will know, feel and receive of it. It will help every individual to break free from his own bondage in his own way. I am the Divine Beloved who loves you more than you can ever love yourself. The breaking of my silence will help you to help yourself in knowing your real self."

But instead of breaking his silence, Meher Baba "dropped his body." And now his followers debate whether their leader will yet break his silence.

Although Baba did not speak, he did write. Among the books that contain his thinking are a five-volume work entitled *Discourses,* a more philosophical work outlining the history of God and the universe entitled *God Speaks,* and a third, *Listen Humanity,* which is an assortment of essays by Baba on various subjects.

Some of the American Baba-lovers follow him only on the basis of emotion. And that is a considerable basis. In *The New Religions,* Jacob Needleman thinks that Baba-lovers live their feelings and strongly rely on intuition as a source of knowledge. In other words, the heart, rather than the mind, is the center of knowledge.

In his *Discourses* Baba affirmed: "Love and Happiness are the only important things in life, and they are both absent in the dry and factual knowledge which is accessible to the intellect."

According to Baba, the mind should not dictate the ends of life, but should only help "to realize those ends which are given by the heart. . . . In other words, it surrenders its role of judge. . . . The mind has a place in practical life, but its role begins after the heart has had its say."

To illustrate his point, Meher Baba says, the planet Earth has two sister planets that feed it with reincarnated souls. On one of the planets the people have 100 percent intelligence and no love, and on the other, the people have 75 percent intellect and 25 percent love. But only when these souls reincarnate on this earth can they learn "true love in all its forms and relationships."

Often when Baba talks (we should use the word "writes") about the importance of love, he makes good sense, but as he elaborates on his total system of belief, it is obvious that his teaching is a weird hodgepodge adapted from various religions, but mostly from Buddhism.

The soul of man is not only reincarnated in other human beings, but actually begins its journey upward as a stone, then as a metal.

The official spokesman of the movement in America explains this by saying: "Certain cars or machines you buy seem jinxed, mostly because the people who made them fought or cursed over them. If you strike a sheet of metal, you will notice it quivers. A lady once told me that she hated polishing silver, and she was surprised when I replied that she should be happy to make the silver shine, as it wants to be itself. It, too, has a soul. However dim its consciousness, it is far ahead of the stone.

"Having exhausted all the metal forms, the soul next takes its abode in the vegetable forms, and when it runs out of these, in the insect and reptile forms. Each time there is a progression, and certain types are more awake than others. For instance, flies and mosquitoes can be killed if necessary without too much qualm, as it hurries their evolution, but spiders, bees and ants have a very complex and interesting life—and they should be allowed to finish their cycle if possible, so as to develop the most from their experiences."

You would think the soul would be exhausted by this time, but boldly it continues its evolutionary journey, according to Baba-lovers, into fish, birds and animals.

Now Meher Baba himself reports that "the kangaroo is the first animal form in which the soul incarnates after passing through the last bird form and that is why its front two legs are so very small." However, after experiencing life as various animals, the soul finally takes the fateful jump from the form of a monkey to "the perfection of form and that is the human form."

Connected with this evolutionary process is the Oriental doctrine of karma, which means that actions in previous incarnations have caused our present circumstances and predicaments. In the same way, what we do now will shape our future destiny.

But even when the soul has taken on human form its evolutionary path is not completed. There are seven planes of existence or awareness for mortals, beginning with the gross materialistic plane. Gradually, as you master your desires, you move up toward sainthood, which is the fifth plane, but if you misuse some of your newly discovered spiritual powers en route to plane five, you are liable to end up as a stone again and have to start all over again like a game of Parchesi. Finally, the sixth plane, the plane of illumination is reached: after that there is Nirvana and merger into the mind of God.

Moving along the path of spiritual progress can be accomplished in several ways, according to Meher Baba. In keeping with normal Buddhist teaching, he refers to the ways of knowledge, of action and of mental and physical discipline as being acceptable. But the best way, according to this modern Avatar, is to surrender completely to Meher Baba. The Hindus would call it Bhakti yoga, or the path of devotion. "Of all the high roads which take the pilgrim directly to his divine destination the quickest lies through the God-man. In the God-man, God reveals Himself in all His glory, with His infinite power, unfathomable knowledge, inexpressible bliss and eternal existence. The path through the God-man is available to all those who approach Him in complete surrenderance and unwavering faith."

Christians would not argue with that last statement by Meher Baba if he were talking about Jesus Christ. The only problem is that Baba is talking about himself and not about Jesus Christ.

Like Meher Baba, Jesus Christ also made some bold claims two thousand years ago. Jesus said, "I and my Father are one. . . . I am the way, the truth, and the life; no man cometh unto the Father but by me. . . . Before Abraham was, I am. . . . He that believeth not on me is condemned already because he believeth not on the only begotten Son of God."

So both Baba and Jesus Christ made fantastic claims, but the difference rests not so much in what they said as in what they did. Jesus Christ performed miracles, died a sacrificial death for those who believe (and that's a far cry from shedding blood in an Oklahoma car crash), and then three days later rose from the dead. It was the Resurrection of Jesus Christ that convinced His followers that what He said was true.

If Jesus Christ had not risen, "our faith would be in vain," as the Apostle Paul stated. But He did rise from the tomb, and even doubting Thomas was convinced when he saw the nail prints in His hands. Somehow Meher Baba's claims seem to fall far short when compared to such demonstrated proof by Jesus Christ.

Meher Baba offers no hope for the sinner. In fact, the

sinner may revert to being a stone and be condemned to begin the evolutionary climb all over again.

Baba-lovers are urged to suspend all rational thoughts to believe in Meher Baba. This, too, does not compare with Christian belief, which is not irrational. The Apostle Thomas was shown evidence that fostered belief. Baba-lovers are told to disregard what they think, and to trust in spite of reason.

Baba-lovers are also told to lose their identity in Meher Baba, who said, "Lose yourself in Baba and you will find that you eternally were Baba. . . . Only when one loves me and loses one's self in me, am I found."

Some Christian concepts may sound similar to this on the surface, but they are totally different. Oneness with Jesus Christ does not mean a loss of identity. The Christian view is that each individual is different and has a personal dignity. Each person is loved individually by God.

The Good Shepherd not only knows his flock but he also knows his sheep individually by name. Each person has personal individualized worth.

Meher Baba would look at snowflakes and notice their basic similarity. The Christian looks at the same snowflakes and says, "Yes, the similarity proves that there is one Almighty God who loves infinite variety in His creation. He does not want carbon copies nor identical snowflakes. He wants His followers, like the snowflake, to reflect both a common Creator and their individual God-given characteristics."

Guru Maharaj Ji and the Divine Light Mission 13

HOW CAN ANYONE find fault with someone who likes Baskin-Robbins ice cream and Batman comics?

How can anyone be irritated if the teen-age "Lord of the Universe" squirts him in the face with a water pistol?

Wouldn't you expect "the Perfect Master" to splatter you with mud as he roars away on his motorcycle?

And wouldn't it be normal for the "Power of the Universe" to enjoy tinkering with his pair of Mercedes-Benz automobiles and his $30,000 Silver Cloud Rolls-Royce?

Let's face it. The Guru Maharaj Ji was unlike any guru from India you had ever met, until he changed his image.

In 1973 he claimed to have some seven million disciples around the world, including sixty thousand in the United States, His most famous convert was Rennie Davis, militant radical who led the Chicago 7 and preached revolution. Now dimpled and clean-shaven, Davis said, "I'm simply doing what Guru Maharaj Ji has prepared me to do all my life. He is the Perfect Master, the creator of the world, and we are nothing but his perfect puppets."

Born Prem Pal Singh Rawat in Hardwar, India on December 10, 1957, Maharaj Ji joined an Indian "Holy Family," a member of the highest of the high Brahmin caste. According to reporters in India, "his family is quite wealthy." His father went by the name of Param Sant Satgurudev Shri Hans Ji Maharaj, and had built up a following as Satguru, which in Hindu circles meant that he was the only Perfect Master living who could reveal the Ancient Knowledge of the inner-self. The Satguru is said to be God Incarnate.

Shri Hans Ji and his wife had four sons in their "Holy Family," but it was the youngest son, Maharaj Ji, who was selected to be the new Perfect Master to succeed him. Obviously precocious, the heir apparent delivered his first satsang ("holy discourse") at the ripe old age of two, admonishing his father's household of the importance of realizing God. When the boy was only six, his father gave him Knowledge with a capital "K." That is the secret and very special ingredient in Maharaj Ji's religion.

Maharaj Ji was eight (and attending a Roman Catholic mission school in Dehra Dun) when his father died. But before he passed on, his father gave his pranams (meaning prostrations) to his son, saying "He is so great I can but prostrate myself in front of him." The father had previously declared that his son was so great in wisdom and enlightenment that he "would one day shine over the whole world as brightly as the sun shines in the sky."

"I didn't want to be Satguru," Maharaj Ji affirms in the cult's official *Who Is Guru Maharaj Ji?* "I didn't understand why it is me. I would have been satisfied to be the humblest servant of the Satguru." But, after all, when his family crowned him with the crown of Rama and Krishna and put the tilak (the colored spot that Hindus wear) on his forehead, what was he supposed to do? And then he heard an inner voice saying, "You are he. You are to take this Knowledge (with a capital K) into the world." And so he did.

By the time he was twelve, he was making converts by the thousands at his Divine Light Ashram on the banks of the Ganges. That year, 1969, he dispatched his first missionary, Mahatma Guru Charnanand (nee Charles Cameron, an Oxford graduate) to convert pagan London.

At first, Cameron considered the pint-sized mahatma to be a "pocket Napoleon." Two days later when he saw the twelve-year-old guru again he heard a satsang on automatic and manual gears in cars but couldn't make sense out of it.

He handed the young guru a poem he had written, but Maharaj Ji crumpled it and thrust it into his pocket, unread.

Later Cameron saw Maharaj Ji in his car (they learn to drive early in India) and pleaded with him, "Please teach me how to love." Maharaj Ji stepped on the gas, and left the Oxford graduate standing in the driveway with dust on his face.

Finally, however, Cameron, with a wild flower in hand, spotted Maharaj Ji standing on top of a sand dune on the banks of the Ganges. Falling at the Indian youngster's feet, he thrust the flower into the sand in front of him.

Maharaj Ji looked at the flower and said matter of factly, "I think this flower will grow." Hearing those words, Cameron became an ardent disciple.

In 1970, having completed the ninth grade, Maharaj Ji dropped out of school and began to take his Knowledge to the world. He started by riding through Delhi in a golden chariot with a retinue of camels, elephants and devotees. By the time the parade reached the India Gate in New Delhi an estimated one and a half million spectators were paying homage to the young Perfect Master. With the words, "I declare that I will establish peace in this world," he exploded what his disciples call his "Peace Bomb."

The following year, Maharaj Ji left India for the West. Gastonberry, England, was his first public appearance. The site, a Pop Festival. Surprising the promoters as well as the crowd, he invaded the concert by driving in a white Rolls Royce, and preaching for five minutes before someone could pull the plug on the mike.

Meanwhile in Los Angeles, three members of the Divine Light Mission (almost half of the entire U.S. contingent) wired London, begging the satguru to include America in his itinerary. A month later he crossed the Atlantic. The Los Angeles team had distributed flyers inviting "all brothers of Love" to welcome the Guru who would come "in the clouds with great power and glory," at the Los Angeles International Airport. About 200 people formed the welcoming committee, shouting "Bolie Shri, Satgurudev Maharaj ki jar," which freely translated means "Sing the praises of the Lord True-Revealer of Light, inexpressibly all-powerful majesty."

The following summer, 1972, he returned again. This time, the highlight of his trip was the Guru Puda Festival in Montrose, Colorado, which was attended by about 6,000 people. Some 2,000 converts were made. So by the fall of 1972, Divine Light Centers were springing up in most major cities of the country. According to their count they now had forty-five centers, 15,000 members and a national center in Denver, Colorado.

That November, eleven 747s were filled with devotees of Maharaj Ji, making a pilgrimage to India for the Hans Joyanti Festival to honor his departed father.

The way Maharaj Ji's converts kept multiplying was almost unbelievable. By spring of 1973, there were 480

Divine Light Centers around the world and in every continent. The U.S. membership had now grown to 35,000.

From the Denver headquarters, new enterprises were being spun off, each one adding new luster to the claims of Maharaj Ji.

As the *Saturday Review* reported, "It operates thrift shops and a New York vegetarian restaurant, runs a food co-op, offers painting, carpentry, plumbing, housekeeping, lawn care, auto repair, and laundry services. There is a divine airline (everything is divine at the Divine Light Mission) and a firm that markets wholesale electronics equipment." And then there was a record company, a motion picture company, and a publishing company that produces *The Divine Times,* a newspaper, and a magazine called *And It Is Divine* (circulation 130,000).

With all going well the young Guru designed the Divine United Organization, "a master plan for the rediscovery of humanity."

But the really big event—billed by devotees as "the most important event in the history of the world" was Soul-Rush, a three-day festival, better known as Millennium 1973 to be held at the Houston Astrodome in the fall of 1973. It was slated to usher in the Millennium described in Revelation 20. Some 80,000 were expected, although other expectations ranged from 144,000 (also taken from the Book of Revelation) to 200,000. A dozen jumbo jets were supposed to bring 10,000 disciples from India. In every major city of the country, signs were posted heralding the coming of Guru Maharaj Ji. The comet Kohoutek was on its way, and some devotees were predicting that visitors from outer space would also show up at the Astrodome.

But Millennium '73 never got off the ground. Between 12,000 and 20,000 showed up at the meeting, although admission was free of charge and curiosity-seekers were expected by the thousands. The Divine Light Mission had spent thousands and thousands of dollars but could not fill the 70,000 seat Astrodome. Only 100 came on the jets from India. Even the comet Kohoutek was a disappointment.

But the Guru Maharaj Ji (whom his followers call Goom Rodgie—it's a contraction of the longer name) had been running into a few other disappointments too. In India, the Guru's secretary was charged with trying to smuggle $80,000 in jewels, watches and money past customs officials. Rival Hindu groups, perhaps jealous of the Guru's fame in the West, said he was seven years older than claimed. One swami called him "a typical Asian phony."

In the U.S. some of his followers attacked a newspaper reporter who had previously thrown a shaving cream pie in the Guru's face. They fractured the reporter's skull with a blackjack. Today the reporter has a permanent plastic plate over his crushed skull.

Rennie Davis responded, "This is not the age to turn the other cheek. This Savior will not be crucified." Not only did Davis admit that the attackers were devotees, he said that one was a mahatma and the other was considered the reincarnation of St. Peter. *Vogue* magazine reported, "Both are still very much in the Guru's good graces."

One Divine Light Official said, "Holiness is a matter of interpretation." A devotee told a reporter, "We must unquestioningly do whatever Maharaj Ji tells us. If he told us to slit your throat, I would do so in an instant."

Besides that, the young Guru who is allegedly bringing peace to the world had a bleeding duodenal ulcer, the kind that middle-aged businessmen get from too much stress. Neither the ice cream that he loves, nor his Rolls-Royces, Mercedes-Benzes, two private airplanes, cabin cruisers or motorcycles seem to ease his inner-unrest.

In 1974 he married a former airline stewardess in his $80,000 Denver residence. The Mission also provided him with homes in London, Los Angeles, New York and several Indian cities.

Gradually, it became apparent that there was dissension within the ranks of the Holy Family itself. Perhaps it began when he declared his non-Hindu wife by the name of Marilyn Johnson to be the incarnation of the ten-armed, tiger-riding goddess Durga. Perhaps it developed when the newlyweds refused to allow his mother Mataji to stay in their $400,000 Malibu mansion. Certainly it was aggravated when Indian officials of the Divine Light Mission charged that the Lord of the Universe was "haunting night clubs, drinking, dancing" and perhaps, heaven forbid, eating *meat*!

Naturally, something had to be done. So Mataji took the matter into her matronly hands and ousted Maharaj Ji for "falling from the path." Installed in his place was Bal Bhagwan Ji, his oldest brother, whom some DLM members call "the reincarnation of Jesus Christ."

Maharaj Ji vigorously fought his mother's action. He questioned whether it is legal to vote God Incarnate out of office. "Nobody can oust the Lord of the universe," he said.

Eventually after a few lawsuits, it was agreed that Maharaj Ji could run the American franchise while his mother and brother handled the operation in India.

In 1976, the Divine Light Mission cut back its operation until only five U.S. ashrams were operating. The movement was decentralized and democratized. No longer was Maharaj Ji considered God incarnate; now he was only their leader with important teachings. Headquarters was moved from Denver to Miami, while Maharaj Ji moved to a mansion in Malibu, California, overlooking the ocean.

So a shadow has fallen on the Divine Light Mission.

But what is the essence of "Goom Rodgie's" teaching besides Knowledge (with a capital K)?

It has been described as "not vastly different from that of the Vedantists." Man's problem is his mind. It plays tricks on him. It says there is good and evil, pain and pleasure. Evil comes from the mind. Suffering comes when the mind asks too many questions. To get rid of suffering you need Knowledge and Knowledge (with a capital K) does not come by receiving information but rather through an experience. When you receive that experience you enter into Oneness with the Infinite.

However, in one area, the Goom Rodgie's teaching differs from other Eastern religions. Unlike other Indian gurus, he encourages his followers to keep their jobs, enjoy good food and make more money.

While the guru teaches that "material prosperity can never provide constant satisfaction" he does not teach that poverty brings contentment either. Otherwise, he would have to divest himself of a few material possessions himself.

But the crucial question is, *How do you get Knowledge with a capital K?* If you ask this question, you will be told that you can't describe the taste of a banana, you have to eat one to know. Even so, you can't know what the guru's Bliss is without experiencing it.

In the Maharaj Ji's official biography, it is stated, "Knowledge is not a religion. It is the direct experience of God or eternal energy that all religions talk about. It establishes beyond any doubt the intrinsic unity between all living things."

Even before experiencing it, however, you have to undergo pre-conditioning. While this pre-conditioning may last weeks or months, it is often compressed into a few hours.

The movement's star convert, Rennie Davis, explains, "Scientists are just discovering that the pineal gland is light receptive, and that the pineal gland is sort of the thing that directs the flow of the brain. Guru Maharaj Ji shows us how to discover this gland, and how to use this light so that we become a part of Him. And this light shows us the Word, and if we can experience the Word, we'll be saved."

When you are adequately instructed by one of "Goom Rodgie's" disciples, you are ready for the mind-blowing experience of receiving Knowledge and Knowledge comes in four forms.

First, you see divine light. *The New Republic* described the process this way: "The living room lights were extinguished, and after a discourse on the significance of spiritual inner light the mahatma began moving among us. Explaining that the center of the forehead is the center of the body, he showed each person how to press against the side of the forehead with the thumb and middle finger of the right hand and against the lower center of the forehead with the index finger. Sure enough, we pressed and saw light."

Bob Larson in his book *The Guru* explains it as "a neurological light caused by a reaction of the retina." At any rate, the meditators after a while become so proficient that they can close their eyes at almost any time and see this inner light.

Second, you hear divine music. Or as they sometimes say, just as the first step develops a third eye, so the second step develops a third ear. "You hear Divine Music . . . in glorious stereophonics," reported *The*

Saturday Review, "when Mahatma puts his fingers into or under your ears." What is actually heard is debatable. Rennie Davis said he heard "loud rock and roll." Another devotee said it sounded like a train. One "premie" said it was the same sound she had heard before in the womb of her mother as a fetus. Official DLM literature calls it "the sound of the universe in tune with itself."

Third, you taste divine nectar. In this step you curl your tongue back, almost swallowing it, and thereby "receive nutrition from nectar that falls down from the center of the head before birth." They say that Jesus subsisted on divine nectar when he was fasting for forty days in the wilderness. While "premies" extol the qualities of divine nectar, skeptics call it post-nasal drip.

Fourth comes the most important step of all. The first three are merely preparatory for number four. It is "receiving the divine word." While followers of Krishna Consciousness receive "knowledge" through chanting, followers of "Goom Rodgie" get it by meditation on the divine word after being psyched up by three preliminary experiences. They speak of a "primordial vibration," but whatever happens in step four often renders the devotee helpless as he lies in a trance in silent meditation.

The Guru's literature refers to John 1:1, "In the beginning was the Word," as if the Gospel writer were predicting the coming of Maharaj Ji, but it insists that this word has nothing to do with language. It can't be spoken. "This is the ultimate experience; this is what they refer to as being 'blissed out.'" It is claimed, says R. D. Clements in *God and the Gurus,* "that in this experience a man is directly perceiving the oneness of the universe." Thereafter he is told to meditate on his experience as often as possible.

It is this fuse-blowing experience that has made ardent disciples out of some of the most unlikely prospects.

Because they have had a life-changing experience of Knowledge with a capital K, they make extravagant claims for their teen-age Guru. Rennie Davis himself stated, "If I weren't absolutely convinced that this is the greatest event mankind has ever known, if I didn't believe with my entire soul that Guru Maharaj Ji is going to save the planet, then I wouldn't be placing myself so far out on a limb."

A Krishna chanter, however, was reported in the *Houston Chronicle* as saying disdainfully, "Since when does the Supreme Lord recommend that you push in your eyeballs, plug up your ears, and taste spit, all the while sitting under a blanket, as the proper way to receive Him into your hearts?"

Obviously, though, DLM devotees have experienced something, and this makes the movement difficult for many Christians to deal with. Christians often like to tell about their spiritual experience with Jesus Christ, about how they were converted. But they soon become frustrated when they give their testimony to one who has experienced Knowledge. In an article in *His* magazine, R. D. Clements wrote, "By swapping experiences, Christians are playing into the hands of a mystical, experience-centered theology."

Adding to the frustration is the way that Maharaj Ji has woven biblical passages into his teachings. He says that "Jesus taught this Knowledge." If you follow the guru, "you won't be denying, you will be going further on the path, you'll be realizing who Jesus was. . . . When we receive Knowledge, we really know what he gave to those twelve disciples."

He speaks about the Word that was "with God and was God." He says that "the kingdom of God is within you," even as Jesus said. He reminds his followers that the Scriptures teach that God was to come as a child.

And a favorite passage is "Taste and see that the Lord is good," or as it is sometimes paraphrased, "Try it; you'll like it."

The problem is that he accepts all religions, but he modestly says that all religions point to him. The world has been given a final chance; if it rejects him, it is curtains for the universe.

The unity of all religions is a standard Vedanta idea, and the guru goes on to espouse another basic Hindu concept that God is impersonal. "He is energy," he says. "We are little parts of that energy. . . . Little drops of that energy are in us and they are our souls."

This is a far cry from the God of the Bible, who displayed emotions such as love and anger and who sent His only begotten Son in human flesh because of His deep love for mankind. When Maharaj Ji thinks of a personal God, he always refers to a grandfather type figure with two eyes and a nose. He refuses to consider what the Bible teaches that "God is a spirit" and yet a spirit with a personality. When man was created in the image of God, he was stamped with the distinguishing marks of God's personality. We are persons, because God is a person.

Not only is God a person, but He is also distinct from man. Therefore, it is possible to have a personal relationship, a one-to-one relationship, an "I-Thou" relationship with Him. Christians are exhorted to communicate with God and indeed to meditate on Him, what He has done for us and what He means to us.

But for those in the Divine Light Mission, meditation is not "on God's person" but "into His essence." Like other Eastern religions, the goal is oneness or merger with the infinite. The modern computer jargon-word "merge-purge" describes the goal: you merge with the oneness of the universe and thereby your unique personality is purged.

At the Millennium Festival in the Astrodome, Maharaj Ji plainly stated that he was not interested in a relationship with God because "that would mean God is a separate person to relate to."

The biblical view is that man's sin hinders his one-to-one relationship with God. Indeed, that was why the Son of God became flesh, according to Scripture. The sin problem was so serious that it could not be handled by man. According to I John 3:5, the purpose of Christ's coming was "to take away our sins."

The Hindu concept of salvation comes through knowledge or enlightenment. To the Hindu, man's problem is ignorance, not sinfulness. "Evil," says the Guru, "is the ignorance of our mind." The divine is within you.

In Mark 7:21-23, Jesus taught that something else was within man, and it certainly wasn't divine.

But there is another thing that followers of Guru Maharaj Ji don't understand about Jesus Christ. To them, the focal point of Jesus' life is his teaching. After all, if the way of salvation is through imparting knowledge (with or without a capital K) then teaching is all-important.

However the focal point of the gospels is the death and resurrection of Jesus Christ. What He did is treated by the Evangelists as even more important than what He said. If all aspects of Christ's life were detailed as voluminously as the Passion Week and the Resurrection appearances, it would take about forty 300-page tomes to cover his biography.

Why did Jesus feel it was essential to His Mission that He die on a cross? Why wasn't it enough for Him to present His teaching? And if Jesus is only one of a chain of divine teachers from Buddha to Mohammed and to

Maharaj Ji, why did His disciples feel the Resurrection of Jesus Christ was so important?

There is no other way to read the Bible. Writers of Scripture considered Jesus more than a great teacher, more than one of a chain of avatars who would bring enlightenment to man. He was not only the one who created all things, but He was also the one through whom we have redemption through his blood, even the forgiveness of sins. "In him," wrote the Apostle Paul, "dwelleth all the fulness of the godhead bodily," in Colossians 2:9.

When Paul wrote his Epistle to the Colossians, he certainly didn't have the Guru Maharaj Ji and the Divine Light Mission in mind. But the little epistle is certainly apropos.

One of his followers affirmed in 1973, "If he isn't God, this is the biggest fraud ever perpetrated upon the world; but if he is God, he has promised to bring us a thousand years of peace."

Five years later, Maharaj Ji denied that he was God incarnate.

VI

IV

A DASH OF THIS AND A SMIDGEON OF THAT OR RELIGION CAFETERIA-STYLE

14

AT FIRST, people joked about Sun Myung Moon's name. They thought he should have disciples named after the planets: Mercury, Venus, Earth, Mars, all the way down to Pluto.

Then they began dreaming up clever names for his followers: Moon-people, Moonites, Moon-flowers or Moonstruck.

But Sun Myung Moon and members of his Unification Church were not laughing. They were hard at work, tacking up posters, buttonholing busy pedestrians, and urging Americans to forgive, love and join their message of brotherhood.

His clean-cut, well-mannered adherents made friends and influenced people; his full-page newspaper ads blitzed the nation's major dailies; and his mass rallies in America's most prestigious centers made Christians and non-Christians alike sit up and take notice.

Who was this man with the strange-sounding name and the oriental face? What is his teaching that, he says, will unify all branches of Christendom?

Already, the Unification Church has a worldwide membership of approximately three million with about 40,000 members in the United States. Of the 40,000 members 10,000 are dedicated core members who live at one of the church's communal centers and work full-time for the movement. Thus the Unification Church has more full-time evangelists than any Protestant denomination.

Allegedly, Sun Myung Moon is a Christian missionary from Korea to America, preaching brotherhood and re-birth. (One of the slogans on his ubiquitous placards is "This could be your re-birthday.") Mixed in with his religious message is a patriotism that would make the Johnny Mann Singers, Lawrence Welk and John Wayne salute. Vigorously anti-Communist, Moon backed President Nixon to the end with a "God Loves Richard M. Nixon" campaign. And one of his publications which billed itself as "America's fastest growing freedom newspaper" got the endorsement of Barry Goldwater and other conservative congressmen.

Now what about Sun Myung Moon? Who is he? Where did he come from?

His official biography states that he was born in Pyungan Buk-do province of what is now North Korea on January 6, 1920. Although raised in a Presbyterian home, he was interested in spiritualism and mysticism from early in his life.

Then, according to his literature, "On Easter morning in 1936, while sixteen-year-old Sun Myung Moon was in deep prayer on a mountainside in Korea, Jesus Christ appeared to him to tell him he had an important mission to accomplish in the fulfillment of God's providence." He was to complete Christ's unfinished work. The details of this vision are not exactly clear. Some reports indicate that he was told to restore God's "perfect kingdom on earth"; in the early days of the movement, he reported that he not only saw Jesus but also heard a voice from heaven that said, "You will be the completer of man's salvation by being the Second Coming of Christ."

The following seven years were very significant for Sun Myung Moon. Not only did he study electrical engineering in Japan and delve into the Bible on his own, but he also developed what he calls "The Divine Principle." This later was written down for him in book form, and became, to his disciples, what Mary Baker Eddy's writings are to Christian Scientists. During this time, he claims to have spent time with Jesus in the spirit world.

In 1945, he began preaching, and this is where his biography begins to be confusing. He apparently was associated with an underground Pentecostal movement in Pyong Yang, North Korea's capital, until his anti-Communism got him into trouble with the North Korean government. (*The Christian Century* reported that it may have been bigamy and adultery that "done him in," rather than anti-Communism.)

In any case, Moon ended up in a slave labor camp for three years, until he was freed by United Nations forces in 1950.

Moving to South Korea, he worked as a harbor laborer in Pusan until he founded his church, officially called the Holy Spirit Association for the Unification of World Christianity, in 1954. *Time* magazine says the movement developed from an earlier Korean messianic movement. "My mission," says Moon, "is to try to unite all Christians into one family before the Lord arrives."

From the start, the Moon mission was controversial. The year that he founded his Unification Church, his wife left him. Moon explains, "She could not understand my mission."

The Religious News Service says, "It is unclear whether

he has been married twice or four times." Moonies say it has only been twice.

But persistent charges of immorality were lodged against the Korean messiah as well. The *Philadelphia Bulletin* reported, "A third jailing in 1955 reportedly was for 'causing social disorder' and having bad morals stemming from ritual sex with women in his church."

According to the Rev. Won Il Chei, a leading Presbyterian minister in Seoul, "If we believe those who have gone into the group and come out, they say that one has to receive Sun Myung Moon's blood to receive salvation. That blood is ordinarily received by three periods of sexual intercourse. But this fact they themselves keep absolutely secret."

A Japanese book, *The Madness in Japan* by Arao Arai, charges that Moon used to teach that "in order to purify oneself of the Satanic blood we inherited and in order to go to heaven after death, humans must have intercourse with those who have God's blessings. This is what they call the ritual of blood-sharing or ritual of holy spirit exchange."

The disciples of Moon vigorously deny the charges. He was arrested in 1955, they say, for draft evasion and was subsequently acquitted. "A fundamental tenet of our church," says its former chief, Neil Salonen, "is chastity and the absolute sanctity of the marriage relationship. . . . No sexual misconduct is tolerated." Others say that what was practiced in the early days of the movement in Korea is not taught today because it would not be acceptable in America.

Nevertheless, the Presbyterian church in Korea ruled the Unification Church as heretical for three reasons: (1) Sun Myung Moon had placed himself, more than Jesus Christ, as the object of faith; (2) their doctrine violated the morals of modern society; and (3) they would destroy the church by deceiving pure and sincere Christians.

But the facts are, that whatever the charges were against him in 1955, he was acquitted. In the following years, besides developing his new religion, he began building a multi-million-dollar network of industries including pharmaceuticals, titanium production, ginseng tea, air rifles and stone vases. Today his holdings are valued at fifteen million dollars.

As Moon climbed the financial ladder in Korea, the government began to look at him more kindly. By the mid-1960s Moon had launched a few anti-Communist front groups, including the International Federation for Victory over Communism. Because of his militant anti-Communism and his vigorous support of South Korean strong man, Park Chung Hee, the Korean government, according to *Time,* "bestows favors on Moon." "Every year," says *Newsweek,* "the government sends provincial officials, militia leaders, teachers and village chiefs to his center outside Seoul for instruction."

The next phase of the worldwide advance of the Unification Church started on January 1, 1972, when God appeared to Moon and told him to come to America and prepare the people for the Second Coming of Christ. The American headquarters was established on a twenty-two acre estate in Tarrytown, New York, which the Church purchased for $850,000. The estate includes a mansion for Moon and his family as well as an elaborate training center for his followers.

Moon's American message was this: the Messiah is on his way and the salvation of the world will depend on whether America repents and turns to God in this decade. In early 1974, during a thirty-two-city blitz tour of America, Moon, speaking through a Korean interpreter, said over and over again, "God's hope for the world relies on America" and "God has chosen Richard Nixon as President." In July he led a rally in support of President Nixon on the steps of the Capitol. Full-page ads appeared across the country in many leading newspapers: "God inspires a man and then confirms him as President through the will of the people. . . . At this time in history God has chosen Richard Nixon to be President of the United States." Not long afterwards, Nixon resigned. Undaunted, Sun Myung Moon continued his coast-to-coast crusade. In New York City, two days after Moon had addressed a rally of more than twenty thousand people in Madison Square Garden, the church bought a two-page spread in the *New York Times* at a cost of more than thirteen thousand dollars in which his sermon was presented in condensed form.

In most cities, he attracted large crowds, but often half the audience left the Moon rallies before his two-hour message was completed. American audiences are apparently not as patient as those in the Orient.

Reinhold J. Kerstan described the Chicago rally in *The Christian Leader.* " 'I'm here to ready the world for the coming of the Lord,' continued the short but husky evangelist with his not so humble claims. A few minutes into his speech, and Moon was in full swing, or as he would call it 'in the full stream of prophecy.' To put across his message, Rev. Moon stabbed and chopped at the air with pudgy hands and used his complete command of Oriental drama to growl, shout, whisper, bark and occasionally spit out his words.

"Rev. Moon repeated his statement: 'I have been in heaven and I have been given the power to see and understand the plan of God.' . . . As the monologue swung from Rev. Moon to interpreter Pak and back again, an alternating current of words was created with occasionally hypnotic effects."

Ever since Sun Myung Moon came to America, his Unification Church has been embroiled in controversy for its devious methods, its recruiting procedures, its techniques of indoctrinating disciples, its fund-raising practices, its mushrooming financial empire, its political machinations and much, much more. In fact, hardly anything that the Unification Church has done has been without a bit of hubbub.

Since "heavenly deception" is practiced by the Moonies, it is somewhat difficult to know truth in their dealings with the outside world. Unification Church officials say that about twenty million dollars was raised in 1978, most of which came from street solicitations. A former member says the true figure may have been ten times that much. But when "heavenly deception" is in vogue, who knows?

To get a degree of acceptance by the establishment, the Unification Church has been courting U.S. senators and representatives, wooing Nobel-prize-winning scientists and making dates with Protestant and Catholic theologians. How they do their romancing is not always above board.

Besides politics, theology and academia, the Unification Church is also interested in business—big business. So they have launched major newspapers, including one in Washington, D.C. which they hope will rival the *Christian Science Monitor,* a chain of convenience markets called Go 'N Joy Food Stores, a tuna fishing fleet in Massachusetts, and seafood processing industries in Alabama.

Overseas, the Moonies have spread to Latin America and Europe with vigor and the usual controversy. In Uruguay, for instance, the cult brought $65 million into the country, launched a newspaper, bought a five-star hotel with a state gambling casino in it and quickly made friends with the anti-Communist military junta in power.

Moon's money-making ventures and political intentions have not gone unnoticed by the U.S. Government. In 1982, the U.S. District Court found him guilty of filing false returns on his income tax. Church leaders termed it religious persecution and called their leader the most abused and misunderstood religious leader of the twentieth century. The jury didn't agree.

The big question, however, is not in politics or business but in the contents of his message. What does Moon teach? What is the doctrine of the Unification Church?

Though there is some indication that the Moonies' theology is still in flux, there are three main sources of information. The best source of information on his teachings comes from the book *Divine Principle,* first published in 1957. The next best source is a commentary by Young Oon Kim called *Divine Principle and Its Application.* The third primary source is the sermons of Moon as they are reprinted in Unification Church literature and sometimes in newspapers.

In 1973, *Time* magazine called *Divine Principle* "a curious mixture of Christian fundamentalism, Taoist-like dualism, numerology, and even metaphors from Moon's electrical engineering. The book points to a new Savior from Korea, whose timing is remarkably similar to Moon's."

Moonies believe that it is impossible to decode the Bible without the use of *The Divine Principle.* Much of the teaching is woven around a proper understanding of the "three Adams."

According to Moon, the first Adam, way back in the Garden of Eden, was supposed to have married Eve and together they would have had perfect children to build the kingdom. Together with God, Adam and Eve would then have formed "the trinity." But instead God's desires were frustrated when, according to Moon's teaching, Eve was sexually seduced by Lucifer (Satan). This started a new trinity with Adam and Eve and Satan.

Frustration also came to God again because of John the Baptist. The goal of Jesus' coming was to marry and have children. While Moonies do not believe that Jesus was God, they do hold that He was a perfect man. Jesus' mission was unfulfilled because he was prevented from marrying the perfect wife and fathering perfect children.

And the culprit in fouling up God's plan was John the Baptist. Here are some quotations: "If John had kept the faith, Jesus would have become king, and John, his prime minister." . . . "Because John failed, he had to die, Jesus had to settle for the lowest class on earth and finally die a premature death."

Too bad about John. He was demoted to being less than the least in the Kingdom of Heaven because of his lack of faith, and eventually he lost his head, Moon says, "because he became involved in the personal love scandal of King Herod—an affair that was none of his business." And, as a result, Moon declares in the book, *Divine Principle*, Jesus failed too.

He failed, of course, because he was crucified before he could marry and produce holy offspring. So God had to settle for second best and devised an alternate plan. According to Moon, "The crucifixion was not at all the original mission of the Son of God, but represented an alteration of his intended course—a secondary mission."

God's second best was the resurrection, which produced only a spiritual salvation, not a physical salvation as would have been accomplished if Jesus had physical offspring. Not having a physical wife, Jesus was given the Holy Spirit, who, as Moon explains, can be termed the spiritual mother of mankind.

But Moon says that what Jesus or the Second Adam accomplished is only a half-salvation. A third Adam is needed to bring full salvation.

Dean Peerman, writing in *Christian Century*, outlines the role of the third Adam this way: "Physical redemption, Moon maintains, will come about through the third Adam—the new Messiah, the Christ of the Second Advent. This savior will marry a perfect woman and they will form a trinity with God; they will have perfect offspring; the blood of all humankind—tainted since Satan seduced the original Eve—will somehow thus be purified and heaven will come upon earth. 'All mankind will be restored to God by forming trinities with him.' Korea is to be the New Israel—and Moon has charts to prove that the new Messiah was born in that country around 1920."

Reinhold Kerstan, in *The Christian Leader*, spells out a little more clearly some interesting comparisons. "Moon holds that the 'third Adam' is needed to succeed where the first and second Adams failed. He neither affirms nor denies that he indeed might be that third Adam, who supposedly was born in Korea ('the new Israel') between 1917 and 1930 (Moon was born in 1920), was married in the 1960s in the marriage of the Lamb as prophesied in Revelation 19 (Moon married his second wife Hak Ja Han in 1960 after his first wife had left him in 1954), and will make his visible domicile in America (where Moon moved in 1972)."

Moon is coy about whether he is the third Adam. In the early days of the movement he seemed to be bolder about it, and even today the Unification Church passes out literature which tells of how Sun Myung Moon has been worshiped by Jesus. When asked if some day

Moon might admit to being Adam III, the church's American president replied, "It's possible."

Despite Moon's history and record of two to four marriages, there is no doubt that the family unit is a key in his teaching. *The Manchester Guardian*, the English newspaper, commented: "The sect's members follow Spartan rules: long hours of work or study, no smoking, no sex outside marriage. . . . It is the sect's leaders who arrange marriages between Unification Church members: men, as well as women, must submit a list of five potential marriage partners, and the final choice is made by the sect's leaders after consultation." *Newsweek* reported that families are encouraged "to raise as many children as possible. The faithful, Moon teaches, will enter the Kingdom of God in family units, which makes his religion hell on bachelors."

One unusual feature of the Unification Church is the rite of mass marriage. Since the church does not practice either baptism or communion, it may be said to be its only sacrament. During a mass marriage, several hundred couples may be united in matrimony. More than 1,000 couples were married at one such ceremony in Korea. Divorce, however, is allowed if a husband or wife strays from the fold.

It is often recommended that couples not live together for a while after marriage. A reporter for the *Sunday Mainichi* of Tokyo asked whether couples are required to live separately for three years after marriage. The answer that he was given was, "There are no regulations. . . . It's just that it is better to serve society for some time before settling down in homes immediately."

While Moon's teachings seem to be a take-off on traditional Christian doctrine, there are strong overtones of Taoism, mysticism and spiritualism as well. As the *Christian Herald* commented, "The male-female dualism common to Oriental philosophies plays an important part in Unification thought." When Moon talks about Jesus and the Holy Spirit, you are reminded of the yin and yang concept of Taoism. All things come in pairs and polarities, such as God and man, male and female, inward and outward, positive and negative, receptive and initiating. The fair appraisal of Robert S. Ellwood, Jr., associate professor of religion, at the University of Southern California, is that the movement "has all the marks of a Far Eastern new religion of the Japanese type" and shows "strong traces of the traditional shamanism of the Korean countryside."

But, as Ellwood goes on to say, "it places no small emphasis on clairvoyance, clairaudience, healing and spiritualistic phenomena." Because of this, when Moon launched his New York campaign at the Waldorf-Astoria in September 1974, Jeane Dixon, the noted astrologer and seer, was seated at the head table. She commended Moon and declared, "The day of hope that most people are waiting for is a lot closer than most people realize."

Several years ago, Arthur Ford, the well known Spiritualist medium, had a séance with Moon. Ford's spirit guide praised Moon as "a most important spiritual light that shines in the darkness of your confused world. . . . Mr. Moon in deep meditation can project himself and be seen just as Jesus has been able to project himself and be seen by the saints. This is one of the marks of the messiahs always."

The book *Divine Principle and Its Application* by Young Oon Kim tells of a group that Moon formed in Korea in which various spiritualistic techniques were practiced. She writes, "Among this group several communicate with the highest realms of the spirit world, and some converse with Jesus and God under any conditions. . . . The Blessed Mother Mary, Gautama Buddha, and Confucius are among those in the spirit world who are directing certain of their followers to this group."

Moon, who is continually getting new "revelations" from God, calls himself "an expert on the spirit world."

So while the Holy Spirit Association for the Unification of World Christianity is a very "Christian" sounding name, it is just as much a part of the occult and a part of Oriental religious philosophy as it is of Christianity. It is obvious that Mr. Moon's orbit is not around the Son.

How does the Christian respond to Mr. Moon's movement?

1. The first danger signal is the fact that the Bible isn't enough for the Unification Church. It is a mark of a cult that it needs an authoritative book to interpret the Bible. For Moon-followers, it is *Divine Principle* written by Yee Hye Wen, a disciple of Sun Myung Moon, which contains, in the words of Charles M. Austin, "Oriental philosophy, Christian terminology, historical analysis and offbeat interpretations of Scripture."

Granted, the Bible isn't always the easiest book to understand, and modern versions and scriptural commentaries may be helpful, but when you say, as Moon does, that the Bible is "written in code" and can only be understood when it is deciphered through the Divine Principle, this is a giveaway as a mark of a cult.

2. The second danger signal is the fact that Moon claims to have had direct revelations from God. While prayer is a Christian privilege and a vital relationship with God is assured through Jesus Christ, new revelations have always been suspect.

Writers in both the Old and New Testaments warned against false prophets. One of the tests to determine whether a prophet was really from God was whether his prophecies were fulfilled; another was to see if they matched up with what God had previously declared in

His written Word. It will be obvious to see whether Moon fulfills the first test within the next ten years; he is already in trouble with regard to the second test.

Despite the fact that Moon claims to have talked with "all the leaders in the Bible," he still has a habit of contradicting them over and over again.

He claims to accept the Bible and yet he indulges in spiritualistic practices, which are expressly forbidden in such passages as Deuteronomy 18:11 and Isaiah 8:19-20. He says that the crucifixion was not in God's plan, although Isaiah had foretold it in Isaiah 53, and Peter at Pentecost declared that Jesus had been "delivered up according to the definite plan and foreknowledge of God" (Acts 2:23). Indeed all the sacrifices of the Old Testament foreshadowed the coming of the One whom John the Baptist said was "the Lamb of God, who takes away the sin of the world" (John 1:29).

3. The third danger signal is that Moon presents a different Jesus Christ from the one referred to in the Bible. The Bible says that "This Jesus will come again in like manner as ye have seen him go into heaven." Moon says Jesus Christ will be physically born again in Korea, which is the descendant of the ten lost tribes of biblical Israel. According to Moon, it is not really Jesus who will return, but rather the same messianic spirit that manifested itself in Jesus Christ will come to earth. As the *Divine Principle* says, "Jesus, as a man having fulfilled the purpose of creation, is one body with God. . . . Nevertheless, he can by no means be God himself." Or, if you prefer, consider these three quotations from Moon: "Man is incarnate God. . . . Man is the visible form of God. . . . Jesus was a man, not God himself."

4. The fourth danger signal in Moon's teaching regards salvation. Man's ultimate redemption will come when Adam III, the Korean-born Messiah, marries and

begets holy offspring. "Except a man be married, he cannot enter into the Kingdom of God," could well be the motto of the Unification Church. Yet anyone who has read what the Apostle Paul wrote in I Corinthians 7 can hardly believe that marriage is essential to salvation.

Besides that, the Bible nowhere suggests that Jesus Christ will return to marry a woman. The New Testament does mention "the bride of Christ"; this is not a particular woman but rather the Christian Church, all those who are true followers of the Messiah. Moon does not have a very high regard for the Christian Church. Young Oon Kim in her *Divine Principle and Its Application* explains why: "Since God has started His new dispensation and the era of the Christian Church is over, He is removing His direct guidance from existing churches." And in *Divine Principle*, it is written, "Christianity, though it professed God's love, has turned out to be in reality a dead body of clergy trailing empty slogans."

What does Moon have in mind to replace Christianity?

In 1978, the United States House subcommittee on International Organizations released a report saying in part, "Among the goals [of Sun Myung Moon] is the establishment of a worldwide government in which the separation of church and state would be abolished and which would be governed over by Moon and his followers."

Each year, the Moonies garner millions more for their Master's coffers. Each year, the Unification Church becomes more powerful as well as more wealthy.

Sun Myung Moon's Unification Church has become a prototype of a successful cult that knows how to move into the intellectual, business and political worlds.

In fact, it's hard to say whether it's more a religion or a business or a political organization.

That's something the U.S. Government would like to know, too.

SOME SAY that George I. Gurdjieff was a kook.

Others believe him to be one of the greatest philosophers of all time. One writer called him "one of the great enigmas of our time." Another called him "an actual incarnation of knowledge."

At any rate, he was a remarkable man with a remarkable mind, and many young people today are discovering him and trying to figure out what he meant. And that isn't easy.

In 1978, a film entitled *Meetings with Remarkable Men* was released. It was based on a book by Gurdjieff. The film director called Gurdjieff "the most immediate, the most valid and most totally representative figure of our times."

Peter Rowley, in *New Gods in America*, estimates that there are about five thousand disciples of Gurdjieff in America today. That in itself is a remarkable figure considering the fact that Gurdjieff's unusual ideas were supposedly dead and buried when Gurdjieff himself died in 1949. And considering the fact that his followers spend more time arguing about what Gurdjieff meant than in evangelizing.

The recent occult explosion has not only revived Gurdjieff (figuratively speaking of course) but has also made him a popular fad on quite a few college campuses. Up until now, his movement has been made up of quality and not quantity.

Among his devotees have been people like Architect Frank Lloyd Wright, P. L. Travers of Mary Poppins fame, Kathryn Hulje, writer of *The Nun's Story*, Colin Wilson, author of *The Outsider*, Katherine Mansfield, well known short-story writer, and an equal number of outstanding artists.

Though dying of tuberculosis, Katherine Mansfield went to Fontainebleau, near Paris, where Gurdjieff had opened an International Study Colony. Her struggles for inner reality are chronicled in her *Journal*.

Today America has its own Gurdjieff Foundation and groups are meeting in most of the major cities of America, as well as on numerous university campuses. But if you haven't heard of Gurdjieff yet, it's understandable, for his disciples are opposed to evangelizing and proselytizing. In fact, they make a fetish out of being secretive about their religion, if you want to call it a religion, and they don't. This stands in the way of it becoming a mass movement. Another thing that hinders its expansion is that it is so difficult to understand. The followers are afraid that if a journalist writes about it he might oversimplify it and thus corrupt it, so they tend to be a bit snobbish about discussing it with others. And finally, once you do begin to understand it, you realize that Gurdjieff's way is not an easy way.

Often the groups are known as "G-O" groups, the "G" for Gurdjieff and the "O" for a mathematician named P. D. Ouspensky. Ouspensky's book about his years with Gurdjieff, *In Search of the Miraculous*, is termed "the best systematic presentation of Gurdjieff's thought." One reason for that is that there hasn't been too much competition.

The meetings of the G-O people are filled with discussions, music and Eastern-style sacred dancing. Gurdjieff derived his emphasis on dancing from Asian mystery schools, and the steps require excruciating self-awareness, such as "counting off constantly changing rhythm cycles while waving your arms in opposing circles." This is supposed to develop your "waking state."

It's important to develop your "waking state." If you don't train yourself to be fully awake, you will sleepwalk your way through life. That's why exercises are necessary. Another simple exercise is to look at the minute hand of your watch while concentrating deeply on the profound thought: "My name is _____ and I am here right now."

G-O meetings are harder to crash than a Presidential reception. You have to be a "sincere disciple" to attend. And practically the only way to become a sincere disciple is by reading, digesting and assimilating a few of the books by Gurdjieff and Ouspensky.

George Ivanovitch Gurdjieff, "stocky, bald and with a handle-bar moustache," was even more puzzling than the modern-day groups that bear his name. A good guess is that he was born in 1877 of Greek-Armenian parentage along Russia's distant Persian border. The nearest big town was a place called Alexandropol.

His father was a local bard and independent thinker who instilled an appreciation for the occult within his son. The local cleric became Gurdjieff's first tutor, "the founder and creator of my present individuality, and, so to say, the third aspect of my inner God."

He became fascinated with astrology and spiritualism at an early age, and studied all types of supernatural phenomena. He sought answers in the church and even considered studying for the priesthood, but, influenced by a disgruntled seminarian, was disillusioned with Christianity and began to seek his answers in ancient mystical religions.

During the following years, he roamed through central Asia, salaried as an assistant to a railroad engineer, but much more interested in investigating the exotic Asian mystery schools and chatting with seers trying to get them to divulge their secrets. His fascinating book entitled *Meetings with Remarkable Men* tells a bit about this segment of his life, but you are never sure in reading it how strictly historical it is.

A jack-of-all-trades, Gurdjieff was also a very keen businessman and made money in everything he did. As he explains it: "I carried out private and government contracts for the supply and construction of railways and roads; I opened a number of stores, restaurants and cinemas and sold them when I got them going well; I organized various rural enterprises and the driving of cattle into Russia from several countries, chiefly from Kashgar; I participated in oil wells and fisheries; and sometimes, I carried on several of these enterprises simultaneously. But the business I preferred above all others, which never required my specially devoting to it any definite time or needed any fixed place of residence, and which moreover was very profitable, was the trade in carpets and antiques of all kinds."

Some of his business dealings were what Gurdjieff would call "sly"; no doubt others would call them downright dishonest. But while hunting esoteric secrets, Gurdjieff was also making a fortune.

All of this was before he was thirty-five years old. Then he moved to Moscow to share his philosophical ideas with the world. The problem was that Gurdjieff didn't seem to have a good sense of political timing. It was just before World War I and just before the Bolshevik Revolution. Gurdjieff arrived in Moscow with a million rubles, two valuable collections—one of carpets and the other of porcelain—and a fresh philosophy: "I wished to create around myself conditions in which man would be continually reminded of the sense and aim of his existence by an unavoidable friction between his conscience and the automatic manifestations of his nature."

Despite the fact that Muscovites must have had other things on their minds in those turbulent years, somehow this zany man attracted a considerable following. In *The Occult Explosion*, Nat Freedland reports, "Since his whole teaching method was based on the mind's being kept in a continuous state of imbalance, he often seemed to be—or perhaps really was—acting erratically."

But between Moscow and St. Petersburg (now Leningrad), his lectures attracted an impressive assortment of philosophers, scientists and other intellectuals. One of them was Peter Demianovich Ouspensky, a man about the same age as Gurdjieff, who had just returned from a trek that had taken him from Egypt to India searching for the "ultimate truths he sensed were hidden behind the symbols of occult tradition." Ouspensky, a precise, bespectacled man, had already achieved fame for his book, *The Fourth Dimension* which established him as an expert in the field of abstract mathematical theory. Ouspensky valued Gurdjieff's ideas highly, though at times his personality rubbed him the wrong way. Gurdjieff was intuitively unpredictable; Ouspensky was logical and systematic.

As Gurdjieff was working on his plans to develop his new organization, the Revolution broke out and he left for his home territory in the Caucasian Mountains. Soon some of his disciples clustered around him and begged him to instruct them. But the obscure Caucasian village of Essentuki wasn't obscure enough for Gurdjieff.

How could you teach philosophy in the middle of a civil war? "Towns passed from hand to hand," Gurdjieff reported, "one day to the Bolsheviks, the next day to the Cossacks, and the day after to the White Army, or to some newly formed party. Sometimes on getting up in the morning we would not know under which government we were that day and only on going out into the street would discover what politics had to be professed."

Remembering a proverb from a wise old Muslim Mullah, "In every circumstance of life always strive to combine the useful with the agreeable," Gurdjieff decided overnight to organize a scientific expedition. The next morning, he received permission from the government that happened to be in power and he conscripted several young disciples of his to join him. Three years later they arrived in Istanbul, almost destitute, and from there they eventually went to France, where Gurdjieff bought his Fontainebleau estate and developed his Institute for the Harmonious Development of Man.

Only a couple of years later, however, when Gurdjieff was nearly killed in an automobile accident, he cut back his rather ambitious program at Fontainebleau and spent more time in writing.

Because of the esoteric nature of his teachings (meant to be understood by the select few) his writings were shared only with his ardent followers until 1959, ten years after his death. The first book to be released was *All and Everything,* or *Beelzebub's Tales to His Grandson,* which Gurdjieff says was written "to destroy mercilessly the beliefs and views rooted for centuries in the mind and feelings of man" by arousing in the mind of the reader a stream of unfamiliar thoughts.

The second book, *Meetings with Remarkable Men,*

was first published in English in 1963. A third book, entitled *Life Is Real Only When I Am*, is still slated for publication and is the object of much speculation. His purpose in the third book, he said, was "to assist the arising in a man's thought and feeling of a true representation of the real world, instead of the illusory world he now perceives."

Gurdjieff's disciples don't want to tell too much to the outside world. They would prefer tantalizing with bits and pieces of information and knowledge so that only those who are serious about pursuing what Gurdjieff sometimes called the Universal Brotherhood will enter it.

Gurdjieff's *Meetings with Remarkable Men* ends with the fascinating sentence: "From then on there gradually arose in me that 'something' which has brought the whole of me to the unshakable conviction that apart from the vanities of life, there exists a 'something else' which must be the aim and ideal of every more or less thinking man, and that it is only this 'something else' which may make a man really happy and give him real values, instead of the illusory goods with which in ordinary life he is always and in everything full."

Writer Peter Rowley presumes that the secrets of this "something else" will be revealed in Gurdjieff's third book if his disciples ever get around to publishing it.

But part of the intriguing thing about Gurdjieff's system is that there is something secretive about it. So why should anyone be in a hurry to publicize Gurdjieff?

Gurdjieff himself was something of an anomaly. He had a difficult time trying to live by his own teachings. He violated his own stress on secret esotericism by publicly staging ballets in Russia. It was this inconsistency that aggravated the methodical Mr. Ouspensky. Ouspensky stated at one point: "There began to take place in me a separation between G. himself and his ideas."

At times, Gurdjieff seemed little more than a sly pragmatist, a shrewd and brilliant Armenian businessman. It was Ouspensky who took the fragments from Gurdjieff and pieced them together into a system.

Ouspensky wrote in *The Fourth Way:* "In the beginning in Russia, Mr. Gurdjieff always insisted that it was not a system; it was just fragments and one had to make a system out of them. And he insisted that it should be given in this way. Now I make it more of a system, because we have more people. But when it was only a small group it was just conversations and not lectures."

Almost like a Zen Master, Gurdjieff frightened most people he met. A translator, A. R. Orage, wrote "To meet him was always a test. In his presence every attitude seemed artificial. Whether too deferential, or on the contrary pretentious, from the first moment it was shattered; and nothing remained but a human creature stripped of his mask and revealed for an instant as he truly was. This was a merciless experience—and for some impossible to bear."

To many of his followers, Gurdjieff was the founder of a world philosophy, not the initiator of a new religion. Once, in Leningrad, when he was asked the relationship of his teaching to Christianity, he hedged at first and then responded, "If you like, this is esoteric Christianity."

But what is unique about Gurdjieff's philosophy is that it is full-blown. Orage states, "He calls us to open our eyes. He asks us why we are here, what we wish for, what forces we obey. He asks us, above all, if we understand what we are. He wants us to bring everything back into question."

According to Gurdjieff and Ouspensky, there are four levels of human consciousness and most people live in only two of them. They are either awake or they are asleep. But Gurdjieff urges his disciples to explore higher levels of consciousness, levels which he calls self-consciousness and objective consciousness.

While most people assume they have a degree of self-consciousness, Gurdjieff is convinced that we don't know ourselves at all. Our sense of I-ness must be present in the whole of our being.

Ouspensky in true mathematical fashion outlines numerous other lists. There are seven categories of man, four kinds of energy, four degrees of schools, the Law of Three and the Law of Seven, Three octaves of Food (a fantastic conglomeration of music theory and nutrition), Seven forces of the Universe (which takes you into astronomy) and sundry other enumerations of ideas.

Many people live in the first three categories of man, they say, but the teachings of Gurdjieff help people to move into the fourth, fifth, sixth and seventh categories of man.

You make the move up the ladder, not by adding logical knowledge to your mind, but by adding psychological wisdom. As Ouspensky would say, most people live in the basement of their house without ever realizing there is an upstairs. "If people tell us about what this house has upstairs we do not believe them, or we laugh at them, or we call it superstition or fairy tales or fables."

When Gurdjieff and Ouspensky speak of psychology, they are not referring to Freud and Jung, but merely to the study of oneself, "I." That "I" is extremely prominent in their teaching. As progress is made, it comes through self-study, self-awareness and self-remembering. The problem with people is that they do not really know themselves; they have no aim. Sin, they say, is being aimless, or missing your goal. Because the "I" of most people is constantly changing (in other words, your "I" today may be different from your "I" yesterday), people have no permanent "I" and this causes personal confusion. In a sense, salvation to a follower of Gurdjieff is finding your permanent "I."

What complicates the whole system is that Gurdjieff and Ouspensky often make words mean what they want them to mean. Yet despite Gurdjieff's obfuscation and farfetched hypotheses, there is some truth to what he says. Man's "I" is out of kilter, and man does live in the basement of his being, little realizing the glories of the mansion in which he resides. Moreover, most people go through life learning about a great deal, but always as interested bystanders and spectators, and hardly ever as participants. Life is to be experienced.

Some of what Gurdjieff says reminds you of what Jesus said, "I am come that you might have life and that you might have it more abundantly."

While Scripture is sometimes quoted or alluded to, you soon realize that Gurdjieff's esoteric Christianity is not Christianity at all. Gurdjieff's thinking has been culled from a variety of sources: Christian, Sufi, Buddhist and occult are all mixed together.

But the emphasis is all man-centered. And it is for an exclusive type of man, the elite man, the man who considers himself able to understand the meandering of Gurdjieff. At best, certain men are able to be helped by it; others are either beyond help or will find help in some other way.

One of the first heresies that struck the Christian Church in the first century was embryonic Gnosticism which was an esoteric Christianity. The Apostle Paul wrote his letter to the Colossian Christians warning them against the elaborate philosophical system that only initiates could possibly understand. Like Gurdjieff's teachings, it contained complicated lists and demanded utter concentration and work.

Paul emphasized to these Christians that Jesus Christ

was the eternal Son of God as well as the suffering Savior. "By him were all things created, that are in heaven, and that are in earth, visible and invisible, whether they be thrones, or dominions, or principalities or powers—all things were created by him, and for him; and he is before all things, and by him all things consist. . . . For it pleased the Father that in him should all fulness dwell."

Later in the same letter, Paul tells the Colossians, who were flirting with the secret philosophies of Gnosticism, "God's secret plan, now at last made known, is Christ Himself. In Him lie hidden all the mighty untapped treasures of wisdom and knowledge. I am saying this because I am afraid that someone may fool you with smooth talk . . ." (Colossians 2:2-4, Living Bible).

Then the Apostle moves in harder: "Don't let others spoil your faith and joy with their philosophies, their wrong and shallow answers built on men's thoughts and ideas, instead of on what Christ has said" (Col. 2:8).

Nor is the Christian gospel available only to the elite, Paul says. "In this new life one's nationality or race or education or social position is unimportant; such things mean nothing. Whether a person has Christ is what matters, and He is equally available to all" (Col. 3:11, Living Bible).

Granted, there is a mystical awareness that Christians need to discover to lift them out of their materialistic morass, but the key to Christian mysticism is Jesus Christ and the framework is the Word of God. Jesus taught his disciples to seek knowledge in Scripture, not in any secret mystical revelation.

If there is no vertical dimension, esoteric thinking soon degenerates into self-centeredness and egocentricity. And this may be the basic difference between Gurdjieff and Jesus Christ. Gurdjieff taught that the most important of all was to know yourself, to have self-knowledge. Jesus Christ taught that the most important of all was to know God, to have God-knowledge. With God-knowledge, you have an entirely new perspective in looking at life. Only with God-knowledge can you have true self-knowledge.

LUTHER BURBANK, one of the world's first flower people, declared, "The religion of peace is the religion we need . . . and in this Bahai is more truly the religion of peace than any other."

Tolstoy wrote that it presented "the highest and purest form of religious teaching."

Not long ago, Historian Arnold Toynbee compared Bahai's growth to that of Christianity in the Roman Empire and predicted that it might become the religion of world unity in the future.

If it is the testimony of great people that you want, Bahai has it, but if you are looking for thousands of adherents, look somewhere else.

Until recently.

Though Bahai is more than one hundred years old, it has struggled for membership, and in America as recently as 1960, its membership was a "shade less than ten thousand." But since that time, largely because of its strong interracial emphasis, the membership has shot upwards, especially on college campuses.

While not giving exact membership figures, Colonel

Salvatore Pelle, director of information for the Bahai in the United States, reports: "The growth has been spectacular in certain areas—one quarter of our new converts are in California. There has been rapid growth in greater Chicago and surrounding states, the New York area, and very recently in the deep South—Louisiana, Georgia, Mississippi, and the Carolinas—where the newcomers are 99 percent black. . . . In the past ten years there has been a steady increase in youths under twenty-five; some years this group increases more than the adult growth."

The number of Bahai Centers (they are also called assemblies, but not churches) was only about 200 in 1960, had increased to 517 by 1970 and is nearing the 1,000 mark today, with Bahai clubs now active on nearly 300 college campuses. The amazing revival of interest in Bahai has propelled membership from under 10,000 to more than 100,000 in slightly more than ten years.

In one year alone, 20,000 new believers in Bahai, mostly blacks, were recruited in the South, "in addition to hundreds of Spanish-speaking people and scores of American Indians."

The strange thing about this belated resurgence is that the Bahais have always had a missionary concern. As soon as a new convert is made, he is told to go and teach. He is told not to wait until he learns more about Bahai, but immediately to declare whatever he has learned.

In the past decade, however, the Bahais have become much more aggressive in their evangelism.

For instance, Jessyca Russell Gaver reports: "One of the unique teaching campaigns inaugurated by the Bahais was started in California in September 1965, when the believers there decided to treat their state as though it were a foreign country, using all kinds of ideas and materials to invade the various townships and cities of California in order to strengthen their numbers."

Soon the aggressive evangelism of California Bahais was copied across the country. Publicity started exploding throughout the United States. CBS-TV showed a "Lamp Unto My Feet" program that included films taken at the World Center and the Wilmette National Headquarters during a Bahai Convention. The NBC-TV "Today" show featured the Faith in a long interview segment. ABC-Radio Network carried a half-hour program. Magazines and newspapers set stories in motion, and the name Bahai was no longer something strange and foreign to many Americans previously unacquainted with it.

But undeniably, the publicity has been abetted by the fact that Bahais not only talk about racial integration, they also practice it. One cardinal principle followed by Bahais in every country is the Oneness of Mankind. Despite prejudice in many parts of America, the Bahai assemblies have fervently adhered to this principle. Instead of becoming a liability for growth, it has become an asset.

Thus, Bahai has been termed "the world's fastest growing religion." And since it emphasizes peace, universal justice and racial brotherhood, it certainly appears to be what Toynbee predicted it might be: "The world religion of the future."

So we had better become well-acquainted with it.

The movement was born in 1844, when a devout Persian named Mulla Husayn started hunting for a Messiah. He belonged to a Muslim sect known as the Shaykbis, who believed in "the imminent appearance of a Divine Messenger." The nation of Persia was sorely in need of a Messiah at the time, because of government corruption, religious bigotry, hatred, moral decadence and degrading poverty.

Mulla Husayn was approaching the city of Shiraz a few hours before sunset when he met a green-turbaned youth who invited him to stay at his house for the night.

That evening as they talked, Mulla Husayn told the young man that he was looking for the Messiah.

"How will you know when you find him?" asked the young man, whose name was Mirza Mohammed Ali ibn-Radhik.

Mulla Husayn gave the description: "Between twenty and thirty years old, medium height, doesn't smoke, without physical defects, but has great knowledge and is descended from Fatimi."

"That's me," said Mirza Mohammed Ali, in effect.

The Mulla checked him out further, and when the young man passed all the tests, he knew the divine messenger had been found. Before the evening was over, Mirza was declaring, "Verily, I say, I am the Bab, the Gate of God."

The date was May 23, 1844. May 23 is still revered by the Bahais as the Anniversary of the Declaration of the Bab.

The Bab, as he began to be known ("Bab" means channel or gate), claimed to rank as the founder of a new great religion, like Mohammed, Moses, Zoroaster and Jesus before him. But gradually, it became known that while the Bab himself was a "Manifestation of God," he was also a John the Baptist, the herald of a greater Messiah yet to come.

"I am a dewdrop," the Bab once wrote in his voluminous writings, "from that limitless ocean, and when He (the great Manifestation of the Sun of Truth) shall appear, my true nature, my mysteries, riddles and intimations will become evident, and the embryo of this religion shall develop through the grades of its being and ascent, attain to the station of 'the most comely of forms' and become adorned with the robe of 'Blessed Be God the Best of Creators.' "

Followers were not hard to get in Persia at the time. But persecution dogged the new religion relentlessly. J. E. Esslemont, in his book *Baha'u'llah and the New Era*, says, "Great numbers of the believers were put to death. Many were beheaded, hanged, blown from the mouths of cannons, burnt or chopped to pieces."

Yet the religion gained strength until the Bab himself, only thirty-one years old, was arrested in 1850 and led to a scaffold in Tabriz. According to the reports of the Bahais, there was a regiment of 750 Armenian soldiers who aimed their rifles at the Bab, hanging from the scaffold. All 750 soldiers missed the Bab, but one hit the rope from which he was suspended and so he dropped to the ground unscathed. Believing it a miracle, the Armenian soldiers walked off the job; but a new regiment was recruited, and this time the Bab's body was riddled with bullets.

Though despondent over the death of their leader, the Babi's, as the followers of the Bab were known, clung to the hope that the Promised One would yet come. More than ten thousand Babi's were martyred for their faith, and thousands more were imprisoned in dank dungeons.

One of these was a wealthy nobleman from Teheran named Mirza Husayn Ali. While suffering in agony and on the verge of death in the Black Hole of Teheran, Mirza was allegedly informed by an angel who he really was and what he was supposed to do. So he assumed the name Baha'u'llah, which means "The Glory and Splendor of God."

Released from prison through the intervention of the

Russian embassy and exiled to Baghdad, Baha'u'llah became an instant hero to the Babi's. For several years he devoted his time to writing the Bahai Scriptures, and to instructing the Baghdad Babi's about their faith. But he still kept his identity secret.

Finally, in 1863, news came that the government was going to exile him again, this time to Constantinople, which was a three-month journey from Baghdad, and about as far away in the Muslim world as he could be exiled. The Babi's were stunned by the news, so Baha'u'llah thought it was about time he gave them some good news to think about. Thus it came to pass that in 1863 in a garden near Baghdad Baha'u'llah made his grand pronouncement that he was the Promised One.

Most of the Babi's liked the idea that this wealthy nobleman was the Promised One. An exception was his brother, Mirza Yahya, who started a religious war to oust Baha'u'llah from power. In disgust, the Turkish government sent Baha'u'llah to the penal colony of Acre, just north of Haifa in Palestine, and exiled his brother to the island of Cyprus.

Though technically a prisoner for the rest of his life (he died in 1892), Baha'u'llah was allowed to roam the Acre, Haifa, Mount Carmel area almost at will, and actually lived several years in a rather luxurious mansion. Said Baha'u'llah, "Verily, verily, the most wretched prison has been converted into a Paradise of Eden." Today that mansion remains as one of the Bahai world shrines.

When Baha'u'llah died (despite his claims to immortality), his son Abbas Effendi assumed control of the Bahai movement. He took the title of Abdul Baha ("Servant of Baha"), and spread the new religion worldwide. He made no great claims for himself, since his father had declared that no more manifestations of deity would appear for another thousand years. Abdul Baha's main job was to be the interpreter of his father's 200 books and tablets and to share with the world the Bahai blueprint for world peace and unity.

Mrs. Phoebe Hearst, of the Hearst publishing clan, was the key to getting Abdul Baha to come to America. She sought out Abdul Baha on a special pilgrimage to the Haifa mansion, but left her Negro butler outside. Abdul brought him inside and served him before the others; the butler became the first black Bahai.

In 1912, Abdul Baha and his Bahai entourage of servants, secretaries and devotees arrived in the United States for an eight-month tour, going everywhere from Montclair, New Jersey, to Kenosha, Wisconsin, to Palo Alto, California, with numerous stops in between. On the barnstorming tour he laid the foundation stone of the Bahai Temple at Wilmette, Illinois, on the shores of Lake Michigan. Actually, the now famous nine-sided structure wasn't designed for several years afterwards and wasn't completed until 1953. Each of the nine sides contains a portal through which adherents of the nine major world religions may enter into the Bahai brotherhood of man. Said the architect, Louis Bourgeois: "The teachings of Baha'u'llah unify the religions of the world into one universal religion, and as we know that all great historic religions developed a new architecture, so the Bahai Temple is the plastic teachings of Baha'u'llah. In the Bahai Temple is used a composite architecture, expressing the essence in line of each of the great architectural styles, harmonizing them into one whole."

Now more than one hundred thousand people a year visit the $3 million structure and the Bahais use it and adjacent buildings as their national headquarters and publishing office.

Today the worldwide Bahai movement is ruled by nine men in Haifa called Hands of the Cause and a representative body called the Universal House of Justice.

Justice is a key word in the Bahai movement. For instance, over one of the doors in the Wilmette Temple are inscribed the words of Baha'u'llah, "The best beloved of all things in My sight is Justice." Yet this justice is not to be administered by the individual but by the group.

While the Bahai movement started out as a reform movement within Islam and still reflects a leaning toward that faith and particularly to two ancient Muslim sects known as the Twelvers and the Seveners, yet more and more it is becoming a faith of its own. In *Bahai Faith* Jessyca Gaver spells out the differences: "The purpose . . . of Judaism was to teach concepts of divine law, of Christianity to teach a relationship between God, man, and salvation, and of Islam to teach submission to the Will of God. The Bahais feel their Faith is here to bring unity to mankind and to demonstrate the unity of all the divine prophets and religions."

On the surface, says Bahai, the religions all look different, but underneath "in all the important things they are in complete agreement." The externals of religion are unimportant, says Bahai; these practices divide, rather than unite. But Bahais themselves have their own externals to which their adherents must subscribe. And some dissidents within the Bahai movement have divided because of them. Easy divorce, no gambling, no narcotics, no drinking, no membership in lodges, no political involvement at all, and strict subservience to the government—these are all rules of Bahai.

Besides that, Bahai also has a distinctive calendar of nineteen months, each containing nineteen days. One of these months is a nineteen-day fast, concluding on March 20. Bahais also observe nineteen feast days, which are held on the first day of each of the nineteen Bahais months. This is "the very heart of their spiritual activity."

There are also nine Holy Days each year that Bahais and their children are expected to observe. Obviously the numbers "nine" and "nineteen" have sacred significance to Bahais.

Bahais are also obliged to draw up a written will and testament. This is certainly a wise policy, but it is especially wise for the Bahais, because they have built into this obligation the importance of "providing for the Faith" in your will.

Of course, the supreme obligation of the Bahai is to recognize Baha'u'llah as the great manifestation of God. As Esslemont says, "He reverences Christ and Mohammed and all God's former Messengers to mankind, but he recognizes Baha'u'llah as the bearer of God's message for the new age in which we live, as the Great World-teacher who has come to carry on and consummate the work of his predecessors."

According to Baha'u'llah, the purpose of man's creation is that he may know God and adore Him. And how does a man come to know and love God? Only by coming to know and love the Manifestation of God, Baha'u'llah himself.

It is one thing to accept the moral and ethical teachings of Baha'u'llah; it is another thing to accept him as the ultimate Manifestation of God and the only way of salvation. It is one thing to affirm the importance of world peace and racial brotherhood; it is another to enthrone a Persian prophet as the capstone of all religion.

Bahai collides head-on with Christianity; it isn't a pleasant merger. Jesus Christ claims to be the exclusive Son of God, the Way, the Truth and the Life. He said, "No one comes to the Father but through Me." His followers declared, "Neither is there salvation in any other," and

"There is one God and one Mediator between God and man." Baha'u'llah makes the same claims for himself; both can't be right.

Bahais try to avoid such clashes. They show how the teachings of Baha'u'llah are similar to what Jesus Christ said in the Sermon on the Mount and to what Moses said in the Old Testament.

When a Christian minister asked Abdul Baha in 1912 how he could help the Bahai movement bring universal peace and brotherhood, the son of the Bahai founder said, "Teach the pure gospel of Jesus without dogmatic additions or limitations."

Not long afterward a university professor asked, "If I become a Bahai, can I keep the religion of my saintly Christian mother?" Abdul Baha answered, "Of course you may keep it. If you become a Bahai you will apply it."

Yet it is precisely in these two answers that Abdul Baha revealed that he did not understand Christianity. The "pure gospel of Jesus" is based on the atoning death and the bodily resurrection of the Lord.

Christ was not a noble martyr like the Bab. Christ died to pay the penalty of man's sinfulness. His death was absolutely unique in all of history. And so, of course, was His resurrection. There is no way that this gospel and its universal implications can be harmonized with Bahai.

Bahai recognizes this, too, even when it doesn't want to admit it. When you join a Bahai assembly, you are required to withdraw from membership in any church or religious organization. You cannot be a Bahai and a member of a Christian church at the same time.

To the Bahai, there is really no such thing as evil. "Error," said Abdul Baha, "is lack of guidance; darkness is absence of light ... falsehood is lack of truthfulness." So all that you need to do is to develop man's goodness and evil will disappear.

Thus, man does not need salvation; he only needs enlightenment.

In fact, Abdul Baha calls his father Baha'u'llah "the foremost teacher and educator of mankind."

But education does not negate man's sinfulness; some of the most educated nations of all time have been the most dastardly.

While Bahai emphasizes non-resistance for its individual members, it urges righteous warfare for communities and nations. "If one nation oppresses or injures another," writes J. E. Esslemont, "it is the duty of all other nations to prevent such oppression."

And that is just about what has made the twentieth century a century of world wars.

Although Bahai seems to be picking up steam in the United States, its worldwide influence is not living up to the predictions made by its founders.

In 1892, Persia (now Iran) had between five hundred thousand and a million Bahais and other Babi's. But since that time the movement has not grown in that land but rather has shrunk, rent by numerous schisms and rifts.

Abdul Baha called the twentieth century the century of the Sun of Truth. "This century is the century of the establishment of the Kingdom of God upon the earth. . . . All the people of the world will become believers."

At another time he made the bold declaration, "Universal peace will be firmly established, a universal language promoted. [He had high hopes of Esperanto.] Misunderstanding will pass away. The Bahai Cause will be promulgated in all parts and the oneness of mankind established. It will be most glorious."

When will all this happen?

Abdul Baha predicted that too.

Take the 1,335 days that the Prophet Daniel mentioned in his prophecy and add them to the time of Mohammed's flight from Medina to Mecca, or the beginning of the Mohammedan era (the Hijrat), or to quote Abdul Baha, "These 1,335 days mean 1335 solar years from the Hijrat." And since the Hijrat occurred in 622, you come to the conclusion that the Millennium begins in 1957.

It didn't.

But Bahais aren't giving up. They still believe that they will bring in the kingdom of God by their diligence.

As Jessyca Gaver wrote, "The Bahais feel that they can accomplish the goals set for mankind by the coming of Baha'u'llah. These are the creation of world peace and unity among the nations of the world, not only through love but because the Bahais have the special ideals, rules and plans for making these a reality."

V

BECOME WHAT YOU WANT TO BE OR AMERICA'S HOME-MADE RELIGIONS

::

WERNER ERHARD had his Damascus Road experience on a California freeway, as he was approaching the Golden Gate Bridge.

On the original Damascus Road, the Apostle Paul found Christ; on the California freeway, Erhard got "it," which has now become "est."

Before he stumbled on est with a small e, Werner Erhard was obviously an unhappy man. He had been unhappy with his name. Previously, he had used the names John Paul Rosenberg (which was the one he was born with) and Jack Frost. But he liked the name Werner Erhard better. He took the first name from a German physicist and the last name from a German ex-chancellor.

Erhard has a way of appropriating things.

He is a self-confessed imposter, a former car salesman and business executive. In 1960 he left his wife and four children and their East Coast home to go west with a girl friend in an appropriated car.

On the West Coast, he was "into" psycho-cybernetics, Scientology, telepathy, human potential, abilitism, Subud, martial arts, Zen, gestalt, encounter training, yoga, Dale Carnegie, Albert Einstein and more. He also went from Nietzsche to Wittgenstein to Maxwell Maltz, which sounds vaguely like a double play combination in baseball.

You might say that Werner Erhard, or whatever his name was at the time, was trying to find himself.

Then, somewhere on a California freeway near the Golden Gate Bridge, he had a life-transforming experience. He found out who he was, and he discovered his OKness. That was the day that est was born.

In an article in *Christianity Today*, Kevin Garvey summarizes, "Erhard learned in his freeway conversion that 'What is, is; what ain't ain't.' He denies the past; its reminders encumber 'the now.' And he thinks we should ignore the future consequences of our actions. Having removed moral and ethical considerations, Erhard decided he was 'God in my universe.' According to est, each of us is God in his own universe."

The name est, always spelled in lower case letters, is short for Erhard Seminars Training. Between 1975 and 1981, more than 300,000 people took the course which costs around $400 and lasts sixty hours. More than 500 magazine articles have been written on est, and more than a dozen books, each selling more than a million copies, have been printed.

Erhard has now appropriated fame and fortune.

He would no doubt deny that est is a religious cult. Technically, it's an educational corporation.

But Erhard speaks in religious terms and his followers utter some amazing things about the founder of est. Singer John Denver called Erhard a "god." Writer Adelaide Bry said, "I see him as totally powerful . . . unlike anyone else who inhabits my planet."

Granted, you won't find any est churches, but that

doesn't stop their evangelistic efforts or their fanatical commitment to their beliefs.

Because many of the est graduates are in education, business and communications, the philosophy of the movement has been spreading rapidly. Says Erhard, "The real thrust and goal of est is to put it in education." Apparently, he is succeeding. Some 15 percent of the graduates are educators. On the est advisory board is a president of NBC radio; and so many Warner Brothers executives have taken the training that the studio has been jokingly referred to as "Werner" Brothers.

Some folks don't think it's a laughing matter. *San Francisco* magazine has stated: "Est is making a serious bid to affect basic American institutions, and Werner Erhard's increasing influence has many people concerned. They see an effective growing organization that has a strong political base."

Federal funding has been received to teach est at the elementary school level—both to students and teachers. In addition, Erhard has been aiming at est in law enforcement, and has been teaching both criminals and police. And he has a special interest in reaching clergymen—they receive a fifty percent discount.

In est, the medium is a major part of the message, and the medium is normally a sixty-hour four-day seminar. Usually the seminar is conducted in the ballroom of a major hotel and usually the training is conducted over two consecutive weekends. About 250 to 300 people may compose the group, and at $400 a head that brings $100,000 to $120,000 (less expenses) into the coffers of est.

What happens is psychologically powerful and often devastating.

You submit to the est trainer totally and utterly. You can't go to the bathroom without his approval. You can't talk to anyone else in the group. Guards are posted at the door. Theoretically you may leave; but practically speaking, you feel intimidated. You don't know the time, because you have surrendered your watch. Sometimes the est trainer may remind you of a Marine Corps sergeant. The language is strong and earthy, and soon you find yourself repeating it. At other times the leader is like a successful businessman or a sage philosopher, but always, he is the leader to whom you have submitted.

John Weldon in an article "The Strange World of est" says, "The experience transforms people because it uses intensive and at times fairly brutal physical and mental conditioning. . . ." One est trainer put it this way: "We're gonna throw away your whole belief system. . . . We're gonna tear you down and put you back together again."

R.C. Devon Heck and Jennifer L. Thompson concur. They say: "A major step in the est training is negating any pre-existing belief system."

That's why an article in *Psychology Today* described the est technique and then charged, "Such efforts, of course, are commonly known as brainwashing, which is precisely what the est experience is."

In est terms, the seminar is simply the process by which a siege is laid on the mind. Mind, according to est, is "uncorrected cybernetic machinery." Normally, Mind "makes you become more and more what you always have been." You take self-improvement courses and read how-to books and you become more proficient, but basically nothing is changed. You need to lay siege on Mind and confront it openly. You need to "identify with Self. Mind restricts you; Self frees you." So says est.

Est would paraphrase Romans 12:1: "And be not conformed to the Mind, but be transformed by identifying with Self."

Basically, Erhard was laden with guilt of past failures and could find no way out of his guilt. He tried many disciplines but all of these failed and inevitably these failures added to his feelings of guilt. His Mind told him he was a failure.

Eventually Erhard had his conversion experience on the way to the Golden Gate Bridge. And the gist of the experience was simply, "I was already all right," and now he tells others, "I happen to think you are perfect exactly the way you are."

Life's problems don't matter. You don't have to worry about "ought-to's." You can remove yourself from anger-causing situations. All you need to do is imagine yourself twenty feet away and concentrate until you get the serenity you desire. Problems are illusions, so don't take them too seriously.

Let's go back to the Mind and the Self which are central to est's philosophy. According to est, it was Self that invented Mind to help it survive, but the invention has become a Frankenstein. Mind is always trying to make itself look right and everyone else wrong. To avoid being dominated it tries to dominate. It builds a belief structure to justify itself and beliefs are enslaving. Whenever we let Mind dominate, est says, we sacrifice aliveness for rightness. You can't trust the Mind's beliefs. They are lies. Only experience is real."

"Life has no rules," Erhard says in capital letters, and since life has no rules, rules are only illusions and you don't have to feel guilty about breaking illusions. You are freed of responsibility and hence you are freed of guilt.

In order to achieve this new outlook on life you need a radical conversion experience, and that's why the est seminars have to be intensive and extensive.

Erhard says, "We want nothing short of a total

transformation—an alteration of substance, not a change in form."

And he gets it.

Some people call it brainwashing, and certainly by a dictionary definition it seems an appropriate description: "To indoctrinate so intensively and thoroughly as to effect a radical transformation of beliefs and mental attitudes." Est denies the approbrium of brainwashing, but even Erhard describes est as "mind-blowing."

Regardless of what you call the process, Erhard gets conversions.

A priest received the training and testified, "The supposed-to is gone from my life."

A female executive took the course, discovered she was frigid and left her "well-paying job to work full-time producing pornographic films."

Another graduate of est said, "I experienced no sadness when I was told that my father had died. My father's death really wasn't significant. Things have lost their significance, so I probably don't notice a lot of things. . . . Things are going to be the way they are. The est training tells you 'what you have to do about things is nothing.' "

A young man said, "Est teaches you that if you have problems, you've chosen to have them." After he took the course, he began having problems at the university he was attending. He decided to "choose not to have those problems," adopted a "so-what" attitude and flunked out of school.

What people "get" from the seminar is quite varied, and because "there are no rules," Erhard expects that est will produce different results in different people.

But est's dramatic conversion—a direct experience of the self along with a new world view—usually produces a "euphoric freedom from past encumbrances, the ability to be open, straightforward and honest, an increased ability to assert themselves and a general enthusiasm about life."

Est makes most of its converts feel better and many of them function better. As one businessman stated, "I don't take responsibility any more for the people that let me step on them, and I don't feel guilty."

Est does remove the burden of guilt from the shoulders of many, and in a society where psychiatrists, psychologists and counselors have to put "Standing Room Only" signs next to their couches we should be thankful for all the guilt removers we can find. Right?

Wrong.

Est may be a placebo, but it's no panacea.

What's wrong with it?

First of all, let's hit at some obvious misconceptions.

All beliefs are illusions, says est, so you can choose your own illusion. The Mind must be transcended. But isn't est's own teaching—that of a transcendent Self outside of time and space that we must identify with— isn't that also a belief, and therefore an illusion? No, says Erhard, it is not a belief, but a notion.

What's the difference? Beliefs are static; notions are pragmatic. A notion is a concept which is valid if it produces "aliveness" in us.

Now if you are getting suspicious that Erhard is adept at playing with words, you are close to the truth.

The fact is that the belief structure of est is derived from Eastern religions and philosophies, and they are the firmly held beliefs that form a new philosophy of life for est devotees.

Another misconception is that est is not a religion and does not interfere with anyone's religious beliefs. That's what Erhard says.

On the other hand, Erhard has also said, "I believe

that 'belief' in God is the greatest barrier to God in the universe. . . . I would prefer someone who is ignorant to someone who believes in God. . . . There isn't anything but spirituality, which is just another word for God, because God is everything."

Or again, "In est training you are God. . . . Therefore, you cannot look to any supreme being for special treatment, goodness or award."

Looking for answers outside yourself is bad, according to est. In est, Erhard says, people get "an experience of enlightenment, which is different from the belief system called salvation. If I get the idea that God is going to save me, therefore I'm all right, that's salvation; if I get the idea that nothing's going to save me, therefore I'm all right, that's enlightenment."

And no matter what Erhard says, that makes est a religion. It also makes est a religion that is moving in an opposite direction from Christianity.

John Weldon compares the two this way: "Est is a system of self salvation that appeals to human ego and imagined personal divinity. Christianity recognizes only an agent outside of humanity, Jesus Christ, as its sole instrument of salvation. Erhard teaches self-glorification; Jesus teaches self-sacrifice."

Now that we understand that est is both a belief system and a religion despite Erhard's semantic denials, we have to ask "What kind of a religion is it?"

Erhard's god is Self—with a capital S. And he means by that much more than the ego of psychology. Unless you "identify with Self, you don't feel OK inside because you haven't experienced your OKness." That OKness is salvation.

"Self," says Erhard, "is the ground of all being, that from which everything arises. . . . When I get in touch with myself and you get in touch with yourself, we will see the same self. Self is all there is."

The more Erhard talks about Self, the more you realize that it is simply Vedantic Hinduism. The vocabulary of est draws heavily on words like illusion and enlightenment which are key words in Eastern religions. Man is part of the oneness of the universal soul or self. Man's problem is in not realizing this oneness, which comes only through enlightenment. Various Hindu based cults receive this enlightenment in different ways. Krishna Consciousness gets it from chanting; the Divine Light Mission prescribes an initiation ceremony called "taking knowledge"; Transcendental Meditation gets it from meditating on a mantra. Est gets it from an intensive seminar.

Like other Hindu cults, est has another drawback. By saying that a problem is an illusion and by denying morality in any absolute sense, est consciously creates a "so what?" attitude in its followers.

Saying "so what?" may make you feel better when engulfed by the world's problems, but it certainly doesn't solve anything. John Weldon charges, "Erhard and his est graduates say 'so what?' to evil, greed, hate, and suffering in the world. Erhard plays his game . . . while millions starve to death."

To counter such charges, Erhard sponsored a Trans-American Bike Team in 1981. End World Hunger was the theme promoted by the cyclists on their 4,219 mile ride from Fort Lauderdale to the Golden Gate Bridge. Each of the 33 riders had to raise $5,000 before joining the ride. The Bike Team capped off the est Hunger Project begun in 1977.

As Actress Valerie Harper explained, the concept would "create a critical mass of agreement about an idea, and then out of that, things will manifest."

Lester Brown, an authority on world hunger said that

the Hunger Project founded by Erhard "probably collected more money in the name of hunger and has done the least about hunger than any group I can think of. . . ."

Mother Jones magazine in an article "Let Them Eat est" reported that approximately one million dollars was raised but almost none of it helped the hungry. Rather, the funds were used to tell Americans about the Hunger Project. Americans were told about the Hunger Project by means of seminars, the proceeds of which went to est.

Is it then a fraud? Not exactly, explains Dave Hunt in *The Cult Explosion*. In est philosophy, "we are each Gods who create our own universe and are therefore fully responsible for what happens to us. . . . Those who live in areas of the world where crops have failed because of drought year after year have caused their own starvation by not thinking the right thoughts about food."

All that's needed is a little positive thinking.

In the *New York Review,* Jonathan Lieberson wrote, "Est theory has no moral spine. Morality requires a position, but this is condemned by est as 'coming from' the Mind-state."

Adolf Hitler, Judas Iscariot, Machiavelli—est wouldn't dare point a finger at any of them. According to one est book, Jesus kept telling everyone over and over that "everybody was like he was—perfect."

That is not even close to what Jesus told people.

On the other hand, it is what Werner Erhard tells everyone over and over. And people keep on paying him $400 for the privilege of attending his seminars in which he tells them about their OKness.

You are OK as is, says the Hindu philosophy that

Erhard appropriated as he neared the San Francisco Bridge.

You are separated from God, says the Bible, and the gulf is too great for you to leap. Jesus Christ is the divinely appointed bridge, the Golden Gate, to salvation.

Erhard stopped before crossing that Bridge.

Scientology and L. Ron Hubbard   18

AT LEAST one thing makes sense about Scientology. Its founder, L. Ron Hubbard, was a science-fiction writer. In fact, it was in a science fiction magazine, *Astounding Science Fiction,* that Hubbard chose to unveil his "dianetics" in May 1950.

Today Scientology has membership, as well as law suits, around the world. It claims to have up to five million members in thirty countries. Three million of them are in the United States. Included among its members are doctors, lawyers, professors and actors, and also many, many college-age young people. But the way Scientology has been expanding, it is difficult to keep up to date on its statistics.

The story of Scientology has always centered around its colorful and controversial leader. Born in 1911, the son of a career Navy officer, Lafayette Ronald Hubbard spent his teen-age years in the Far East, but returned to America to enter college in 1930. He flunked out of his science courses at George Washington University, but eventually was given a Ph.D degree from Sequoia University, a school that operates out of a post-office box in Los Angeles.

While he is described in the Scientology brochures as "explorer, travel writer, Lt., U.S. Naval Reserve, commanding escort vessels during World War II, and screenwriter," he also may be credited with other exploits.

In the late 1930s, Hubbard trekked the jungles of Central America to gain his explorer's badge. During World War II, he served in the South Pacific. Once, in a lifeboat for several days, he was severely injured and blinded by the hot Pacific sun. According to one report, he became critically ill after five years of naval duty. "Crippled, blind and twice declared dead by doctors, he rebounded to perfect health," by applying his self-discovered principles of Scientology.

After the war, he was divorced and remarried, wrote seventy-eight science-fiction stories and was developing an idea that he called "dianetics." A 1976 *Time* magazine article said that Hubbard had counseled an audience in 1949, "Writing for a penny a word is ridiculous. If a man really wanted to make a million dollars, the best way would be to start his own religion." And that's exactly what Hubbard did. Within three months of its publication in 1950, his book on dianetics had sold 100,000 copies, and Hubbard was launched on a new career.

The complete title of the 435-page book was *Dianetics: The Modern Science of Mental Health,* and basically it was a do-it-yourself psychoanalysis manual. Dianetics clubs sprang up across the country and thousands of people were probing into one another's prenatal influences. (One of Hubbard's theories was that one's present problems are caused by prenatal experiences.)

Within a year Hubbard set up dianetic foundations, institutes and organizations in several states. One by one, however, they fell by the wayside, the victim of bankruptcy proceedings, personality conflicts or disputes with physicians. Dr. J. A. Winter, for instance, who had earlier befriended Hubbard's dianetics, publicly criticized Hubbard's methods and said that dianetics was causing people to go psychotic. The New Jersey Board of Medical Examiners charged Hubbard with operating an unlicensed medical school in that state. Hubbard had been allegedly giving out M.D. degrees; only he meant Master of Dianetics, not doctor of medicine.

With such a negative reaction from the scientific community, Hubbard decided to turn dianetics from a science to a religion, for after all, freedom of religion is guaranteed by the Constitution. And so Scientology hatched full-grown from the egg of dianetics.

Meanwhile, the thrice-married Hubbard was becoming wealthier than ever. He doesn't receive the church's tithes, but Deputy Guardian Arthur Gaiman says he could have them if he wanted them. "We have millions. Money is no problem. The only people who ever get very excited about money are those who don't have it."

That is not Hubbard's problem. According to *Time* magazine, he has boasted to friends that he has $7 million "stashed away in two numbered Swiss bank accounts."

While Hubbard is not exactly a man without a country, he spends much of his time in international waters sailing the high seas in his 3,300-ton 320-foot yacht with its blue-uniformed crew of 200 sailors and students. Most of the crew on the "Sea Org," Scientology's administrative branch sailing the high seas in a trio of three ships including Hubbard's yacht, have signed billion-year contracts with Hubbard to work for him for a weekly sustenance pay of between $10 and $60.

You can easily see why Hubbard himself is controversial; just as controversial is the religion itself. One expert on comparative religions termed Scientology "the most sinister of all modern cults."

An Australian official report called it, "The world's largest organization of unqualified persons engaged in the practice of dangerous techniques, which masquerades as mental therapy."

It has also been described as "a curious amalgamation of crude psychoanalysis, positive thinking, sensitivity training and indoctrination."

An article in *Today's Health* magazine called it a "dangerous cult" which "claims to help mentally or emotionally disturbed persons, for sizable fees."

Yet if you talk to Scientologists, you will be told that it is the greatest discovery ever made and that "tens of thousands of case histories" attest to its worth.

To understand Scientology, you have to know its distinctive vocabulary. Otherwise, you will get bogged down in "Orgs," "E-meters," "clears," "pre-clears," "engrams," "Boo-hoos," and "Thetans." The terminology could have been dreamed up only by a science-fiction writer.

In her exposé, *The Scandal of Scientology,* Paulette Cooper explains: "The Church of Scientology . . . no longer claims to cure people of their emotional and physical problems. Instead, they say it's people's spiritual well-being that concerns them now. The method is still basically the same, resembling a combination of psychotherapy and the Catholic confession. . . ."

The beginning Scientologist is called a pre-clear—someone who is not yet free from his problems and difficulties as is a clear Scientologist.

And how do you progress from a pre-clear to a clear?

Slowly, very slowly.

First, you are introduced to an auditor or a private counselor. Most auditors are young men with only a modicum of training. Hubbard says you don't need any more training to be a counselor.

The private counseling session is called "auditing" or processing, and the magic device that Hubbard uses to make it work is an E-meter which some have compared to a lie detector. Actually it is an electrogalvanometer measuring fluctuations in skin resistance. It consists of two empty tin cans—usually soup or V-8 juice—which are connected to a simple galvanometer. As a pre-clear, you grasp the tin cans while the auditor asks you personal questions.

Why is all this necessary? To help you get rid of the engrams that are fouling up your life. You didn't know you had any engrams? That's because they are stored in your unconscious, or as they say in Scientology, in your reactive mind.

According to their primer called *What Is Scientology?* "Ron Hubbard started his research on the premise that man is basically good." But stored up in man's reactive mind are compulsions and inhibitions that cause "unreasonable and uncontrolled behavior." So the primer goes on to say: "Ron Hubbard's most remarkable discovery (and one which is changing the course of mankind) is this: The source of man's reactive mind can be contacted and erased."

To make sure you reveal all the details of your sordid past, the auditor probes your psyche with such questions as "Have you done anything your mother would be ashamed to find out?" And when you have both hands on the two tin cans of the E-meter and when you are looking eyeball to eyeball at your auditor the truth comes out.

The problems that are haunting your reactive mind are called engrams. And some of these engrams were planted there even before you were born. "Some Scientologists," according to Paulette Cooper, "are able to remember being a sperm or even the egg eagerly waiting to be met by the sperm." So if you can remember how your father beat your mother while she was pregnant with you, you are well on the road to becoming clear.

But that isn't all. In his book *Have You Lived Before This Life?* L. Ron Hubbard encourages his flock to probe into previous existences for those troublesome engrams. One Scientologist claimed to have fallen out of a spaceship fifty-five quintillion years ago and to have become a manta ray fish after he was killed by one. Hubbard, who is a bit more modest in his claims, only says that the Thetan (or immortal spirit) has been around for seventy-four trillion years. Sometimes it takes a while for a Thetan to find a body to inhabit, so it may have a wait of a few million years before reappearing on earth.

As you are gradually cleared of engrams that have afflicted you in your current existence because of prenatal influences or previous existences, you move up through eight grades of clearness until you are finally pronounced clear. Out of the fifteen million people who have been exposed to Scientology training only three thousand (or one-fiftieth of 1 percent) have made it through the grades.

Now, Scientologists go beyond "clear" status and can proceed through other levels to become an Operating Thetan. The definition of an OT is "a Thetan exterior who can have but doesn't have to have a body in order to control or operate thought, life, matter, energy, space and time."

Naturally, this costs a little money. Fees for auditing (called donations) vary. They usually range from $50 to $80. Many report that they have spent $10,000 to $15,000. A few have spent over $100,000. One young man claims that he spent $23,000 in nine months and hadn't even completed his second course.

But Hubbard says, "It would be worth ten thousand additional hours of time to recover and be able to use and apply the knowledge, experience and skills of a lifetime. One receives a bonus of increased health, happiness and longevity, an increase in longevity which is at least a hundred to one for every hour of therapy. Yet therapy all the way to a clear takes far, far less than ten thousand hours of work. . . . If it takes a thousand hours, then blame the parents, not therapy. Yet few cases should consume a thousand hours even in unskilled hands and the bulk of them should take at most two or three hundred."

Because of the huge sums of money that go into Scientology coffers and because much of it was alleged to have gone into the pockets of L. Ron Hubbard, the Internal Revenue Service withheld tax-exempt status from the Church of Scientology for several years. In recent years, the ruling has been reversed, state by state.

While the federal government has had its doubts about whether Scientology is a religion, Scientologists don't question it. Their ministers are garbed in full clerical garb, with a large cross, although the Church of Scientology calls itself a "nonsectarian religious corporation." Church services are conducted on Sundays, but Paulette Cooper says that they are "more of a pitch for Scientology than they are for God." Sometimes a taped lecture from "Ron," as their leader is affectionately called, is included. The Bible is seldom used.

Scientology also has its rituals for marriage, christenings and funerals. None of these rituals include prayer or any reference to God. The Australian Report on Scientology called one of the christening rituals a "travesty."

When you examine Scientology as a religion you find

it is a mixed bag. *Time* magazine described it as "a sort of religion of religions, combining parts of Hindu Veda and Dharma, Taoism, Old Testament wisdom, Buddhist principles of brotherly love and compassion, the early Greeks, Lucretius, Spinoza, Nietzsche, Schopenhauer, Spencer and Freud." But probably the strongest influence on Scientology is Hinayana Buddhism, the traditional form of that religion.

While originally Scientology made great claims of healings, gaining and losing weight and the raising of IQ's ("about one point per hour" of processing), more and more the testimonials concern spiritual matters. Today, as one of their ministers said, "We do not treat or cure physical ills. But through professional medical attention addressed to the body and pastoral counseling addressed to the spirit, we do guarantee health and happiness as a final obtainable result."

What you want most of all in life is to survive. This lies at the basis of Hubbard's eight dynamics, the first four of which stemmed from dianetics and the last four of which evolved through Scientology. Here are the eight: (1) To survive as an individual; (2) To survive through sex and family; (3) To survive as a group (school, society, town and nation); (4) To survive as mankind; (5) To preserve animal and plant life; (6) To preserve the physical universe, including matter, energy, space and time; (7) To preserve spiritual existence; and (8) To preserve immortal existence. While the eighth dynamic is called the Infinity or God dynamic, Hubbard states, "It is carefully observed here that the science of Scientology does not intrude into the Dynamic of the Supreme Being."

Does Scientology help you know God?

No, say its followers. Its only interest is to help you know and understand yourself.

However, Scientology does peddle a book, called

Scientology and the Bible, in which quotations from Hubbard and from the Bible are set in parallel columns. But the problem is that there often is no correlation between the two. For instance, opposite the verse from John 10:28: "And I give unto them eternal life, and they shall never perish, neither shall any man pluck them out of my hand," is the Hubbardian quotation: "Life is basically a static. Definition: A Life Static has no mass, no motion, no wave length, no location in space or in time. It has the ability to postulate and to perceive."

But how, then, can Scientology be evaluated by biblical Christianity?

First, its primary assumption that man is basically good is not biblical. Familiar Scriptures such as "For all have sinned and come short of the glory of God," and "All our righteousnesses are as filthy rags," indicate quite clearly that the Bible and Hubbard are not in the same corner.

Second, Scientology's highest authority is not Jesus Christ or the Christian Bible but a science-fiction writer named L. Ron Hubbard. The way in which Hubbard is idolized is ridiculous, and the iron-clad control under which members are kept is frightening. It's a far cry from "Ye shall know the truth and the truth shall make you free." In some ways, the Scientology organization is disturbingly similar to Orwell's *Nineteen Eighty-Four* with Ron Hubbard as "Big Brother."

Third, to Scientology God is irrelevant. Scientology alone is relevant. Whether God exists or not is not a matter of concern. The entire working of Scientology does not take God into consideration.

Fourth, Scientology has no salvation to offer the poor. It may have programs to help drug addicts or the mentally retarded, but such people can never become good Scientology members unless they have money. Books are sold, counseling sessions are expensive. Joseph Martin Hopkins wrote in *Christianity Today*, "The door to salvation is not open to those who cannot afford to pay the price of processing." Nothing is said about the plight of the poor, the sick, the homeless and oppressed. According to *Time* magazine, one woman said, "It's the only church I've seen with a cashier's booth." Contrast that to biblical Christianity which offers salvation "without money and without price."

Fifth, Scientology has a warped code of ethics. In the Scientology code are such statements as "Never fear to hurt another in a just cause," and "To punish to the fullest extent of my power anyone misusing or degrading Scientology to harmful ends." Such statements bear no resemblance to the words of Jesus: "Turn the other cheek," and "Love your enemies, bless them that curse you, do good to them that hate you and pray for them that despitefully use you and persecute you." Scientology has harassed its critics through the courts and often outside of the courts. During the 1970s Scientology filed about sixty lawsuits against federal agencies, including one against the FBI, and more than a hundred against publishers and authors.

And sixth, Scientology deifies man. In fact, in its writings, man is often capitalized. Not only is man good, but his sentient mind "is utterly incapable of error." Man's reason will produce perfect behavior and therefore solve all the problems of the human predicament.

"In 50,000 years of history," writes L. Ron Hubbard, "on this planet alone, Man never evolved a workable system." But Hubbard himself came up with Scientology, which he calls "a workable system. It is doubtful, if in foreseeable history, he will ever evolve another. . . . Man is caught in a high and complex labyrinth. To get out of it requires that he follow the closely taped path of Scientology.''

But while Scientology may lead out of a labyrinth, it may also lead into a straightjacket. It is neither good science nor good religion; it is neither good ethics nor good philosophy.

Is it good for anything?

Yes, it is good business.

Black Muslims 19

CAN A CULT CHANGE ITS SPOTS?

Yes, if it's the Black Muslim movement.

You probably first became acquainted with the Black Muslims a couple of decades ago. No doubt, it was in a bus station or a train depot where they were hawking their newspaper *Muhammad Speaks*. Or it might have been on a street corner where they were preaching their incendiary gospel of hatred against the white race. Or it could have been that you noticed their billboard notices, "Hear the Honorable Elijah Muhammad, Messenger of Allah, Speak on Freedom, Justice and Equality."

In those days every Black Muslim was an ardent missionary, and it would have been quite unlikely had you been unaware of their presence.

Each issue of *Muhammad Speaks* sold 600,000 copies, and the leader of the group, Elijah Muhammad, claimed to have "half a million believers." Probably a true head count would have totalled only about fifteen thousand disciples with nearly a hundred thousand more hangers-on. But in the big cities of America they were a force that dramatically affected urban life.

Perhaps even more significant was the fact that nearly eighty percent of their membership was between seventeen and thirty-five years old.

Not everything has changed, but the changes have been striking.

Elijah Muhammad had been shaping his followers for forty years and they had become a paramilitary, pro-Arab, anti-white cult. Within the black community of America, they had almost become the separate nation that he had intended them to be.

Then in 1975, Elijah Muhammad died and his son Wallace took over. The changes he made in his father's Nation of Islam were monumental and by no means pleased all of his father's followers. In fact, there has been bloodshed over the matter.

But let's get a little more background on the movement.

While the Black Muslim movement goes back fifty years or more, it had been foundering in the black community with only modest effectiveness, gaining a few hundred converts a year until national publicity swept it into prominence in 1960. Its policy of racial separation, its bombastic rhetoric and its strange rituals and costumes made it front-page copy. Muhammad and his chief lieutenant Malcolm X were easily protrayed as menacing public enemies. While this vilified them with many whites, it glamorized them among young blacks.

Quickly the ranks of the Muslims began to swell.

It was the radical approach of the Muslims that appealed to frustrated blacks. While Martin Luther King had fought long and hard for integration, Black Muslim leaders spoke eloquently for separation.

The FBI began to watch the activities of the Black Muslims and to keep the leaders under surveillance. After all, Muhammad was teaching that the entire Caucasian race would be destroyed and that black people would no longer have the white man to rule over them. Besides that, he was saying that Allah had revealed that the United States would be destroyed in 1970, and then the Black Nation would emerge as the sole ruler of the world under Allah's guidance.

For a hundred years since the Civil War, long-suffering black Americans had yearned for equality and dignity, and they had faced disappointment after disappointment. They patiently tried to make it in the white man's America. Martin Luther King and others told them that it was possible. Their Negro Baptist and Methodist ministers told them it was possible. But in their own experience they were finding that it wasn't possible. They were told to be patient, but some of them were getting tired of being patient. Martin Luther King told them that he had a dream, but some of them had been dreaming for years, and the dream had faded.

For those whose dream had faded, Elijah Muhammad was the Messiah. His followers enlisted others like themselves who had lost all faith in the white man and his promises and who no longer could dream the American dream. And in the early 1960s hundreds of black people, formerly Baptist and Methodist, marched to the arenas of major cities to hear Malcolm X speak. And Malcolm X planted within them a different dream.

The speech would go something like this:

"I want you, when you leave this hall, to see the white man as he really is—a devil. Oh yes, he's a devil. I just want you to start watching him, in his places where he doesn't want you around, watch him reveling in his preciousness, and his exclusiveness, and his vanity, while he continues to subjugate you and me.

"Every time you see a white man, think about the devil you're seeing. Think of how it was on your slave foreparents' bloody, sweaty backs that he built this empire that's today the richest of all nations—while his evil and his greed cause him to be hated around the world."

Then Malcolm X would pause briefly, look squarely at his congregation and ask: "If you believe what you have heard, would you please stand to your feet?"

Everyone would stand up.

Then he would tell them to sit down again.

Malcolm X would pause again before asking another question. "How many of you are willing to follow the Honorable Elijah Muhammad?"

This time not everyone would respond. They would know that to be a follower of Elijah Muhammad demanded total commitment. They would know it wasn't like walking down the aisle in a revival meeting. But some would respond. And soon there would be enough followers to begin a new temple.

Then Malcolm X would give the benediction: "In the name of Allah, the beneficent, the merciful, all praise is due to Allah, the Lord of all the worlds, the beneficent, merciful master of the day of judgment in which we all now live—Thee alone do we serve, and Thee alone do we beseech for Thine aid. Guide us on the right path, the path of those upon whom Thou hast bestowed favors—not of those upon whom Thy wrath is brought down, nor the path of those who go astray after they have heard Thy teaching. I bear witness that there is no God but Thee and the honorable Elijah Muhammad is Thy Servant and Apostle."

They claimed to be Muslims and invoked the name of Allah, but most foreign Muslims would have nothing to do with them. They were black brothers, but most black leaders avoided them. Yet the movement grew.

It grew, of course, not so much because it was a religion, but because it was a nationalist movement. Christianity was called the "white man's religion"; only in Islam could a black man find his true racial dignity and pride.

The history of the Black Muslims can be traced back through four leaders, Timothy Drew, Wallace Fard, Elijah Poole, and Malcolm Little.

Born in North Carolina in 1886, Timothy Drew founded the first Moorish American Science Temple in Newark, when he was twenty-seven years old. Though he had little education, he grasped parts of Islamic teaching and became convinced that Islam was the only way out for Negroes. Taking the name Noble Drew Ali, prophet of Islam, he taught that American Negroes were really Moors whose forefathers had inhabited Morocco. Therefore they should no longer be called Negroes but Moors. Christianity, he charged, was for the white-skinned Europeans, and Islam was for olive-skinned persons. Until each group followed its peculiar religion, there would never be peace on earth.

Mysteriously, he died in 1929, shortly after he had been released on bond awaiting trial for the murder of a rival. During his lifetime, membership in the movement climbed as high as twenty to thirty thousand.

When the cult split into several factions after his death, one group was led by Wallace D. Fard, who called himself the reincarnation of Noble Drew Ali. Mystery surrounds the background of Fard. He was a peddler of silks and raincoats door-to-door in Detroit's Negro neighborhoods, but claimed to have been educated in England and at the University of Southern California. He also said he was born in Mecca, from the same tribe that Prophet Mohammed had come twelve centuries earlier. But, no one really knew if Fard was an Arab or a black man.

At first, Master Fard, as he was most often known, spoke against Christianity and then against the white man himself. The black people, he told them, were gods themselves; and in their midst was one who was the God of gods, although a human being like themselves. The white man, he said, was the serpent devil, and in the Last Days at the end of time, God would separate His black people from their enemies. He led Detroit's Allah Temple of Islam for only three years, between 1930 and 1933, and then disappeared from the scene as mysteriously as he had entered.

Soon some of his followers were claiming that Master Fard was not only the reincarnation of Noble Drew Ali, but was in fact Allah personified.

The chief spokesman for that view was Elijah Poole, better known later as Elijah Muhammad. Under his leadership the movement became officially known as the Nation of Islam. Born in 1897, the son of a poor Baptist pastor in Georgia, Elijah Poole worked at a variety of jobs until he moved to Detroit in 1923. Then, after losing his Chevrolet assembly-line job at the start of the Depression, he met Master Fard, and became his assistant minister. Dropping his slave master's name of Poole, he became known from then on as Elijah Muhammad.

A small, frail man with a fairly light complexion, Muhammad found that his role as the chief prophet of the reincarnated Allah wasn't easy. In 1934, he was arrested and charged with contributing to the delinquency of a minor. He had tried to start parochial schools for Muslim children and along with his members refused to send his children to public schools. For this "offense" he was arrested, tried and put on six-months probation.

But the movement didn't grow. Only a few hundred Negroes identified with it. Some violently opposed it. When the going got too difficult in Detroit, he moved to Chicago, started a second temple and faced more persecution. The severest blow to the Nation of Islam came shortly after World War II began. When Elijah Muhammad announced to his membership that Allah forbade them to bear arms or to do violence to anyone whom He had not ordered to be killed, he was arrested and convicted of inciting his followers to resist the draft. Seventy-one of his followers were imprisoned for three years. Elijah Muhammad himself stayed in a federal prison until 1946.

That imprisonment "turned out to be a blessing in disguise," according to E. U. Essien-Udom in *Black Nationalism*. It undeniably helped Elijah establish his leadership. And it also opened a new door for evangelism—the prisons themselves.

Eric Lincoln, in his study *The Black Muslims in America*, wrote: "The prisons are made to order for Muhammad. Nine times out of ten, the potential convert was arrested by a white policeman, sentenced by a white judge, directed by a white prison guard under a white warden. The prison chaplain was white, and he knew when he got out that he could not go to a white church for help. The Negro church was not interested, but there was Elijah waiting."

One of those convicts who was converted to Islam was Malcolm Little, better known as Malcolm X. (Muslims drop their slave master's name, and use X to represent their unknown true name. If they have a common first name, they may be known as John 6X. Sometimes, however, they take Arabic last names instead. Boxer Cassius Clay, for instance, became Muhammad Ali, basketball star Lew Alcindor became Kareem Abdul Jabbar.) Like Elijah Muhammad, Malcolm was the son of a Baptist minister. During his second incarceration for larceny, he began corresponding with Elijah, and by the time he was released he was a zealous Muslim.

Although Elijah's son, Wallace, was the heir apparent

in the Nation of Islam, Malcolm X soon became the chief prophet and most widely known Black Muslim. With Malcolm as the fiery evangelist, the Black Muslim movement shook itself out of the doldrums and grew rapidly to 30,000 members.

Though a strong-minded firebrand, Malcolm was a dedicated disciple of Muhammad. He testified, "I owe my present moral structure to Mr. Muhammad for whom I would give my life so that he may live. He has done so much for me."

When late in the 1950s Mike Wallace did a TV documentary on the Black Muslims, called "The Hate That Hate Produced," major national magazines devoted articles to this black nationalist movement and news reporters trailed Malcolm X for samples of his flamboyant rhetoric.

By 1961, the Nation of Islam had nearly seventy temples (now they call them mosques) in the United States.

Perhaps the movement reached its peak when heavyweight boxing champion Cassius Clay announced his conversion to the movement. But shortly after that, there was a rift between Elijah Muhammad and his strongest evangelist Malcolm X. It threatened to bring down the entire organization.

I. F. Stone in an article, "The Pilgrimage of Malcolm X," reported: "On the one side envy and on the other disillusionment were to drive the two men apart."

Elijah Muhammad and his family were envious of Malcolm's charismatic attractiveness and organizing success; on the other hand Malcolm was shocked "when former secretaries of Elijah Muhammad filed paternity suits against the prophet." So Malcolm X resigned from the movement saying that the real reason was "jealousy in Chicago, and I had objected to the immorality of the man who professed to be more moral than anybody."

From that point on, Malcolm X knew that he was a marked man. Though he broke with Elijah Muhammad and the Black Muslim movement, he did not break with Islam. Instead, in the spring of 1964, he made a pilgrimage to Mecca, acquired a new name (El-Hajj Malik El-Shabazz) and returned with the announcement: "My trip to Mecca has opened my eyes. I no longer subscribe to racism. I have adjusted my thinking to the point where I believe that whites are human beings—as long as this is borne out by their humane attitude toward Negroes."

Then on February 21, 1965, Malcolm X was murdered. Elijah Muhammad said his organization had nothing to do with the violent assassination, though the murderers were apparently former members of the movement. After that time, the Black Muslim movement had struggled to hold on to its membership, waiting for a new Malcolm X to do some more evangelizing.

In February, 1975, Elijah Muhammad died, after heading the movement for more than forty years. His son, Wallace, was selected to be the new spiritual leader.

Wallace was not a charismatic leader, but no one can accuse him of not being willing to take a few chances. And during his thirty months in office he completely altered the Black Muslim organization.

He changed the name from the Nation of Islam to the World Community of Al-Islam in the West. Women were allowed to share the leadership with men. Followers could join the U.S. Armed Forces and vote in elections. He even opened the doors of his mosques to whites as well as blacks. Eventually, the 208 mosques were turned over to laymen who were told to support them by free will offerings. And before he resigned in

1978, he stopped using the word black. Instead Negroes became known as Bilalians, named after an ancient Islamic warrior.

He was against the worship of his father or of Fard, so rather than appointing another leader to succeed him, he turned the leadership of the movement over to a council of six regional imams.

Strict dress codes were relaxed, and no longer was separate nationhood the goal of the movement.

It was revolutionary indeed.

But all has not gone smoothly in the Nation of Islam, whether the Nation is an earthly kingdom as Elijah Muhammad taught or a spiritual kingdom as Wallace Muhammad taught.

Abdul Haleem Farrakhan of Harlem is a fiery orator of the Malcolm X school and leads a rival faction. He strongly believes that Wallace distorted his father's teaching. Unlike Wallace, he is a separatist. Allah to him is a Supreme Black Man among a nation of divine black men.

As a result the Black Muslim movement is in flux today and it is difficult to assess.

But it remains a force in black America. Black Muslims take pride in owning their own businesses and attaching distinctively Arab-sounding names to them. So you may find Schabazz Kosher Market, Omar's Ice Cream Parlor, or the Kaabu Haberdashery with prominent signs in front of their respective establishments.

But what has traditionally impressed most blacks as well as whites is the high code of cleanliness, morality (although there may be a few blind spots in this area) and discipline among the Black Muslims.

Louis Lomax writes in *The Negro Revolt*: "You never see a Muslim without a clean shirt, tie and coat. You never see him drink, smoke, dance, use dope or be with a woman other than his wife. Nor will you ever see a Muslim without some means of income."

Five times a day they pray toward Mecca; and they refuse to eat pork in keeping with traditional Muslim practice. Until the dress codes were relaxed in 1977, Black Muslim women always had their heads covered and wore long, flowing white skirts in public.

But most impressive is what Black Muslims have done in rehabilitating convicts.

Louis Lomax reports: "They start out by convincing the ex-convict that he fell into crime because he was ashamed of being black, that the white man had so psychologically conditioned him that he was unable to respect himself. Then they convince the one-time prisoner that being black is a blessing, not a curse, and that in keeping with that blessing, he, the ex-convict, must clean himself up and live a life of decency and respect."

A lawyer reports that he has known of only four Muslims who have returned to crime in the past five years. And, remember, 600 convicts a year are converted to the Nation of Islam. Parole officers and the police say that the Black Muslims are the best rehabilitation agency at work among Negro criminals today. They arrange parole for their converts and then carefully watch over them.

"I'd feel better," said one Chicago policeman, "if one of them would just get drunk or get in a fight or something."

But as Lomax says: "The crucial issue is that these criminals are rehabilitated . . . in a faith that denies and condemns everything American. . . . Instead of working to improve conditions within the framework of American society, as do other Negro leadership organizations, the Black Muslims react by turning their backs on that society entirely. Their one positive aspect is that they work to make Negroes proud of being Negro."

What Elijah Muhammad taught was this: "The white man is by nature evil, a snake who is incapable of doing right, a devil who is soon to be destroyed. Therefore, the black man, who is by nature divine and good, must separate from the white man as soon as possible, lest he share the white man's hour of total destruction."

According to Muhammad, the black man originally lived on the moon sixty-six trillion years ago until a huge explosion (generated by a black scientist, incidentally) separated the earth from the moon. The black men on the newly-formed earth settled in Mecca, until they migrated to the Nile Valley fifty-five thousand years ago.

Incidentally, it should be remembered that Muhammad, like the Pope, was infallible in his ex cathedra pronouncements.

Six thousand years ago a brilliant but evil genius named Yakub, who wanted to destroy the other blacks, crossbred the weaker lighter-skinned blacks until eventually by this degenerating process, the white strain was evolved to create a Hell on earth for six thousand years. Two thousand years after Yakub came Moses, who was a "prophet sent to civilize the Caucasian devil." Then two thousand years later came Jesus "to civilize the Jews." The Christian era will expire no later than A.D. 2000, with America the first to be judged around 1970.

The God of the Muslims is Prophet W. D. Fard, who is also called Son of Man and the Saviour. Muhammad said, "Allah came to us from the Holy City of Mecca, Arabia on July 4, 1930." In fact, he said that Fard's birth is alluded to in Revelation 18:1 of the Bible. Thus, Muslims affirm that Allah is a black man, although Fard's race is still undetermined. Muhammad explained that

Fard's light skin was necessary to make him acceptable to both whites and blacks.

Furthermore, Muhammad taught that Negroes in America were Lost Sheep and that Master Fard had come to redeem and return the Negro to his true religion. While many of the old Negro spirituals talk about heaven in the future, the Black Muslims affirm that heaven is not up in the sky someplace nor is hell down there someplace. Instead, heaven and hell are conditions in which we live on earth right now. For four hundred years, American Negroes have been living in hell, according to Master Fard, and he would take them to heaven in their own nation, away from the devil white man.

While the movement under Elijah Muhammad was called the Nation of Islam, it bore little resemblance to orthodox Islam. Most foreign Muslims gave no recognition to Elijah Muhammad at all and would have been the first to label his group a cult.

What Wallace Muhammad sought to do was to move the Nation of Islam away from its cult status and make it a legitimate sect of Islam. Orthodox Muslim leaders were especially concerned about its teachings on race. Islam teaches racial equality. Its founder Muhammad took a Negro to be one of his wives in the early part of the seventh century, and he gave his daughter in marriage to a Negro. It is because of such a belief that orthodox Islam is so effective in making converts in Africa as well as in Asia.

Of course, the Black Muslim movement bears no resemblance to Christianity either, even though the Bible is referred to just as often as the Koran.

The story that Jesus told about the Good Samaritan was a direct slap at racial superiority (Luke 10). When Jesus admonished his followers, "Thou shalt love thy neighbor as thyself," it wasn't limited to people of the same race.

When the Old Testament Prophet Jeremiah had been thrown into a dank dungeon, fortunately there was an Ethiopian who forgot about racial differences to rescue him.

In the New Testament, the Apostle Peter had the idea for a while that Christianity should be reserved for the Jewish people, until God gave him a dramatic vision (Acts 10) and indicated that salvation was just as available to a Roman army captain as it was for Jewish fishermen.

And Paul's classic sermon on Mars Hill in Athens declared that God "hath made of one blood all nations of men." All are made in the image of God, and that makes us all blood brothers. Paul taught that we all stand in equal need of God's salvation.

But Christianity can hardly condemn the traditional Black Muslim movement for its racial doctrines. It is inevitable that such a movement has sprung up in reaction to decades of white racist views. White Christians have too often made Jesus Christ to appear as a white Anglo-Saxon with a cultural overlay similar to our own. Seldom do we appreciate that Jesus was a rugged swarthy-complexioned Jew who might not be accepted in some of the "better" churches of America.

It is hard to tell what direction the Nation of Islam, now the World Community of Al-Islam in the West, will take in the next decade. If it continues to follow the course set by Wallace Muhammad, then it can legitimately be called a branch of Islam and will have to be dealt with on that basis.

If, however, some of the more fiery and charismatic orators of the movement revert to the movement's original character, it will once again be racist, separatist and bitterly full of hatred.

Several years ago Martin Niemoller said that when the Heidelberg Confession was being written centuries ago, the central issue was "Who can find a merciful God?" Today, he said, the key question is this: "Who can find a merciful neighbor?"

And the question needs to be asked in the white community as well as the black community.

VI

DANGEROUS DETOURS OR TAKING SHORTCUTS THAT AREN'T ON THE MAP

Herbert Armstrong and The Worldwide Church of God

20

IT'S AMAZING how much Herbert W. Armstrong has in common with the Black Muslims. But more on that in a moment.

First, we ought to answer the question, Who is Herbert W. Armstrong?

Chances are, you don't recognize the name of the denomination which he founded, the Worldwide Church of God. Once it was called the Radio Church of God, but now it has 250 churches and approximately seventy-five thousand members, including some in Africa, Europe and Asia, so it was about time it changed its name. Like some other sects, it claims to have a corner on the truth and that all other denominations are spurious.

You may be a bit more familiar with its publication, *The Plain Truth,* which has a circulation of about 4.3 million. Two and a half million people subscribe to it, and nearly two million others pick it up free of charge at supermarkets and newsstands. Armstrong has taken every precaution possible to avoid asking for money. Occasionally readers are warned that if they try to pay for the magazine their checks will be returned. All Armstrong says is that there are 125,000 co-workers who undergird "the Work."

However, the best known of all Armstrong's enterprises is his radio broadcast. In fact, everything else—the denomination, his magazines, even his two colleges—have sprouted from the seed of Armstrong's radio microphone. According to Armstrong's figures, more than fifty million people a week hear his radio program. "The World Tomorrow " is currently heard on about a hundred radio stations; his TV broadcast goes out over nearly one hundred fifty television stations each week. Overseas the radio and television outreach is even greater. For several years the broadcasts were handled by Herbert W. Armstrong's son, Garner Ted, whose smooth radio voice (he sounds like news commentator Paul Harvey) had attracted hundreds of thousands to write in for the free literature offered at the close of the program. (more about Garner Ted's defection later.)

Frankly, you wouldn't pick out Herbert W. Armstrong as a likely religious prophet. Born in Des Moines, Iowa, in 1892, he describes himself as a precocious youth who wanted to be rich, prominent and learned. But he shunned college to go into sales and advertising, while brushing up on his philosophy and business administration at the local library on the side. By the time he was forty, however, he had failed in three business ventures. His official autobiography explains that his businesses failed due to "forces beyond Mr. Armstrong's control."

He was also a failure in regard to religion. His earliest religious training was among the Quakers, in Iowa. Then he joined a Methodist church in Illinois shortly after he married a Methodist girl. When he was thirty-four and living in Salem, Oregon, a neighbor had convinced his wife that all good Christians should observe Saturday instead of Sunday. Armstrong himself was convinced, and together he and his wife joined the Church of God (Seventh Day).

For the first time Armstrong began to study the Bible seriously, so seriously that he decided to give up on the advertising business and to go full-time into the ministry. In 1931 he was ordained. But soon he was having difficulty with his tiny denomination. The denominational editors kept rejecting his writings as too fanciful and sensational, especially when he wrote about biblical prophecy, and a sensational notion that he had about Anglo-Israelism.

Finally, Armstrong was so critical of two Church of God evangelists (including one that had ordained him) that he was expelled from the ministers' fellowship, and was asked to leave the denomination.

And since he couldn't be happy in anyone else's denomination, he started his own. At the age of forty-one, a failure in business three times over and a failure in religion at least that many times, he gave a series of lectures in a little one-room country schoolhouse, on the biblical formula for success and prosperity, and that was the incredible beginning of his vast religious empire today. Before this series was six months old, he began broadcasting his message out of Eugene, Oregon's little (100-watt) radio station KORE, and decided to crank out a couple of pages of material on a borrowed mimeograph to pass along without charge to interested listeners. He called the paper *The Plain Truth*.

What happened that first Sunday in 1934? Armstrong, who has never been noted for understatement, says, characteristically, "On the first Sunday in 1934, God's time had come. God opened a DOOR. Jesus Christ Himself had foretold this event. Millions have read His prophecy. . . . What really occurred that Sunday morning, precisely at 10 o'clock, was a momentous event. It was the fulfilling of a definite cornerstone prophecy of Jesus. More than that, it was the initial, start-off event of the fulfilling of some 90 percent of all the prophecies in the Bible. And approximately a third of the whole Bible is prophecy."

Not only that, but it was also the first time since A.D. 69 that the true gospel of Jesus Christ had been preached. In A.D. 69, the Romans "were successful in stamping out the organized preaching of the gospel"; the following year Jerusalem was destroyed by the Roman general Titus. In all the intervening years, a "counterfeit gospel" was preached, according to Armstrong, but then the church made its appearance once again on the first Sunday in 1934 when "The World Tomorrow" began broadcasting and *The Plain Truth* began publication.

By 1947 Armstrong was ready to begin his Ambassador College, which today has a campus in Texas as well as one in Pasadena, California, with some seven hundred students, and a Bible correspondence course program which prints and mails approximately 80,000 lessons each month. The lushly landscaped California college also holds title to two jet airplanes, which are used freely by the founder.

Obviously, Herbert W. Armstrong is no longer a failure. Though over ninety, he still has an active role in the organization. Today the big question is, Who will succeed him when he passes on?

His son Garner Ted had been groomed to take over. Besides being the preacher-commentator on the daily "The World of Tomorrow" radio program and the weekly television show, he had also been vice-president of the denomination, executive editor of *The Plain Truth,* and vice-chancellor of the two-campus college.

Then the shocking news came. Early in 1972 it was reported that Garner Ted went on an indefinite leave of absence "for purely personal reasons." The *Los Angeles Times* said that Herbert Armstrong had written a letter to all congregations informing them that Garner Ted was "in the bonds of Satan." The letter was to be destroyed as soon as it had been read. According to the *Los Angeles Times,* however, one source said that Garner Ted had confessed to having "sinned against my wife, my children and the church," and that he considered himself a reprobate like other sons of the prophets in the Bible.

Then as suddenly as he was placed in exile, he was restored—or at least partially restored. Perhaps it was that the income of the organization was falling off by a reputed 40 percent. But four months in exile was long enough, and Garner Ted returned to take his post as radio, television and conference speaker for the Church of God. He was not restored, however, as executive editor of *The Plain Truth* or as vice-chancellor of the college.

Herbert W. might have imagined that things could return to normal, but apparently his prophetic vision had dimmed. 1972 had merely been the beginning of sorrows for him. By 1974 there were new charges that Garner Ted had committed adultery; some even suggested that Herbert W. was concealing the evidence. The new rumors caused several leading ministers to resign; once again income was dipping. But Garner Ted's leadership brought new ideas that distressed the old-timers just as much as the rumors did.

Under Garner Ted's rule, church regulations were relaxed. The third tithe became less important. No longer was makeup banned. No longer was it illegal to celebrate birthdays. Meanwhile unrest and rumors multiplied. Nearly 5,000 members were "disfellowshipped" in 1974 and 1975. It was obvious that certain elements of Herbert W.'s teachings were being watered down.

And in 1978, Herbert W. could take it no longer. In an agonizing eight-page letter to his faithful followers, Herbert W. announced that he was "disfellowshipping" his own son and heir apparent, Garner Ted. "My son spread the rumor that my mind had gone senile. He is guilty of what he accuses—his mind has become filled with HATE, ANTAGONISM and has become UNSTABLE."

Garner Ted went off to start his own church and Herbert W. was left to battle charges of financial fraud within the church and pick up the pieces of an unsettled following.

Not all of the disruption in the Worldwide Church of God can be laid at the feet of Garner Ted. Not by any means. The state of California has had some embarrassing financial questions to ask, and Herbert W. Armstrong himself has been doing some fancy footwork to make it appear that he wasn't betraying his biblical principles. You wonder how many jolts his following can stand.

Here's one example: Throughout his ministry Herbert W. has been so adamantly opposed to divorce that hundred of his members who had been wed to divorcees had to dissolve their marriages. Then in 1976 the rule was relaxed. The following year, Herbert W., whose first wife had died ten years earlier, married a divorced woman forty-six years younger than he. And in 1982, after five years of marriage, Herbert W. announced that he himself was filing for divorce.

Perhaps Herbert W. Armstrong's Worldwide Church of God, like several other new cults, is entering a transition period, but at the moment it still bears the unique marks of its founder. Its rapid growth—and Herbert W. says that "it GREW and GREW with God's blessing" for the thirty-five years up to 1969—has to be credited in part to its Madison Avenue techniques. Herbert Henry Ehrenstein in *Eternity* magazine wrote, "Armstrong is a sensationalist. Consider his sermon titles, for example: 'Three Years Ahead of Schedule— the United States of Europe'; 'Was Jesus Christ Born Again?' 'Millions Who Believe in Christ Have No Salvation at All.'

"These spectacular themes are generally coupled with equally tantalizing subtitles or introductory sentences: Don't be too sure you know ... Millions seem unable to understand. ... A tremendous delusion is gripping the world. ... Scriptures that baffle most Christians. ... Astonishing facts which will shock you."

Armstrong's favorite words seem to be "shock," "astound" and "amaze." Here's a typical sentence: "Astounding as it may seem, there is no other work on earth proclaiming to the whole world this very same gospel that Jesus taught and proclaimed." Armstrong may have left Madison Avenue, but Madison Avenue hasn't left Armstrong.

But beyond his sensationalism, Joseph Martin Hopkins, writing in *Christianity Today,* lists five reasons for Armstrong's climb to success:

1. When many Christian denominations have wavered in their religious commitment, Armstrong projects an image of "unwavering orthodoxy" and supports the inspiration and authority of Scripture.

2. When America is reeling from moral decay, protest movements and licentiousness, Armstrong strongly condemns all of these, calling them signs of the decadence of American society.

3. When old-time virtues are being mocked, Armstrong crusades for a return to traditional moral values.

4. When people are losing all hope, Armstrong speaks

of a future with God in a "bright, new beautiful World Tomorrow." As the Bible prophecies he has spoken about are being fulfilled, his followers are more sure than ever that the Battle of Armageddon is just around the corner.

5. When religious hucksters are begging for money, Armstrong gives away everything. There is no pressure to join anything, to contribute anything. His operation seems completely devoid of mercenary interests. In fact, his church is harder to join than the Secret Service.

But then, what's the catch? How is he able to support such a multifaceted operation? Where does all the money come from?

Armstrong explains that the money comes from "co-workers." These co-workers are those who have been converted to the Armstrong gospel and tithe their money to him, explains a former disciple.

And Armstrong makes it quite clear that his followers are to give to him and to him alone. "Only one church must receive your tithes and offerings. Which Church? God's Church. . . . To give to a different church would be worse than not giving at all."

Members of the Worldwide Church of God are reminded of a second tithe and a third tithe and occasionally even offerings beyond that.

What fools many people, though, is what Armstrong believes. On the surface, he seems like an alert, timely evangelical minister, a bit sensational at times, a bit eccentric at times, and a bit dogmatic on Bible prophecy. But certainly nothing heretical as far as Christianity is concerned.

Like his teaching of British-Israelism, for instance. It's certainly bizarre, but it isn't scurrilous. According to this notion, the so-called "ten lost tribes of Israel" are the fore-runners of the British and American people. If you remember your Old Testament history, you will recall that the Hebrew people were taken into captivity in two grabs. First, ten tribes were taken by the Assyrians about 721 B.C.; later—125 years or so—the two remaining tribes were taken by the Babylonians.

According to Armstrong, the people we call Jews today came from the two tribes who went into Babylonian captivity; the remaining ten tribes meandered across Europe leaving such telltale signs as a river named Danube and a country named Denmark (Dan's mark, according to Armstrong), until they ended up in Great Britain. So the true descendants of the ten lost tribes are the peoples of England and America, says Armstrong. For proof, he cites the word "Saxon" which allegedly is derived from Isaac's Sons. Moreover, *The Plain Truth* once declared that the Old Testament Prophet Jeremiah escorted the daughter of Judah's last king to Ireland in 569 B.C., where she married the son of the king of Ireland. Jeremiah carried with him the stone which Jacob had used as a pillow in the Book of Genesis, and today that stone is called the Stone of Scone, now a part of the Coronation Chair in Westminster Abbey.

Armstrong apparently has never considered the geological evidence that indicates the Stone is of Scottish origin. Nor the linguistic evidence that English bears no resemblance at all to Hebrew.

Of course, if you equate England and America with the ten lost tribes of Israel or more specifically with the Israelite tribes of Ephraim and Manasseh, it gives you a lot of fascinating Bible prophecies to play with. (Armstrong's book, *The United States and the British Commonwealth in Prophecy,* milks the Ephraim and Manasseh references in Scriptures for everything that could possibly relate to today.) It also gives to England and America an exclusive status. Like the Black Muslims who claim to be a part of the great Nation of Islam, Armstrong's followers believe that they too have an exclusive claim on Bible prophecy.

But there is no scientific or anthropological evidence to support Armstrong's theory of British-Israelism. In fact, there is no reason to suspect that any of the Israelite tribes were ever lost. To be sure, some Hebrew families did not return from their captivity and chose to continue their family life far from Jerusalem. But many of these made annual treks back to Jerusalem at Passover time each year. By the time of the New Testament (see Acts 2) the Jews were scattered among at least fourteen different lands (and probably many more), but they did not forsake their Jewishness nor their allegiance to Jerusalem.

Like the Orthodox Jews, whose descendants they claim to be, Armstrong's Worldwide Church of God members also keep Saturday as the Sabbath, honor Old Testament feast days as special holy days and adhere to Old Testament dietary laws. Like the Black Muslims, they do not eat pork, for instance. They are strictly kosher. Many of these views Armstrong derived from his early association with the Church of God (Seventh Day), and of course, these views are also shared by Seventh-day Adventists.

But these are mild, though fanciful, aberrations from biblical Christianity.

The most extreme aberrations are in the areas of who God is, who Jesus Christ is and how a man obtains salvation. And no matter how you look at it, these are mighty important areas.

When you listen to Armstrong, his beliefs seem very biblical and proper at first, but gradually you hear such phrases as "I suppose most people think of God as one single individual Person. Or as a trinity. This is not true."

A key idea in Armstrong's theology is that God is a family. "Yes," he says, "the name of God is a name like family, church, or team."

But who is a part of that team? While the traditional Christian doctrine of the trinity connotes Father, Son and Holy Spirit, it is certainly not considered a team effort in the Scriptures; it is a unity. Armstrong, however, is not thinking at all of the Holy Spirit, who has been downgraded to a "divine force."

What then does Armstrong mean when he says that God is a team?

Here's how he explains it. "That one God is a kingdom. There is but one true church—one church but many members (I Corinthians 12:20). So it is with God.

"Do you really grasp it? The purpose of your being alive is that finally you will be born into the kingdom of God when you will actually be God even as Jesus was and is God and His Father, a different person, also is God. You are setting out on a training to become Creator, to become God."

Of course, Herbert W. Armstrong is distorting the Hebrew meaning of God, but he declares it so positively that his followers accept his definition without batting an eyelash. Walter R. Martin, author of *The Kingdom of the Cults,* says that Armstrong's teachings about Man becoming God is nothing new. "Satan first taught the 'God family' doctrine to Adam and Eve."

It may seem commendable that Jesus Christ is retained in the God family by Herbert Armstrong. Yet even Armstrong's view of Jesus Christ is far from orthodox. "Jesus alone, of all humans," he says, "has so far been saved. By the resurrection power of God . . . He was the first human ever to achieve it—to be perfected, finished as a perfect character."

The third major area where Armstrong's teaching is at

odds with orthodox Christianity is the doctrine of salvation. Armstrong teaches that "None is yet saved. . . . The popular denominations have taught just believe, that's all there is to it, believe on the Lord Jesus Christ and you are that instant saved. That teaching is false . . . the blood of Christ does not finally save any man. The death of Christ merely paid the penalty of sin in our stead and wipes the slate clean of past sins. It is only those who during this Christian spirit-begotten life have grown in knowledge and grace, have overcome, have developed spiritually, done the works of Christ and endured to the end who shall finally be given immortality."

Only as you keep the Ten Commandments, Armstrong says, can you be saved. If you keep obeying God's laws for the rest of your life, you will be born again when Jesus returns to earth.

For some reason, Herbert W. Armstrong seems to have neglected reading Paul's Epistle to the Galatians in the New Testament. There the Apostle says such things as "By the work of the law shall no flesh be justified. . . . If righteousness come by the law, then Christ is dead in·vain. . . . The law was our schoolmaster to bring us unto Christ, that we might be justified by faith. But after faith is come, we are no longer under a schoolmaster."

While the Bible speaks of past, present and future aspects of salvation, Armstrong stresses only the future. And even that is contingent on the good works you do between now and then.

Of course, the other similarity between the Black Muslims and the Worldwide Church of God is that just as the Black Muslims claim that Elijah Muhammad was God's authoritative mouthpiece, so Worldwide Church of God members believe that just as "Jesus chose Paul, who was highly educated, for spreading the gospel to the Gentiles," even so in these last days, when the gospel must go around the world, "Jesus chose a man amply trained in the advertising and business fields to shoulder the mission." That man, of course, is Herbert W. Armstrong.

An interesting tangent of Armstrong's belief is that God works in nineteen-year segments. According to Armstrong, Jesus Christ died in 31 B.C., and "for two nineteen-year cycles the original apostles did proclaim this Gospel . . . but in A.D. 69 they fled." Then he says, "the ministers of Satan wormed their way" into the church, and so for eighteen and a half centuries the gospel was not preached. "Today Christ has raised up His work and once again allotted two nineteen-year time cycles for proclaiming the same Gospel, preparatory to His Second Coming. . . . Yes, His message is shocking today. Once again it is the voice in the wilderness of religious confusion."

Armstrong's first nineteen-year cycle began in 1934 and concluded in 1953. His second began in 1953 and presumably it was to have concluded with the return of Christ on January 7, 1972. At least that's what Herman L. Hoeh's *A True History of the True Church,* published by the Ambassador College Press, intimated. The only thing that happened in January of 1972 was the exile of his son Garner Ted.

Actually, since 1937, Armstrong had predicted three different dates for the return of Christ. When faced with the disturbing inaccuracy, a Seattle pastor in the Worldwide Church of God explained that this is because "Herbert W. Armstrong is an Apostle and not a prophet."

The pastor was only quoting what Armstrong himself had suggested in the February 1972 issue of *Tomorrow's World*: "I have definitely not been called to be a prophet. . . . I have never claimed to be."

Around 1972, Armstrong withdrew from circulation

his booklet *1975 in Prophecy,* which predicted Christ's return in 1975, half-way through the tribulation. He has downplayed the nineteen-year cycle ever since that time.

Despite these denials, Armstrong spends much of his time examining current events to see whether or not they dovetail into what he thinks the Bible has to say. Like a great many conservative Bible scholars, he believes that the European Common Market foreshadows a revived Roman Empire in Europe, that rebellion, crime, lawlessness and sexual permissiveness speak of conditions that are described as prevalent in the Last Days, and that the return of the Jews to Israel indicates that soon the temple will be rebuilt and Old Testament sacrifices will again be instituted there. (In 1969, a young Australian who had been influenced by Armstrong's writings allegedly tried to take matters into his own hands by trying to burn down Jerusalem's Al Aksa Mosque, so that the temple could be rebuilt on the site.)

It was in February 1972, one month after the Tribulation was scheduled to begin and one month after the Worldwide Church of God was slated to be "raptured" to the desert fortress of Petra in Jordan, that Herbert W. Armstrong admitted, "I feel at present that the whole question of chronology is in confusion, and no one can be positively SURE of dates."

It was a begrudging admission for Armstrong to make because he had spent his life being positively SURE and making SURE that everyone else believed he was positively SURE.

By using capital letters, Mr. Armstrong makes you positively SURE that he is positively UNSURE.

Perhaps there is more in confusion in Mr. Armstrong's thinking than the question of chronology, and perhaps there are other matters besides dates on which he is not positively sure.

The Children of God or The Family of Love 21

MOSES LED the Children of Israel out of slavery in Egypt, across the Red Sea, and through the wilderness, to the borders of the Promised Land.

Where "Mo" is leading the Children of God is anyone's guess.

They have certainly wandered far, in more ways than one, and they are deeper into the wilderness than they were a decade ago.

They have been praised—by Libya's Colonel Muammar Kaddafi, whom they consider "one of God's chosen ones." But, after Kaddafi, you have to go a long way to find anyone else who will say much that is good about them.

In fact, as Joseph Carruth says in the SCP *Newsletter* (Summer, 1980), "their mobility has appeared to be less a pilgrimage than a flight from criticism and repudiation."

Back in 1972, as angry parents began forming coalitions against them, the Children of God began leaving America. They went to England, then Italy, then North Africa, Spain, the Canary Islands and South America.

Wherever they traveled, they started new communes

called "colonies" and enticed new disciples to join. Enticed is a good word to use, for one of their most notorious evangelistic strategies is "flirty fishing," better known as prostitution.

But the Children of God have changed far more than merely their home base. They have also changed their name. They now call themselves the Family of Love. And their leader, "Mo," now prefers to be called Father David.

Though their total number probably doesn't exceed 6,000, they are spread through more than eighty countries and very few parts of the world have been unaffected by them.

The Children of God—Family of Love cult is led by David Brandt Berg, better known as "Mo," Moses David or Father David. His regular letters to his flock, which are called "Mo" letters, have the same authority as Holy Writ. In fact, he encourages his faithful to "read what God said today in preference to what He said two thousand or four thousand years ago." After all, he calls himself God's end-time prophet, and the job of his followers is to share not what the Bible teaches but what is revealed through their prophet.

And who is this latter day Moses who has gotten lost in his own wilderness?

David Berg was born February 18, 1919 in Oakland, California. His parents were evangelists and he traveled with them. One year he attended nine different schools. Though quite shy, he decided to become an evangelist when he grew up. And so he did.

Ordained a minister in the Christian and Missionary Alliance church, he served a congregation in Arizona for a short time. But it was only a short time and when he left, he was bitter about the organized Christian church. Since that time, he has never had a kind word to say about the organized church. He took a position with Evangelist Fred Jordan of the American Soul Clinic in California. Jordan was an aggressive Pentecostal evangelist and radio-TV preacher who needed a public relations man to enlarge his work. Berg seemed to fill the bill.

But while relations with the public improved and the Soul Clinic acquired a Texas ranch to train missionaries, relations between Jordan and Berg rapidly deteriorated. Finally Berg quit.

He next appears as the director of a coffeehouse in Huntington Beach, California in 1968. Calling his ministry "Teens for Christ," Berg taught intensive Bible study sessions and established a communal pattern of living among a small closely-knit group of followers. These followers, encouraged by their leader, soon quit their jobs, dropped out of the system and became dedicated disciples of David Berg.

Then came the turning point.

In 1969, about the time of his fiftieth birthday, Berg received a prophecy that California would soon fall into the ocean during an earthquake and that in Moses-like fashion, he should lead the Children of God through the wilderness to safety.

But before departing from "Egypt" they tried to plague their captors.

The *National Observer* tells how they "roamed streets and beaches in sackcloth, faces daubed with ashes, yokes hanging from their necks, exhorting the unsaved to come to Jesus before it was too late." But they also delighted in interrupting church services, marching in barefoot while the services were in progress and sitting in the first rows, or on the floor in front. When newspapers got wind of their tactics, COG got free publicity.

But soon the Children of God left California, "not

knowing whither they went," wandering 100 to 150 strong throughout the southwest. Some of their veterans say that they had to eat grass at times in order to survive but finally Fred Jordan, the Soul Clinic radio preacher, took mercy upon them and allowed them to stay indefinitely at his Texas ranch. It became their base from which to prepare the world for the second coming of Christ.

In the 400-acre Soul Clinic ranch near Mingus, Texas, Berg's two sons-in-law, Arnold Dietrich and John Treadwell, called Joshua and Jethro by the Children of God, took increased responsibility as Berg's lieutenants.

In return for the privilege of living on the ranch, COG members appeared on Jordan's television program without charge. Jordan was able to raise money for his ministries by using the Children of God, and COG was able to have a 400-acre ranch for nothing. But the love affair soon soured. Jordan says that he finally realized that the group was "teaching hate," so he kicked them off his property in September 1971.

By that time, however, COG had national publicity, and new recruits were joining the radical army at a rapid pace. So they dispersed from the ranch and started more than one hundred colonies across the country. But by mid-1972 COG was on the move again. More than thirty of its colonies in America had been closed and the members had been dispatched to England and northern Europe. A few were also scattered to more than a dozen other countries from Mexico to Japan.

Richard Holmes, who has adopted the biblical name of Cornelius, explained that the exodus resulted from two convictions: (1) that the gospel must be preached throughout the world and (2) that the United States would soon fall under the judgment of God.

What would be the nature of this judgment? Cornelius

wasn't sure. "It may be an invasion or may be the rise of a reactionary political movement. America has heard the message but it has not really repented. We don't intend to spend a lot more time here."

Once some COG members marched into San Francisco's Grace Cathedral on Nob Hill. During the entire service they stood silently and forebodingly in the center aisle; then at the close of the service they shouted, "Repent," in a unison voice that reverberated throughout the cathedral leaving the worshipers almost shell-shocked.

That probably didn't gain many recruits, but it did attract attention. COG's recruitment procedures have always raised eyebrows. The authors of *The Jesus People* tell of a nursing student who was shopping in downtown Los Angeles one day when she met the COG witnesses. Upset because she could not find the shoes she wanted, she was easy prey. "Why don't you come and live with us?" the witnesses asked her. "We don't worry about needing to get shoes. We have plenty of shoes and plenty of everything else that we need."

Then with proof-texts from Scripture, they scared her about impending doom; she was resisting the will of God if she refused to accompany them back to the colony. Finally, she agreed to go with them. At the colony, they tried to talk the student nurse into selling all her belongings and giving them the money. (In the early days that was the way that the Children of God movement survived. Each new convert surrendered all money and possessions to the movement.) When she tried to leave they circled around her and prayed loudly for her. Finally, however, when she was adamant about leaving, they allowed her to go.

While some recruits were gained in shopping centers, even more were garnered from college campuses. The

Children of God delighted in invading a campus during final examinations, even going room to room in the dormitories. Uptight during exam week, students were susceptible to COG witnessing. Many of them willingly accepted the invitation to stay a weekend with their brothers and sisters at COG. And many never returned to the campus.

At the colony, the new converts studied the Bible for about eight hours a day, were given a new biblical name, and learned a trade on the side. Each new convert was supposed to memorize three hundred Bible verses in his first two months with the colony. After basic training, they were required to learn two additional verses a day. By the end of their first year, they knew nine hundred verses. On the surface, it appeared as if it were an intensely biblical group.

But with the verses, the new converts also learned Moses David's unique interpretation of the Bible, complete with his prophecies and visions. And soon they were introduced to his "Mo" letters.

For many of the "Jesus people" of the early 1970s, it was an attractive and effective group to join. One of those early converts was David Hoyt. Though converted in California from a life of narcotics smuggling, he made his mark on the Jesus movement in Atlanta where he had launched eighteen communes. What discouraged him about his own efforts, however, was the fact that his communes didn't hold on to their members. The colonies associated with the Children of God seemed to be able to keep those who joined. Soon Hoyt became a convert.

Russ Griggs of Vancouver was another prize catch of COG from the Jesus movement. A prominent organizer of communes in British Columbia, he felt that tighter discipline and increased legalism were necessary to keep the flock in line. He too joined the Children of God.

Both Hoyt and Griggs, like many others, left the cult after a few years and became engaged in legitimate Christian ministries.

From the beginning the Children of God have been extremely controversial. In 1974, for instance, the Attorney General of the State of New York wrote a sixty-five page report in which he described the "apparent metamorphosis of the Children of God from a religious Bible-oriented group to a cult subservient to the whims or desires of the Berg family and other leaders." The report went on to charge the cult with a variety of offenses from sexual abuse, including rape, to abduction and fraud in gaining recruits and soliciting funds. None of these offenses was prosecutable because of possible encroachment on America's religious freedoms.

But the Attorney General was correct. Both the doctrines and the practices of the group have degenerated. At first, it seemed an anti-establishment cult that fit in with the anti-country, anti-church and anti-parents mood of the late 1960s. But gradually it became more obsessed with sex and the spirit world.

Since the cult began, Berg has had an involvement with the occult. In 1970, after visiting with a band of Gypsies near Houston, Texas, Berg spoke of receiving revelations from God through spirit helpers. He said his main spiritual counselor was Abrahim, a supposed Gypsy king who died about seven hundred years ago. Others from whom he claims to have received subsequent spirit communications include Rasputin, the Pied Piper, Joan of Arc, Oliver Cromwell, Merlin the Magician, William Jennings Bryan and Martin Luther. It is certainly an ecumenical list. Sometimes, Berg says, it helps you make contact with the spirit world if you "prime the pump" by first drinking a little wine and getting drunk.

Through the years his favorite spirit guide has been Abrahim, who speaks through Berg's mouth with a broken-English accent and interlaces his conversation and revelation with blasphemies and filth.

It must be said that Berg's spirit guides aren't batting a thousand in regard to their revelations. California hasn't yet dropped into the sea; Kohoutek, the celebrated comet of 1974, didn't destroy America; and a major East Coast city wasn't demolished during the Bi-centennial.

Berg has instructed his followers how to receive spirit communications; increasingly he has been teaching reincarnation and astrology. "I'm Aquarius," he wrote in 1972. "Jesus told me so."

Perhaps the weirdest aspect of Berg's interest in spiritism is his claim to have had sexual relations with female spirits, whom he calls goddesses. They wait in line outside his door to make love to him, he says.

That is not the only thing about COG's sexual practices that is weird, however. Berg's sexual aberrations stem back at least as far as 1970 when he travelled to Europe with his secretary Maria. He claimed to have had a revelation that authorized him to do it. Just as Jesus spoke of old wine and new wine, so there was an old church and a new church (COG) and, as a symbol of that, God had told him to take a new wife along with his old wife. Since that time, Berg hasn't limited himself to any one woman, nor waited for special revelations to justify his actions. After all, he says that if Abraham, David and Solomon all had concubines, why shouldn't he have his own concubines? And he does.

Since 1973, the "Mo" letters have become increasingly spicy in their sex-orientation. In a 1973 letter, he wrote, "We have a sexy God and a sexy religion with a very sexy leader with an extremely sexy young following."

And if you've got it, you might as well use it, he says. The young women in the cult, whether they are single or married, are called upon to use this sexiness to win converts. It's called Flirty Fishing. Women are told to "hook, trap, net or spear men for Christ." And that includes sexual relations. They are to be the bait.

In one of his "Mo" letters, Berg tells the story of one of his followers who "caught" a Frenchman. "Soon this fine young Frenchman was literally melting under 'flirty fishy's' loving gaze as well as in her warm and tender embrace. . . . He was soon begging for more than she could give him on the dance floor."

Berg wrote an article in his *New Nation News* that rationalized the conduct this way: "We could not withhold any need from the love starved. . . . We soon found there was no stopping place. . . . We soon found our hearts irresistibly drawn into the vacuum of their hearts to satisfy their spirits, even as our bodies were irresistibly drawn together and sucked into each other to satisfy their flesh. There was nowhere to draw the line between the two, flesh and spirit."

Berg is quite explicit in how the girls should conduct their evangelism. "No bras, see-thru blouses! Show them what you've got. . . . If it doesn't tempt the fish, it's not bait, right?"

Besides winning converts, prostitution makes good money. In one week in 1978, he reported that his flirty fisherwomen brought in $3,500. COG has also established discotheques, massage parlors and escort services to ply their trade.

In recent years Berg has encouraged lesbianism and seems to be gradually lowering his previous prohibition against male homosexual conduct.

Theologically, too, Berg's views are straying farther and farther from the doctrines in which he was brought up. The King James Version of the Bible, long revered among COG members, is now called the Word of God for yesterday. The "Mo" letters are the Word of God for today.

While he claims to believe in the God of the Bible, he recognizes the "gods of the spirit world," and certainly those two beliefs are not comfortable with each other. According to Berg, just as God the Father had intercourse with the Virgin Mary in order to have Jesus, so Jesus enjoyed sexual relations with his female followers, including Mary and Martha. His proof? "I saw Mary making love to Him in a vision I once had."

As far as his views about the Holy Spirit are concerned, he calls the third member of the Trinity the Goddess of Love, God the Mother. In COG literature, the Holy Spirit is usually depicted as a very seductive young maiden.

Bible verses that Berg most frequently refers to are taken out of their biblical context. One favorite Scripture has always been: "Think not that I am come to send peace on earth; I came not to send peace, but a sword. For I am come to set a man at variance against his father, and the daughter against her mother, and the daughter-in-law against her mother-in-law. And a man's foes shall be they of his own household. He that loveth father or mother more than me, is not worthy of me" (Matthew 10:34-37).

This passage in Matthew obviously emphasizes the importance of total commitment to Jesus Christ. But Berg makes it a necessity to be totally committed to him and the cult. According to COG, part of "forsaking all" means to give everything to the group, as the early disciples did in the Book of Acts. The Children of God have delighted in chanting together: "And all that believed were together, and had all things common, and sold their possessions and goods, and parted them to all men as every man had need" (Acts 2:44,45). Having "all things common" includes sharing spouses with leadership.

The New Testament describes communal living as a temporary situation in the early Church at Jerusalem, but the Children of God regard it as a permanent injunction. Obviously, other New Testament churches didn't follow the same pattern; instead of surrendering all their possessions to the common treasury, they were asked to give free-will offerings when necessary. The Bible says, "Every man according as he purposeth in his heart, so let him give, not grudgingly, or of necessity" (II Corinthians 9:7).

In other areas as well, the Children of God are not biblical. Perhaps the most obvious is the outspoken hatred for the Christian Church. COG sees little difference between the Church and the world-system of materialism and hypocrisy. In *The Jesus People* the Children of God are characterized like this: "They are as violently opposed to the established church as any group could possibly be. . . . Churches, schools and jobs are part of the Great Whore of Babylon, and to participate in any of these is to commit spiritual fornication with her."

How different this is from the spirit of the Apostle Paul. Churches weren't simon-pure in his day either; the New Testament churches seemed to be plagued with all the maladies that beset churches today. Yet Paul wrote, "Give no offense, neither to the Jews, nor to the Greeks, nor to the church of God" (II Corinthians 10:32). And the Church at Corinth, which seemed to be everything that a church of Jesus Christ shouldn't be, was told by Paul, "Now ye are the body of Christ."

The Children of God call themselves the remnant church, the 144,000 mentioned in Revelation 7 and 14. Moreover they believe that the second coming of Christ will take place in 1993.

Whether the Children of God will survive that long is questionable. The cult is going downhill rapidly, and Berg, who has a weak heart, is aging.

Originally, the Children of God was a protest movement, and while it was extreme and unloving in the way it manifested itself, it almost had the character of an Old Testament prophet about it.

But that's changed.

The name has changed too. But while it is called the Family of Love, the love it manifests is a distortion of biblical love. Increasingly Mo's inspired letters take precedence over Scripture and his spirit guides lead him and his following away from the Bible verses they had earlier committed to memory. Their sexual preoccupation is becoming more perverted each year. And their views of God are getting more and more out of focus.

A book published in Holland asked a question in its title, "Who Are the Children of God?" And it answered: "They are not just an aberrant Jesus movement offshoot. They are a movement very deeply motivated by spiritual personages not of God."

David Berg may change his name from Moses to Moses David to Father David and the group may change its name from the Children of God to the Family of Love. But changing names does not help you find your way out of the wilderness. Nor does changing your name help you find your identity. And this group has lost more than its identity.

The Way 22

THE WAY is the way. So says Victor Paul Wierwille.

But some ways lead nowhere, except to confusion. And the teachings of Victor Paul Wierwille have confused thousands.

Ever since motorcyclist Wierwille started going nationwide in his search for youthful converts in the late 60s and early 70s, The Way has become a boulevard.

Today he has more than 40,000 disciples (some say the number may be 100,000), and with assets of $50 million Wierwille and Company are sending missionaries around the world.

What concerns secular authorities is not The Way's doctrines or missionary practices but the recent interest that the movement has shown in collecting guns. The *Indianapolis Star* labelled The Way as "the largest and most dangerous cult in the country today" and said that "the combination of mind control and gun training with Wierwille's peculiar variety of Christianity could produce a deadly mixture."

Not so, says Wierwille. "We are simply conducting hunter safety classes." Former members of the cult are

271

afraid that it is not as simple as that. "Non-believers are cockroaches," said one. "And what do you do to cockroaches?"

For Weirwille, who was born in 1917, life began at 50. Or to put it more explicitly, his cult began to mushroom when he turned 50.

Raised in a grim, legalistic home, he claimed to have taken correspondence courses from Moody Bible Institute; to have graduated from Mission House College in Wisconsin and to have gotten a degree in practical theology from Princeton Seminary. Moody officials deny that he ever completed any of their courses and Princeton officials deny that he ever specialized in Greek at their school.

In 1948, he got a Th.D. degree from Pikes Peak Seminary in Colorado, a school which according to the Colorado Commission on Higher Education "had no resident instruction, no faculty, no accreditation and no professional supervision." The *Colorado Springs Sun* says that the seminary consisted of a house and a post office box in Manitou Springs, until it closed down under pressure from the I.R.S.

Today his followers reverently call him "the Doctor."

As a minister of the Evangelical and Reformed denomination, serving small churches in Ohio and Indiana, he became disappointed by the few results in his ministry.

Wierwille tells the story himself. "My wife and I began in the Christian ministry, plodding ahead with the things of God; but somehow we lacked an abundant life. Then one time I was especially alerted when I read from the Word of God that Jesus said He had come to give us life more abundant."

Prodded by a missionary who urged him to "search for the greatest thing that would enable Christians to live the abundant life," Wierwille began searching. He re calls, "For six years, I prayed, asked, pleaded and begged God for his spiritual power, I literally travelled thousands of miles just to ask people about the Holy Spirit and the gift. I always returned spiritually lacerated and bleeding. . . . I almost gave up in despair."

In the process, he discarded his 3,000 volume library. He claimed that all the contradictions of his books only confused him. So, ceremoniously he took his books to the city dump, and resolved to read only the Bible.

Finally, he received "the power." It came by learning to speak in tongues.

But that wasn't all. While studying the Bible, he concluded that Jesus Christ was not God, and with that heresy he began to develop his course called "Power for Abundant Living."

Everything he teaches, he says, is based on the Bible, not on other books. "There is absolutely no guesswork."

"I don't want your double talk, your triple talk; all I want is Scripture." That is the way he speaks. And because he speaks positively, dogmatically and charismatically, people listen.

For a number of years, however, not too many were listening.

He began a radio program called "The Way," launched a Biblical Research Center and resigned from his church and denomination. None of these actions caused a national stir. The number of his followers was in the hundreds.

But in 1968, he took to the road, riding a raspberry-colored Harley-Davidson motorcycle and preaching his anti-Trinitarian notions and anti-church views to the turned-off generation. For young people who didn't want to stray too far afield from conventional Christianity, The Way seemed just a step outside the churches that they had rejected. Moreover, it was saying the same thing about the churches that they were feeling—that the churches were ineffective—and it was claiming to provide biblical solutions.

It sounded good.

The "Jesus People" revival prepared an audience for Wierwille's personality and program. Obviously, Wierwille was "with it." How many 50-year-old clergymen rode motorcycles? But more than that he was a man who apparently loved people, enjoyed life, knew the Bible and seemed to be at peace with himself. What more could you ask of a guru?

In the 1970s Wierwille began sponsoring youth get-togethers called "Rock of Ages Festivals" that attracted between 5,000 and 10,000 young people. Here young people met Wierwille personally, and his convincing confidence turned them on.

But Wierwille is more than a charismatic leader; he is also an able organizer. He has organized The Way like a tree. The roots are Victor Paul Wierwille, "from whom all teaching and direction originate." The trunk is the international headquarters in New Knoxville, Ohio. The branches are the twenty statewide organizations; the twigs are the nearly 2,000 home and campus meetings; the leaves are the thousands of disciples. Missionaries do not plant churches; they plant "twigs."

Spreading the movement internationally are his WOW ambassadors. WOW stands for "The Word over the World." Usually the WOW ambassadors reside in houses called Biblical Research Centers and work part-time to support their missionary activities.

Besides the 150-acre Ohio headquarters which houses the movement's printing facilities, The Way has two colleges, one in Emporia, Kansas, and one in Rome City, Indiana, a mountain hideaway in Colorado, and survival camps in New Mexico and Colorado, besides dozens of smaller properties.

To get new recruits, members of The Way often infiltrate Christian groups and invite unwary young people to enjoy their Bible study sessions. The friendliness of The Way-ers is effective. Soon the curious newcomers are introduced to Wierwille's "Power for Abundant Living" course. Twelve three-hour sessions with Wierwille are available for a $100 donation. (The highlight of the PFAL class is the session in which the recruit learns to speak in tongues.)

Speaking in tongues, or as insiders talk of it, S.I.T., is easy. "Rest your head back and breathe in deeply," Wierwille writes in his book, *Receiving the Holy Spirit Today.* "Opening your mouth and breathing in deeply is an act of believing which God honors. . . . You must now by your own will, move your lips, your tongue, your throat; you must make the sounds, form the words. . . . What you speak is God's business; but that you speak is your business."

A person is not born again, Wierwille says, unless he speaks in tongues, and only as you speak in tongues can you produce true worship. This elevates speaking in tongues to be the *sine qua non* of the faith.

If any members of The Way begin to have doubts, they are encouraged to take the PFAL class all over again. One former member testifies he went through the course five times in six years. "You become a spiritual junkie," he said. "It's like *Star Wars*; you see things you didn't see the first time."

"When Wierwille gets done with them, they all talk like him," said one observer. "They all think like him, or rather don't think."

After pledging allegiance to The Way, young converts are encouraged to leave home in order to make their full commitment. Then they sign up as WOW Ambassadors, pledging themselves to a year's service in the movement. At that point they are cut off from friends and relatives.

The elite of Wierwille's disciples are recruited for The Way Corps, Wierwille's leadership trainees. This is the group that concerns many observers. It is quite military in its orientation and is ultra-conservative in its political views. The movement has also been charged with anti-Semitism.

One former member said, "I think Wierwille was genuinely concerned about losing control." Wierwille himself said, "The love of God does not work. We've got to put some teeth into the ministry." Then he started The Way Corps.

Members of The Way Corps learn how to use a gun. It sounds innocent enough when it is taught in a course called "Hunter Safety." But it is disturbing that members of The Way have increasingly had problems with the law regarding gun violations.

In October 1977, Wierwille in Martin Luther-like fashion nailed a document to the door of the United Church of Christ located near the headquarters of The Way. The document stated: "Jesus Christ is not God, never was and never will be." Armed with a P.A. system, surrounded by bus loads of 200 followers wearing Styrofoam hats saying "Jesus is not God," and followed by several P.R. people with cameras, Wierwille took good advantage of the dramatic situation. He got the press coverage he wanted.

In earlier years, Wierwille wasn't so open in his heresy. But that has changed. Wierwille's book *Jesus Christ Is Not God* is his most blatant attack on the fundamental Christian doctrine of the Trinity. It was published in 1975.

Wierwille's blend of Unitarianism, ultra-dispensation-alism ("the Gospels belong in the Old Testament"), charismatic teachings on tongues and healing, and psycho-cybernetics came to him through divine revelation, he says.

But Wierwille claims his authority rests on the Bible and the most authoritative version is the Peshitta, which is used by the Syrian Orthodox Church. Yet when he tries to prove his unique interpretations, he resorts to novel twists of the Greek. Jack Sparks in *The Mind Benders* says, "He speaks as if he were an authority on Greek, Hebrew and Aramaic. No doubt he makes an impression on some who have no knowledge of any of those languages. To those who do, his games are little more than comedy relief. He arbitrarily makes up rules for grammar and assigns meanings to words with caprice."

If you get involved with his followers, they will easily convince you that Jesus was crucified on Wednesday, that four thieves, not two, were crucified with Christ, and Jesus was not a Jew, but a Judean; and that your soul sleeps after death. Once they convince you that they know the Bible better than you do, it is easy to convince you of other things.

The Christian Church has always believed the obvious interpretation when Jesus said, "I and my Father are One," and when John wrote, "In the beginning was the Word and the Word was God. . . . And the Word became flesh and dwelt among us." Of course, Wierwille works his way around those verses with clever mental gymnastics.

If Jesus had used those same mental gymnastics on the first-century Jewish leaders, He would not have had to be crucified.

Having disposed of Jesus as part of the Trinity, Wierwille also gets rid of the Holy Spirit. The Holy Spirit is just another way of saying God. (The Trinity, after all, was merely an invention of the early church, he says.) Christians are not filled with the Holy Spirit, according to Wierwille, but with holy spirit, and the small letters make a big difference.

You are saved when you receive this holy spirit from God, and with your salvation you get a guarantee of successful living. "When this happens," Harris Langford writes in *The Presbyterian Journal*," you have entered a spiritual shopping mall. All you must do is pick out the goodies you want, for this is the purpose of salvation." As Wierwille says, "His will for us is success in everything." The poster, advertising his courses, promises, "You Can Have Whatever You Want."

How do you get in on this?

Only through Wierwille. God has given him the exclusive franchise.

If you think it's strange that a man who didn't study Greek in seminary should be the authority on the interpretation of the Greek New Testament, and that God has withheld the truth from the Christian Church for nearly 2,000 years, so he could reveal it exclusively to a minister in Ohio, then you are entirely too suspicious to be a good prospect for The Way.

Wierwille claims that God audibly told him "He would teach me the Word as it had not been known since the first century."

Ever since the first century, Christianity has been on a detour. So says Wierwille. The Way is the only way. So says Wierwille.

Unless, of course, Wierwille doesn't know how to read the road map.

VII

THREE NEW CULTS TO WATCH

(1) The Church Universal and Triumphant $\quad$ 23

"GURU MA" may seem like an unlikely name for the leader of a new religion. And Camelot may seem an unlikely name for her headquarters.

But unlikely or not, Elizabeth Clare Prophet ("Guru Ma"), also known as "World Mother," is the leader of the Church Universal and Triumphant, once known as the Summit Lighthouse. And her California headquarters is indeed called Camelot.

Guru Ma also has a university, and frankly it is an unlikely university. It's called Summit University and it is not accredited, but who cares?

Listen to what its official literature humbly says about it: "Summit University is sponsored by Gautama Buddha and assisted by . . . the World Teachers, Jesus and Kuthumi. The teachers at Summit University are the individual I AM Presence, and Christ Self, the ascended masters, and the messengers." Guru Ma is a messenger.

It gets better.

Among the courses you can take are "Mother Mary's Scriptural Rosary for the New Age," "Meditations for the Conception of New-Age Children" and "Jonathan Livingston Seagull."

Perhaps the best way to describe the Church Universal and Triumphant is to call it a sophisticated mish-mash. It is a little bit of everything.

In a religious service of the movement, you may hear Handel's Hallelujah Chorus over loudspeakers, receive a "papal" blessing from Guru Ma (it is given over the "third eye"), see an expertly produced multi-media presentation which integrates all religion, hear a sermon delivered by "spirit dictation," visualize your chest cavity as full of light (your own "Holy of Holies") and see dozens of pictures of Buddha.

Mark Albrecht of Spiritual Counterfeits Project calls it an attempt to integrate all forms of spiritual expression into an all-embracing monistic-mystical system of eclectic occultism, resulting in a "systematic inversion of biblical truth through Gnostic reinterpretation of Scripture and carefully orchestrated syncretism."

That sounds complicated; even Ronald Enroth's delineation of it as eclectic and syncretistic is not much better. So you might prefer to stick with sophisticated mish-mash.

The Summit Lighthouse movement was begun in Washington DC in 1958 by a young man, Mark Prophet, who claimed to be a messenger for El Morya, a Tibetan mahatma, who "ascended" in about 1898.

After Mark Prophet died in 1973, his widow Elizabeth Clare Prophet swung into action. That's when things started moving. She announced that the ascended masters of the Great White Brotherhood had summoned her late husband and herself to be the messengers of God, releasing the sacred Scriptures of the Aquarian age to the world. The Great White Brotherhood are spirit guides who use Guru Ma as a mouthpiece. In 1977, she wrote:

"We see all around us the signs of the end times which Jesus described in chapter twenty-four of the book of Matthew, signifying that the end of the age of Pisces is upon us, and the rising sun of a new order of the ages is about to appear."

Her aim, then, is to initiate disciples "for the Coming Revolution in Higher Consciousness."

And her basic teaching is that God is the "Real Self" of every person. In her own words, her role is "by her adoration of the Buddha and the Christ in us all . . . to open the hearts of her children to be the focal point for the glorious release by the Elohim, the Archangels, and the Lords of Creation of the Energies of the Great Central Sun."

To get a little more of the flavor of the teachings of the Great White Brotherhood (and a little more of the religious smorgasbord), read this taken from their official literature: "Long ago the Ancient of Days came to Earth from Venus . . . that you and I might . . . one day know the self as God. . . . Within your heart is the spark of God, your divinity. 'For God so loved the world that he gave his only begotten Son. . . .' This son, the eternal Christos is . . . within your heart . . . the fiery core of cosmic consciousness, the Real Self of all who choose . . . to increase God Self-awareness."

In one of the dictations from El Morya—printed as a 110-page book under the title *The Chela and the Path*— more than 120 Bible verses are referred to.

But it is hardly biblical. Listen to this: "As Jesus walked by the Sea of Galilee . . . and said . . . 'Come ye after me, and I will make you to become fishers of men,' so the call goes forth from the hierarch of the Aquarian age to disciples of the Flaming One of Freedom.

"And those who have the marking of the law upon their souls will straightway forsake their nets and follow him . . . through whose great heart fires all mankind shall be drawn into the net of the Cosmic Christ consciousness. And so the 'fishes' merge into the oneness of the Greater Self into that love which is above all other loves even as the loaves were also formed of the love of the Father—Mother God."

Today the cult is coming on strong all across America. Why?

First, because it exudes an aura of excitement; second because it ties many religious strands together and tries to give coherent meaning to them all; and third because it is filled with mystery and mysticism.

It grossly misrepresents Christianity, but by referring occasionally to the Bible and by appropriating some Christian trappings, it is able to look legitimate to the unwary.

Basically the Church Universal and Triumphant is an offshoot of the Theosophical Society formed in the last century by Madame Helena Blavatsky and Annie Besant. It is based allegedly on the teachings of a great fraternity of mahatmas who made their home in Tibet.

In *The Kingdom of the Cults*, Walter Martin says this about Theosophy and it applies equally to its step-child, The Church Universal and Triumphant: "The entire system is Eastern in its origin; it is Hinduistic and Buddhistic in its theology, Gnostic in its vocabulary, and Christian only in its key terminology, which is specifically designed to imitate the true content of the Gospel."

The Apostle Paul faced some of the same problems in the first century. His Epistle to the Colossians made clear that the religious mish-mash in which some Colossians had gotten bogged down was a far cry from the simple gospel that he had been preaching.

The Bible speaks of prophets, but according to its

definition Elizabeth Clare Prophet is a false one. Like many others before her, she has complicated the very simple plan of salvation and has concocted a left-over stew which is not satisfying to anyone who has ever tasted the real thing.

(2) Eckankar 24

YOU HAVE TO ADMIT that there's something very intriguing about Eckankar. After all, how many religious groups teach you the ancient art of soul travel or out-of-body experiences?

But soul travel is merely one of the thirty-two facets of Eckankar. Other less dramatic tricks are ESP, mind reading, magic, alchemy and weather control.

Ever since Journalist Paul Twitchell developed Eckankar in 1964, it has been growing into a world-wide religion. Today it boasts of more than three million followers around the world; but actual membership may be closer to 50,000.

It's come a long way since Twitchell pulled away from Scientology and placed a small ad in a magazine inviting readers to write in to "learn the separation of spirit from body" by their own volition.

According to the *SCP Journal*, "Eckankar provides us with one of the most interesting case histories of the evolution of a spiritual movement. It embodies almost all of the characteristics of a 'made in America' religion—a recent vintage eclectic movement, combining occult philosophy and mystical experience, big money, misrepresentation of origins, rampant spiritism, manifestations of psychic phenomenas, virtual veneration of the leader as God, syncretism, indoctrination, and a form of attempted mind control.''

To understand Eckankar better, we have to look at its roots and in particular its founder Paul Twitchell.

A Kentuckian by birth, Twitchell became a correspondent with *Our Navy* magazine in 1945 after a three-year stint in the navy. Working out of Washington D.C., he began investigating the occult, eventually joining the Self-Revelation Church of Absolute Monism. In the early 50s he edited their magazine *The Mystic Cross,* until he was asked to leave, allegedly for reasons of misconduct. Soon he became associated with another Eastern cult, Divine Science of the Soul, and then went into Scientology, where he became a disciple of L. Ron Hubbard and a staff member of the movement.

Eventually, however, he discovered that he was a better teacher of "out-of-body" experiences than his mentor L. Ron Hubbard.

Twitchell wrote: "Ron Hubbard was trying to get people out of their body, but frankly he was failing badly. When I was a staff member, occasions came up when I was asked to help. . . . It wasn't hard to do. . . . Hubbard never acknowledged this ability of mine, and after leaving him, I did a lot of experimenting and suddenly discovered a lot of new techniques that made it so much easier for anyone to try and succeed with."

Soon he was a popular lecturer on "Bilocation," which he described as "the secret way that all masters use to reach the ultimate of all universes."

Correspondence courses followed. Then to flesh it out, Paul Twitchell, "author, traveller and lecturer," developed Eckankar, a Hindu word meaning union with God.

His early hand-outs claimed, "He has developed a complete new philosophy" around the concept of soul travel, but within a year the philosophy had become an ancient philosophy, and in two more years Twitchell was hailed by *Mystic World Magazine* as "one of the outstanding, if not the greatest, spiritual leaders of our times."

Soon the emphasis was no longer on soul travel as much as on himself. By 1970, he was known as the Mahanta as well as the only living ECK Master. A Mahanta, he once explained, only "appears in the flesh every few hundred years or so" and is "omnipotent, omniscient and omnipresent."

Unfortunately, he died in 1971, and was quickly succeeded by Darwin Gross, who is not only an ECK Master but also a Mahanta "whose characteristics include the Trinity." None can "be higher in this world and other worlds than the Mahanta, the Divine One."

A writer for the *San Francisco Chronicle* found all of that hard to believe. The new Mahanta, "before his deification, worked in a plywood mill and played the trumpet in North Beach dives." A native of North Dakota, Gross became the 972nd living ECK Master, though Twitchell is the only other one that people knew about. Eckankar writings state, "We cannot consider the ECK Master as an ordinary human person like the rest of us. He is the singular one who is responsible for all the things that go on within the universes of God."

In the ECK scheme of things, "it is not possible to enter into the Kingdom of Heaven except through the teachings of Eckankar." The reason that you need Eckankar is because there are eleven realms in the cult's system of "god-worlds" and you move up to higher realms through soul travel. Spiritual Counterfeits Project likens it to an eleven-layer cake.

Or if you prefer, you could liken it to a multi-tiered game like Monopoly, but a game full of traps (called "Kal traps"). The only way of going ahead in the game is not by rolling dice but by plugging into the cosmic current (ECK—and you learn to do this by submitting to the Eck Master). Then you begin to "flow with the Eck" up through the various "God Worlds." In the process you attain enlightenment.

Eck's God is Sugmad, which is a pantheistic everything, like any standard brand Eastern religion. Twitchell says, "There is nothing in the universe that is not SUGMAD."

There is however a devil named Kal, who is a lower manifestation of god, and a prison warden of the lower echelons.

Eckankar believes in reincarnations, millions of years and thousands of reincarnations to pay off your karmic debt. You start as a mineral and work your way through plant, fish, reptile and mammal reincarnations, until you get to be human.

Twitchell himself was a mineral, so he said, eight million years ago, but of course in his final reincarnation became a Mahanta and was "translated" (died) in 1971. The only shortcut in the process is by meeting an Eck Master or if you are living at the right time a Mahanta. Twitchell and his successor Gross have claimed to be both.

Obviously, there are many problems with the religious system that Twitchell developed.

1. His God SUGMAD has schizophrenia. Twitchell admitted a conflict between the righteousness of God and the evil of Kal and yet because of his total monistic view of God he had to admit that Kal also is God.

2. While some of ECK's vaunted soul travel is simply a matter of imagination and some comes from an altered state of consciousness through such techniques as chanting a mantra and deep meditation, ECK encourages trance states and the use of spiritism for its psychic experiences. Yet even Twitchell realized that playing with the spirit world is hazardous. He admitted that the Kal can be deceptive and "Kal experiences" can be damaging. The Bible is much stronger than that, and denounces any form of spiritism.

As Spiritual Counterfeits Project says, "It is easy to see that any and all of Eckankar's touted mystical travels into other 'realms' are likely to be no more than an implanted spiritual telecast into the blank mind of the Eckist." In fact, the learner is told he must "surrender to the Perfect Master, while throwing his mind blank."

3. Twitchell urged total surrender to the ECK Master. His followers were to put their minds in neutral, chant the word ECK and suspend the "personal activity of thought." That sounds like brainwashing.

Make no mistake about it. Eckankar can generate some unique experiences, but if you want to travel to exotic places, it's best to have an experienced pilot in the plane and a map that gives you an idea where you are flying.

The Bible affirms Jesus as the Way as well as the Shepherd-Pilot. And the Bible itself has been a trusted map for millennia. Twitchell's writings, flawed by contradiction, have been with us for only a couple of decades.

IF YOU LIKE orange and enjoy people with a sense of humor, then you might be fascinated by Bhagwan Shree Rajneesh.

Outside one of Rajneesh's buildings is the clever sign, "Shoes and minds are to be left outside." Rajneesh isn't kidding about that.

Rajneesh is also dead serious in his crusade to become a major factor on America's religious scene. He advertises for disciples in *Time* magazine; he sells a four-volume set of commentaries on his beliefs called *Come, Follow Me;* and he urges his followers to "let go" and become god.

"Letting go" is one reason why he is attracting a strong following among the under-35 set and also attracting some hostility on the part of others. At a Rajneesh ashram, "participants are . . . encouraged to fight, shout, act out violence, anger, rage, sexuality and depression with an absolute maximum of permissiveness and encouragement. This sometimes results in black eyes, broken bones, shattered egos, and an amazing degree of release, growth, change and clarity."

Rajneesh, who arrived in America in 1981, was controversial as soon as he set foot on American soil.

Part of the controversy swirls around his reasons for leaving India. He had opened his ashram in Poona, India, in 1974, and soon found himself in conflict with the government regarding tax matters, with other religious groups because of his hostile attacks on them ("He even attacked the Nobel Prize winner, Mother Teresa," said one), and his admonitions to discard conventional sexual mores.

Soon he became the target of assassination threats, and by 1981, after a rather candid documentary film, *Ashram,* was produced on his movement, Rajneesh came to America. His Poona ashram, he said, was getting too crowded. Of course, other factors may have contributed, at least somewhat, to the move.

His disciples in America bought him 64,000 acres of ranchland in central Oregon, which should allow him some room for growth. The cost for the purchase: a cool six million dollars. And the result: the world's largest ashram. Rajneesh wants to create a spiritual community "isolated from the outside world and unfettered by traditional values."

Neighboring residents are concerned about becoming overrun by cultists, and their fears haven't been eased by the Rajneesh ad in *Time*: "Sex. Never repress it. Never be against it. Rather, go deep into it with great clarity, with great love. Go like an explorer. Search all the nooks and corners of your sexuality. Sex is just the beginning, not the end. But if you miss the beginning, you will miss the end also."

Of course, more than that is taking place back at the ranch.

Included on Rajneesh's agenda at his ranch-ashram are "Gestalt and primal therapies, psychosynthesis, bioenergetics, psychodrama, rebirthing and psychic phenomena, Freudian and Jungian therapy, sex therapist encounters, Reichian and neo-Reichian therapies, Rolfing, postural integration, Alexander work, Traiger work and massage, Shiatsu, acupuncture, Zen Buddhism, Taoism and Sufism.''

It may sound like a psychiatric delicatessen, but of course it's an introduction to a Hindu cult.

Rajneesh has more than 400 centers worldwide, and various estimates of the number of his followers range from 100,000 to 250,000.

Rajneesh is known as "the Blessed One who has recognized himself as God.'' Regarding Christ, he says, "Jesus worked the same way as you feel I am working, but twenty centuries have passed.''

With an attractive personality, big brown eyes and a delightful sense of humor, he melts away the hostility or suspicion of those who meet him face to face. Sometimes he builds his teaching around a joke, as when he talks about an archer who shoots an arrow into a tree and then paints a bull's-eye around it.

Though he himself does not laugh, he affirms that existence "is a cosmic joke,'' and that is why "my religion is rooted in playfulness, in nonseriousness.''

By laughter, Rajneesh's followers can escape from the world's problems. Problems are not meant to be faced.

At his Poona, India, ashram, he discouraged the feeding of beggars at its gate. His followers (called *sannyasin*) are taught to close their minds to the suffering around them. Bliss can be known only by experiencing the infinite unknown beyond the mind. The mind limits us. As life's limitations are removed, we can realize life's limitless potential.

"Only nothingness can be free,'' Rajneesh once lectured. "If you are something, you will be in bondage. If you are, you will be in bondage. Only a void, a vacant space, can be free."

Rajneesh differentiates between the yoga approach and the tantra approach, which he adopts. "Yoga is suppression with awareness; tantra is indulgence with awareness. . . . In yoga you have to fight with yourself to go beyond." You need to "fight, dissolve that which you are so that you can attain that which you can be. Going beyond is a death in yoga. . . ."

On the other hand, "tantra says accept yourself as you are. No death is needed. . . . And only through total acceptance can you grow. . . . Use every energy you have. . . . Everything is holy; nothing is unholy. . . . The ultimate for tantra is to bring about a state where there is no mind."

His *sannyasin* wear orange clothes and necklaces with 108 beads and pictures of Rajneesh. Upon their initiation they are given a new name by Rajneesh which they thereafter use.

As in other Eastern religions, the follower surrenders all to the guru. As Rajneesh once told a group of new disciples, "Now you say, 'Do whatever you like. I am in your hands. Ask me to jump into the well and I will jump.' "

But the disciple does not consider this as bondage to Rajneesh, but rather freedom from personal responsibility. Individual bliss comes from "complete assertion of the self."

"Once you attain to your inner realization," Rajneesh writes, "you are the only begotten son of God—as if the whole existence exists for you and only for you."

"You are gods," he once wrote. "That is your reality."

The Bible disagrees, and anyone who looks at the world with serious eyes must disagree too. Of course,

Rajneesh says that it is a mistake to look at the world seriously.

But to approach life that way, he has to overlook sin and suffering, the needs of others, and the problems of a war-stricken world.

So while he provides an escape from the world, it is truly a short-sighted and self-centered solution.

The Bible speaks of men and women as sinners. But when they find forgiveness through Jesus Christ, they can become salt and light, permeating the structures of this evil world for the glory of God.

"Shoes and minds are to be left outside," the Rajneesh sign reads. Reality has to be left outside as well.

VIII

WHAT MAKES YOU THINK CHRISTIANITY IS ANY DIFFERENT?

Conclusion 26

OF THE MAKING of curious cults, there is no end.

So the Esalen Institute, Soka Gokkai, Rosicrucians, the Church of the Final Judgment, Yoga, Subud and scores of other cults continue to attract young admirers with increasing success. While the soil for cults to grow in seems particularly fertile on the West Coast and in the metropolitan East, no place in the country seems to be exempt.

Yet, in a sense, cults have been springing up like weeds since the dawn of history.

Take, for instance, the Ahmadiyans of Pakistan, the faithful disciples of Mirza Ghulam Ahmad, who lived in the last century. Though a devout Muslim, Mirza had so many dreams and visions he convinced himself that he was not only the Mahdi of the Mohammedan world and the Krishna of the Hindu world, but also the returning Christ of the Christian world.

According to no less an authority than Mirza himself, he got himself crucified like Jesus Christ, but fortunately was taken down from the cross shortly before he "gave up the ghost." Then he wandered to Kashmir, where he discovered the ten lost tribes of Israel, a fitting climax to his ecumenical life.

Since his death, his followers have established several religious centers and a few magazines to try to keep the ten lost tribes from being lost again.

So cults have been cultivated in the soils of all nations and throughout all periods of history. But there is no denying that this is one of the most fertile periods of all.

Why?

Because man is incurably religious? That's true.

But it's more than that.

Coupled with his insatiable religious appetite is the fact that man would rather create God in his own image than be re-created in God's image. Thus, man has created a wax museum full of gods, curious gods—sometimes almost comical gods, schizophrenic gods—each a bit different from the others.

Is there anything that ties all these nuclear-age cults together? Do these strange new beliefs have anything in common that accounts for their popularity today?

The Greeks had a word *apocalypsis*. Loosely, it could be translated "to take the lid off."

If anything could be said to tie all these curious new cults together, it might be this word *apocalypsis*. Technically, the word means revelation or unveiling and is applied to revelations of the secret purposes of God and the end of the world.

Of course, this isn't the only thing that unites these cults. Several of the cults—the Children of God and the witchcraft covens for instance—are built upon the need for community as well. Modern man has forgotten the meaning of that old word fellowship, and all that is left is a smile or a cold handshake.

If a young person has moved his residence at least a half dozen times by his twentieth birthday (and that's usually the case) and if divorce has shattered his family at least once, it is understandable why he would jump at the chance to join a seemingly stable, caring community. Many of the new cults seem to offer a deeper, more intimate fellowship than the young person has ever experienced before.

Another thing that unites many of the cults is escapism. Young people are very susceptible to an occult cop-out. The world's problems are weighty on youth today. Problems have increased in number and have grown in magnitude, and the world has shrunk in size. In addition, television has plopped all these problems right in their living rooms. Ecology, population, war, violence, family tension, bureaucracy, poverty, generation gaps are all problems that appear hopeless and easily bring depression.

It is little wonder that some young people figure that it's senseless to try to cope. Instead they use religion as a cop-out. And many of the Eastern religions are made to order for copping out.

But the main thread that weaves in and out of most of the new cults is the thread of the apocalyptic, the mystical, the taking the lid off, the "other way of grasping nature," the unveiling of God Himself.

Colin Wilson tells the story of the historic meeting of Goethe and Schiller at a scientific gathering in Jena two centuries ago. Goethe, who hated the materialistic direction toward which science was heading, remarked, "There ought to be some other way of grasping nature—as active and living. . . ."

But Schiller pooh-poohed the idea, saying, "That's not scientific. It's just an idea of yours."

Wrote Wilson, "For two hundred years, science has agreed with Schiller. And now, amazing as it seems, it is beginning to agree with Goethe."

Wilson went on to illustrate his point from genetics. He told how some bugs can form a beautiful imitation flower as an evidence of how marvelous genetic programming has been built into the universe. An acorn has been programmed like a computer to become an oak tree. "But who or what," asks Wilson, "programs the computer?" Then he concludes with the prediction, "By the year 2000, the rigid scientific materialism of the nineteenth century will be regarded as a thing of the past."

Is there some other way, as Goethe has suggested, of grasping nature?

We have gone to the moon, and surgeons have transplanted hearts. Everything that was mysterious or sacred or unknown has been explained away. But still young people are not satisfied. Science cannot explain everything; in fact, the new generation says, instead of expanding our vision and opening up new horizons, science has put us in a box. What we need to do is to take the lid off the box. Isn't there some way we can take away the ceiling and see the stars? Isn't there some way we can see the stars without thinking of how many light years they are from us? Drugs can do it, but many young people are looking for a safer way. So they turn to religion.

Of course, the Christian Church has complicated the picture by accommodating itself to its materialistic milieu. Miracles are explained away; everything is explained rationalistically. Even the churches that have retained the miracles have lost the wonder and mystical side of original Christianity. The Bible has often become a document to be studied coldly, scientifically, logically, rather than a revelation to be enjoyed. Christianity has turned into a religion that can be outlined on a three-by-five card, rather than being an experience with the living God.

Christians have become engrossed with their roots when young people are enamored with flowers. Granted, a flower can't live long unless its roots are solidly implanted in soil. But the trouble is that all many young people see in Christianity is a very fancy root system. And very few flowers.

It's strange because the New Testament oozes joy. The word we use to describe the biblical message is "gospel," which means "good news." The historical narrative of the New Testament begins with some angels telling a few dazzled shepherds that they have "good tidings of great joy" for them.

What makes Christianity joyful is that it essentially is an unveiling of God. The Bible begins with God, not man. It says that God takes the initiative in solving the human dilemma. It admits that man is powerless to do much about the miserable mess he's in.

The God of true Christianity is a personal God, a God who can be known, a God who can love. Granted, He is a transcendent God, an awesome God, as Moses discovered in the wilderness. But Moses also discovered that God could be talked to—personally. Most of the new cults don't talk to God that way. To them He is the Ultimate or the Infinite or some other vague philosophical term. It's like trying to catch a fog in a net; you know it's there, but it's not much comfort when you've lost your way.

Carole King's hit song, "You've Got a Friend," said something about what youth is yearning for. Eastern religions can't satisfy it; neither can astrology or witchcraft. But the God of Christianity can be known as a Friend.

The God of Christianity is God who is reaching out,

showing not passive interest but active concern. He is not the cosmic clockmaker, who wound up his timepiece eons ago and is gradually letting it run down. He is not merely an interested spectator in the grandstand rooting for His team to win. He is a God who wants to pull the lid off so He can reveal His love.

And this means hope. Because He is transcendent, He is capable; because He is involved, He brings hope. Frankly, the new cults don't offer much hope. Rather, they assist you in becoming reconciled to despair.

Allen Ginsberg, one of the movement's patriarchs who has led his followers from one new cult to another, wrote: "I feel as if I am at a dead end and so I am finished. . . . I never escape the feeling of being closed in and the sordidness of self, the futility of all that I have seen and done and said."

Even after a generation of searching, Ginsberg still can "never escape the feeling of being closed in." The past is sordid, the present is unbearable and the future is terrifying. In the light of that diagnosis, why not become reconciled to despair?

Against such a black background, the hope of Christianity shines in brilliance. Christianity gives meaning to man's existence. It says that you are important. It gives you personal dignity and worth. Even when you know what kind of a person you really are, it says that God loves you anyhow.

In most of the new cults, man is robbed of his individuality. They say that man is a segment of Ultimate essence, or even, as Radhakrishna says, "Man is God's temporary self-forgetfulness." Salvation comes only when you are liberated from yourself. You need to float along with the tide or to move in conjunction with the stars.

But here again Christianity stands out in contrast.

The God of Christianity makes man important. In fact,

the Bible says that God thought man was so important that He sent His Son Jesus Christ to die for him. God thought man was so important that He invaded human history for him.

Another contrast is what happened after the crucifixion of Jesus Christ. The Resurrection on Easter Sunday demonstrated that God can do something about man's problem.

The curious new cults talk about reincarnation, not resurrection. When you die, they say, you will be reincarnated into a new body, and after many reincarnations you will eventually be absorbed into a cosmic nothingness. Or as Pogo in the comics once defined it: "Absolute zero."

Christianity talks about resurrection. Jesus Christ arose from His tomb as a fact of history. His resurrection means that He is alive today, and that's a statement that no other religion can make about its founder. But His resurrection is also a guarantee that man, as man, has a permanent identity. Man has a future.

That is Christianity. And there's nothing like it in the whole world.

But Christianity isn't something to be admired. It is something, Someone, to be received. Those who only admire it are missing the best part.

Further Reading on the New Cults

All God's Children by Carroll Stoner and Jo Anne Parke. Chilton Book Co.

The Bahai Faith by Jessyca Russell Gaver. Hawthorn Books, Inc.

Black Nationalism by E. U. Essien-Udom. University of Chicago Press.

Buddhism by Peter A. Pardue. The Macmillan Company.

The Case for Astrology by Jim Anthony West and Jan Gerhard Toonder. Coward, McCann & Geoghegan, Inc.

Christianity and the Occult by J. Stafford Wright. Moody Press.

Counter Culture and the Vision of God by Robert L. Johnson. Augsburg Publishing House.

The Cult Explosion by Dave Hunt. Harvest House.

Dianetics by L. Ron Hubbard. Paperback Library.

Eastern Religions in the Electric Age by John H. Garabedian and Orde Coombs. Grosset & Dunlap, Inc.

The Kingdom of the Cults by Walter R. Martin. Bethany Fellowship.

The Lure of the Cults by Ronald Enroth. Christian Herald.

The Making of a Counter Culture by Theodore Roszak. Doubleday & Company, Inc.

The Mind Benders by Jack Sparks. Thomas Nelson

New Gods in America by Peter Rowley. David MacKay Co., Inc.

The New Religions by Jacob Needleman. Doubleday & Company, Inc.

Prison or Paradise by James and Marcia Rudin. Fortress Press.

Religion in the Age of Aquarius by John Charles Cooper. The Westminster Press.

The Religions of Man by Huston Smith. Harper & Row, Publishers.

Religious and Spiritual Groups in Modern America by Robert S. Ellwood, Jr. Prentice-Hall.

The Scandal of Scientology by Paulette Cooper. Tower Publications, Inc.

Scripture Twisting by James W. Sire. Inter-Varsity Press.

The Truth about Witchcraft by Hans Holzer. Doubleday & Company, Inc.

Youth, Brainwashing and the Extremist Cults by Ronald Enroth. Zondervan Publishing.

Zen Buddhism by D. T. Suzuki. Doubleday & Company, Inc.